D0016871

No Mountain High Enough

No Mountain High Enough

RAISING LANCE, RAISING ME

LINDA ARMSTRONG KELLY

with JONI RODGERS

Foreword by Lance Armstrong

BROADWAY BOOKS
NEW YORK

PRINTED IN THE UNITED STATES OF AMERICA

Visit our website at www.broadwaybooks.com.

First edition published 2005

Book design by Michael Collica

Library of Congress Cataloging-in-Publication Data

Kelly, Linda Armstrong.
No mountain high enough : raising Lance, raising me / Linda Armstrong Kelly; with Joni Rodgers; introduction by Lance Armstrong.
p. cm.
1. Armstrong, Lance. 2. Cyclists—United States—Family relationships.
3. Kelly, Linda Armstrong. 4. Mothers—United States—Biography.
I. Rodgers, Joni, 1962– II. Title.

GV1051.A76K45 2005
796.6'2'092—dc22
2004057016

ISBN 0-7679-1855-X

1 3 5 7 9 10 8 6 4 2

This book is dedicated to my family:
My son Lance, my inspiration for life
Ed, my wonderful husband, who gave me the courage,
love, and support to tell my story
My precious grandbabies: Luke, Isabelle, and Grace
My bonus kids: Maureen, Mike, Megan, Jeff, and Jenny
My mom and dad
Debbie and Alan
Sam, always there for me, and Barney, for playing so well with Sam
LAK

For my son, Malachi Blackstone Rodgers
JR

CONTENTS

ACKNOWLEDGMENTS

This is the totally biased, subjective, slanted, rationalized, and confabulated story of my life according to me. Someone else might have a different perspective, and I respect that, but it doesn't change mine. They're free to go out and make a book about their own life, and I encourage them to do so. It was an illuminating experience. Of course, you can't re-create a dead-on verbatim play-by-play of every little thing thirty years after the fact, but I've tried to stay true to the spirit of events as I remember them. Lawyers got in there and changed some of the names, and to make it readable we had to squash some very nice people together into composite characters here and there and telescope events so it wouldn't go on and on like a soap opera. All in all, I think we did a very good job telling the story, and for that, I'd like to thank my coauthor (she prefers the term "memoir guru"), Joni Rodgers. My agent, David Hale Smith, was recently featured in *D Magazine* as one of Dallas's coolest people. I agree. Thanks also to his better half and business partner, Elizabeth Ostrow Smith; our terrific editor, Stacy Creamer, for being such an efficient midwife and all-around-fabulous gal; Marjorie Braman at HarperCollins for allowing Joni to red-rover over to Doubleday/Broadway for this project; Joni's family for letting her travel so much; and Sally Jenkins for her valuable contribution. The only way I know how to thank my wonderful family for their overwhelming love and support is to cook for them, so I'd better get to it.

Linda Armstrong Kelly
Spring 2005

FOREWORD

by Lance Armstrong

How does a supermarket checkout girl produce a son who becomes a Tour de France champion? The theorists and social psychologists can bicker all they want over the nature versus nurture question, but for me, the matter's settled. It's perfectly clear: I owe it all to my mother. What would I have been without her? A barroom brawler maybe. Or an arsonist.

My mother gave me my heart, lungs, arms, legs, and genes. But whatever natural physical abilities I possess were as randomly awarded as the winning numbers on a roulette wheel. Without an organized will and discipline, physical attributes are meaningless. Without the surehanded parenting I received from Linda Mooneyham Armstrong, they would have amounted to nothing. They'd have been just a collection of scattered characteristics, topped off by a smart mouth.

As I've grown older and become a parent myself, it seems to me that rearing a child is the trickiest job in the world. Every word and gesture can have unintended consequences, and a large mistake can mean the difference between a whole, healthy, self-fulfilled human being and a deprived and self-defeating one. Not until I became a father myself did I properly understand what a trying job it is, nor did I understand the full measure of the job my mother did with me. Somehow, a seventeen-year-old single mother managed to fill the roles of two parents at once and made me feel that I had everything I needed or wanted. In the process she instilled a work ethic that has allowed me to make the most of my gifts, to endure the most grueling sporting event in the world, and to cross the finish line first and stand on the podium.

"Make every setback an opportunity," she told me.

We lived by those words as mother and son, and I've never forgotten them.

But what stands out to me, what I'm most struck by, are those things she *didn't* say or do. There were occasions on which she could have given up, but didn't. When she could have lost her patience, but didn't. When she could have discouraged me, but didn't.

Here are a few of the things my mother never said to me:

She never said, "Get off that damn bike and get inside this house."

She never said, "This sport is getting too expensive. I'm not paying for one more spoke on one more wheel."

She never said, "Who do you think you are? You better learn to settle for less, instead of dreaming of the impossible."

She never said, "There's a position open at Kroger's. I think you should quit racing and apply for it."

She never said, "What's wrong with you? Why can't I have a normal kid?"

She never said, "Life's not fair. Why is this happening to me?"

My mother must have been exhausted and even a little desperate at times. She worked two jobs to support us, and there were even occasions when she worked three. She punched a cash register at Kentucky Fried Chicken and sorted packages at the U.S. Post Office to make extra money. But my memories are of a small, uncomplaining dynamo of a woman with seemingly inexhaustible energies. I don't recall her ever complaining about her burdens or fatigue. No matter what, she was my cheerful mother who was never too weary to read to me every evening.

You could chart our progress by the succession of better neighborhoods she moved us to. In Richardson, Texas, she bought me my first good bicycle and signed me up for swimming lessons. In Plano she found a job as a secretary with a telecommunications company and bought us our own home. Over the years she worked her way up to account manager and found herself giving on-the-job training to kids much younger than her, with college degrees.

My mother refused to acknowledge limits, for herself, or for me. We were partners in carving out better lives for ourselves, and we fought for each other, back to back against our obstacles. She gave me a silver dollar as a good-luck piece and suggested that if I put my mind to it, I could become an Olympian. When the local high school objected to the fact that my amateur athletic career caused me to miss too much school and threatened to flunk me, she didn't scold me. Instead, she searched the entire Dallas area for a better school.

In the evenings I would train for my budding career as a triathlete, and sometimes I would ask her to drive behind me as I rode my bike, to check my times and count the miles. She would grab her car keys, and off we would go.

She never said, "I'm too tired."

And she taught me to never say it either. Once, when I was exhausted and on the verge of collapse in a triathlon, my mother walked miles out on the course to find me, limping along. She strode beside me and said, "Son, you never, ever quit. Whatever you do, you stick to it. You may have to walk, but you're going to finish." With her next to me, I did.

When I was diagnosed with cancer, there was something familiar about the sensation of battling once again side by side with my mother. "This isn't going to happen to us," she announced, and I believed her. Her belief was my belief, and I'm convinced it was that belief, in combination with the marvelous abilities of my doctors, that helped me to survive the disease. As my mother once said, "You were a survivor long before you got cancer."

How do you adequately express gratitude for the gifts from a parent? I've tried in various ways to tell her *thank you* over the years. Only once did I come close to succeeding, and even then it was an awkward attempt, as I emerged through the fog of anesthesia from surgery to remove two cancerous lesions from my brain. "Where's my mother?" I asked the nurses. My mother appeared by my bedside.

"I want you to know how much I love my life," I said, "and how much I love you for giving it to me."

At this writing, I wish I could find better, more eloquent words with which to thank her. But I don't seem able to improve on that very simple statement, uttered in gratitude: *I love this life*—and I love and appreciate her for giving it to me.

As you read this book, you'll see that her story is my story, and my story is hers. I'm many things: a cancer survivor, a father, a Tour de France champion. But I'm one thing before all others, and it's a thing I'm so proud of.

I'm a son who seems to have pleased his mother.

ONE

REFLECTIONS

I would like to say right up front—I did not know about the fireballs. Obviously, if I'd known my twelve-year-old son was lighting gasoline-soaked tennis balls on fire and batting them around the yard with oven mitts, I would have been all over his case. No, I read about it in his autobiography, just like the rest of the world, and I guess I'd feel bad about that if I didn't know this: there's not a kid past middle school who hasn't done something that would chill his mother to the bone if she knew about it. And I'll bet I'm not the only mother with a few fireballs of her own—moments from the past that would take her child equally by surprise.

That's the way it is between mother and child. You grow up, grow together, grow apart, grow old, never really knowing the true life story of that other person whose life was so entwined with your own. Mothers see what they want to see. Children see what they need. And that's as it should be. Everyone should have a moment to believe they're the center of someone's universe, and my son and I gave that moment to each other. That's what I want to tell people who ask me about Lance: that he's my son, fireballs and all, and I would think he was the most amazing man in the world even if the world had never heard his name.

Watching him take his sport by storm (and occasionally worrying about the sport taking him), I'm continually astonished at the all-out *beauty* of that boy and the enormous love he brings out of me. It swept us both outward like a riptide from the day he was born to—well, right now. Right here, in the lovely foyer of my lovely home, where TV people are swarming, switching, scurrying around. They flip through my photo albums, searching for the secrets of his success. They mine my memories, stirring up dust and ghosts and odd little gremlins I thought I was done with long ago. (You know how you tuck things away in little dresser drawers in your head.)

Vivaldi was tuned in on the satellite dish when they arrived, but Motown was the music in my mind. It always is when I revisit those days. It was in the air back then, hanging in the humidity, breaking up the exhaust fumes that turned the taste of the heat smoky and brown. When I think of walking down the streets of Dallas, my freshly ironed hair swinging to the Supremes, I hear the drill team chants mingled with a girl group beat, the bluesy lyrics pattering back and forth between the boys in the sweltering alley. The harmonies lifted worn white sheets that waved on wire clotheslines between the tenement buildings, flagging the surrender of the people inside. Motown drifted from shop doors by day, from car windows by night. Now James Brown and Diana Ross and Little Stevie Wonder play alongside my memories like a movie sound track. I can't separate the music from the smell of hot asphalt. It's one of the ways in which my memories have been mellowed—healed by time, rewritten by compassion, surgically enhanced by this dog-with-a-bone optimism that won't let me give up on anyone until a tree falls on me.

My son doesn't like to revisit the past. He is a man perpetually in forward motion. Always has been. Love that kid. Head down, into the wind. No time to look over your shoulder. Nothing back there is as important as what's ahead. But I don't personally mind it. Revisiting. I like that word. That word makes it sound like I'm knocking on the door at Granny's house and she's still there to open it. Or like I'm passing by that Mooneyham girl who sits on the crumbling cement steps in front of some god-awful apartment building, fanning herself with the want ads from the *Dallas Morning News.* If I could drop in on that girl like a fairy godmother, whisper in her ear through the summer breeze, I know just what I'd say.

"Don't give up. You're gonna be okay. Today is the first day of the rest of your life."

I can't remember where I first heard that one, but I used it a lot. Even then I knew some clichés got to be clichés for a reason: because they're true. The false old saws about knowing your place and following the rules—those don't seem to wear as well, and anyway, I never really thought they applied to me. Even then I knew if I was going to make the life I wanted, I was going to have to color outside the lines. But that is so much easier to say at fifty than it is at fifteen.

From this perspective, I feel a great affection for that girl. I don't cringe at the polka-dot bell-bottoms or the daisy-splattered minidress. I'm proud of what I was, where I am, and how I made the trip from there to here. And it frankly boggles my mind that a television crew is setting up their light trees and tripods in the middle of my foyer, having traveled to Plano, Texas, from New York City just to ask me all about it.

"Who'd have ever thought?" says my sister Debbie in absolute wonderment.

"Who ever would've?" I agree.

Back in the days when we played Lawrence Welk Show (Debbie and I were Kathy and Dee Dee Lennon, while our little brother Alan was pressed into service as Myron Floren), we thought, to be on *television,* well, that must make you something pretty special. Poverty has this way of making a child feel invisible, I think. Maybe that's why we dreamed so dearly of being someone worth noticing.

When Lance was fourteen or fifteen, he was interviewed on an ESPN program called *KidSports,* and I'll tell you what, I saw my son on national television and—oh, my *God!* There was *my son* on national *television*! I was immediately on the edge of my seat, trying to coach him through the glass. "Okay, son, stand up straight. Look at the camera—no, wait! Maybe you're supposed to look at the guy with the microphone—no, wait! Look at the crowd. And smile! And—and be sure to thank the—"

Lance was unflappable. He was so caught up in the thrill of

winning, he apparently forgot to be thrilled about being on TV. He'd been riding hard for two hours, so he was breathless and sweaty and still in his Speedos. He bounded to the platform like some big goofy puppy—completely raw, innocent, and radiating a child's liquid joy.

"I'm just so excited to win!" he said happily. "Sometimes I even get *paid* if I win, and my mom doesn't have a lot of money, so that really helps her."

"So I guess it'll feel pretty good to get home and rest up for a few days, huh?" said the guy with the microphone.

"Oh, no," Lance replied, "I'm gonna race again tomorrow! That'll really cap it off." He hoisted a gallon jug of water, slugged some down, and wiped his mouth with the side of his hand, still breathing hard and grinning larger than life. "I was gut-checkin' out there! Had to get away from that other guy. Man, he has a motor on his bike!"

That's all it was about for him. The race was the thing. Winning was the goal. Losing was an opportunity to learn what might help you win next time. Being in that inner circle, being recognized and applauded—that was part of the rush, I suppose, but not enough to make someone go through what he had to go through to make winning happen. He was never nervous about getting up on the platform at the end of a race, smiling for the cameras, talking to the microphones. He was eager to share his joy. Isn't that the heart of celebrity? Celebration? It took us a while to figure out that all those accolades—well, it's like a big ol' peach pie. Wonderfully sweet. But eventually it draws ants. Hornets even, if you don't keep a lid on it.

Nonetheless, ya gotta make hay while the sun shines. That's what I tell my son. There's a window of opportunity for an athlete, and it's nothing so enduring as Motown. Someday in the not-so-distant future it'll all be a scrapbook, so today praise the Lord and pass the Colgate. I'm gonna mug every photo op like a Dallas Cowboy cheerleader. I am a bona-fide *show dawg.* I fix up quite nicely, if I do say so myself, and the camera and I have a mutual understanding: it adds ten pounds but subtracts ten years. I am unutterably proud of my son and happy to do whatever I can to make sure the rest of the world feels the same way. Sign me up. Lights, camera, action.

"Gotta go," I tell Debbie. "They're looking at me like they expect something."

"B'bye," we both say to our stylishly tiny phones.

"Do you mind if we remove the swag?" asks the producer, but apparently this is a rhetorical question. She has already dragged the swag down and yanked the tall drapes closed. Too much sun, I guess. The artificial light is sharper, narrower, easier to harness than all that dayshine. But it irritates me, this lack of regard for the labor of love it was. The interior decorator—a terrific lady who owns a little shih tzu just like Sam—and the window treatment lady—who had a baby last year—reverently fluffed and tugged and smoothed for half an hour to get it just so, and it's hardly been touched since, except with a feather duster.

"Oh, hon, set that on the rug," I tell a young man who has pushed aside a standard of silk gladiolas and is opening a huge metal box on the round mahogany table. I see the glance he exchanges with another crewman, but I don't care. Let them think this is some rich lady's house and she's all uptight about it. I make no apologies for loving my beautiful things. Isn't that terrible? Materialistic or something. But I've worked very hard for what I have and know what it's like to do without. This house is quite literally my dream home. A Technicolor Emerald City, in contrast to the sepia-toned projects of Dallas where I grew up.

And it's not because I'm rich. I've felt the same way about humbler surroundings in the past. A house is never just sticks and bricks to me. It's a sanctuary sometimes, a tornado shelter at others. It's the place where I nurture my family and my cooking skills and my stubborn vision of the life I want to create. A porch where a boy on a red bicycle deposits the morning paper. A door where a daddy leans in, removing his hat for his welcome-home kiss. A bay window with lace curtains on the inside and neatly trimmed hedges on the outside. A table with wedding china and good silver and seconds on beef Stroganoff if you want it. As a child, I studied this dream on television—*Donna Reed* and *Father Knows Best* and all the commercials in between—so I knew it was possible, and I hammered away at that possibility in every room at every address I've had since my son was born. I wanted that for him. And for me. Still do.

"Can we see Lance's room?" asks the producer.

"Well, you'd have to ask him," I tell her. "It's at his house."

"Oh." She seems crestfallen. "This isn't where he grew up?"

I just have to laugh at that.

She seems pleased when I bring out the photo albums. Yes, this is more like it. Lance's third birthday party on the cramped cedar deck of a run-down apartment complex. Lance grinning in the driveway outside the quintessential mid-seventies suburban crackerbox. Lance wheeling down the block in his little Darth Vader costume. A giant's humble beginnings. That makes for good television, I suppose. That's what they're here for. The Legend of Mellow Johnny. They think I somehow made him be the way he is and should be able to tell them how to make their child be that way too, so they can bottle and sell it. They want to know why my little boy loved his bike, and I wonder, why don't they ask a little boy? Someone who hasn't forgotten that a game is to play, a ball is to throw, a bike is to ride.

Of course, these folks have no more patience for that sort of thing than they do for a carefully arranged swag. They're so busy with their flashbulbs popping over his rock-star status, I'm not sure they even see how beautiful this genuine human being is when he moves—what a great idea God had when He sat down at the drawing board and mapped out how He could make the most of two legs, two lungs, a brain, and His own breath.

On days like today I sit on the embroidered silk dais in my foyer, blinking up into the lights, prepared to give them my best sound bites, even if it isn't always what they want to hear. The producer prompts and coaches, suggesting things for me to say, but I know how to speak for myself. They come looking for Vivaldi. Motown is what they find. I won't perpetuate the myth that a parent's role is to relentlessly drive a child in some direction or other—or that it's even *possible* to drive a child in one direction or another. (There was a time when I truly believed Lance's best hope for prosperity was an associate's degree in computer science, and you'll notice he doesn't have one.) If there is some microwavable recipe for raising a wunderkind, I haven't got it. I won't pretend I do. And I simply reject the belief that certain people are born blessed, predestined, lucky—however you want to say it. We were lucky enough to have it tough, I guess. We were blessed with challenges that forced us to grow. But if there is some cosmic master plan, it didn't cut us any slack. I can't let people look past the blood, sweat, and road rash Lance has invested in his accomplishments (or the brains and hard work I have invested in mine). That would let them off the hook when it comes time to invest the same sort of effort in their own dreams.

The sound crew wires me with a little microphone, and I tuck the battery pack into place.

"Okay, I just need you to say something so we can sound-check," the technician tells me.

"Voice check . . . one two three . . ."

"Got it," nods the producer. "So, Linda. Tell us. How did you do it? How did a single teenage mom manage to raise a real live superhero?"

"Well," I smile my best Donna Reed smile, "I always made sure he had a good hot breakfast."

"Breakfast?"

"Biscuits and gravy usually. Eggs and bacon when we could afford it. Waffles maybe. On special occasions."

"Right . . ."

"No, really. I know it sounds unimportant, but—well, think about it. Instead of sleeping in and then tearing around and rushing out the door, we got up early enough so he could sit down and eat this breakfast I made for him, and we'd talk about the day and what was going on with him and what was going on with me and . . . whatever. We had a hectic schedule. I wanted to spend that time with him. I wanted him to know he was the first and best thing in my day. Every day."

"So he had a healthy diet, structured schedule—but so do a lot of kids. What did you *do* that made Lance Armstrong who he is today?"

Funny. They never ask about what I failed to do. What I couldn't give him. But the truth is, those are the things that made him who he is. The things he had to go out and get for himself. He's a child of necessity, and I'm a mother of invention. That's how we got by. A child doesn't build a life on what you give him. He builds his life on what you show him. The good and the bad. And one of the good things I showed my son was how to climb hills. I can think of no firmer foundation for this soap bubble of fame than the broken pavement of the Dallas projects, where I grew up too fast and brought that extraordinary creature into the world.

This is the value of memory, I guess. Grounding. Perspective. And if you're lucky, understanding.

TWO

BALL OF CONFUSION

I am floating.

I worked hard at spin class this morning, and the notion of this moment—drifting in a pontoon chaise between the wide blue sky and the sky-blue water, tall iced tea in one hand, stereo remote in the other—that's the reward that kept me motivated. I'm pleased with the decision to invest in a backyard swimming pool. A nice one, with rocky landscaping to the side and flowers scattered around the perimeter.

My hippie girlfriend is sitting in the shade.

"If you can't stand the heat," she says, "get out of Texas."

But that Texas heat is part of me. Sometimes I feel like it's radiating out of me into the atmosphere instead of the other way around. It's not so much that I like it. It's just what is, and I tend to be a bloom-where-you're-planted kind of person, so it brings out the iguana in me. I stretch in my chaise with that same kind of sanguine purpose—my muscles mellowing, elongating, absorbing warmth, releasing the vague vibration that still lingers from spin class.

That's just one of the ways in which my hippie girlfriend and I are very different. She's liberal. I'm conservative. She shops the woman's sizes, while I shop the petites. Hanging out with hippies was something I never did when hippies were in their heyday, but it seems like the divisions I used to see between people have faded. Like the wind blows over a line in the sand. I used to be very conscious of who was on which side of the tracks, but this very curious person came into my life a while back, and she seems to fit quite nicely.

"Have you lived in Dallas all your life?" asks my hippie girlfriend.

"Pretty much."

"Where were you when Kennedy was shot?"

"Why do people always ask about that when you say you're from Dallas?"

"I don't know," she shrugs. "Watershed moment. Platform for discussion."

"Seems like we were living in Oak Cliff. Or maybe those terrible apartments over on . . . whatever street that was. Anyway, I was home, watching TV. I was always watching TV. I watched so much TV, you wouldn't believe."

Seems like the lady on *As the World Turns* was dusting a pile of books. There was lots of dusting on that show. Nothing was dusty; it was just busywork that kept a person hovering in the room until the doorbell or telephone rang and an ominous blast of organ music signaled something dire was about to happen.

I don't remember what my mother was doing. Maybe she was looking out the window. Debbie was down in the courtyard, playing with Alan, I think. It was cool and crisp outside, one of those glorious Texas autumn days offered in apology for the dog-mouth days of summer. On a day like this you could open the windows and make the whole house feel cleaner. Like you hosed it down with the fresh air. Somebody outside had a radio on. The Marvelettes were singing, "Oh, yes, wait a minute, Mr. Postman," and the girls out on their balcony joined in, "Way-yay-yay-yate, Mr. Po-wost Man!"

Maybe Mother was looking out because of the sirens. Not your usual sirens that come on and pass by and fade to a far-off mosquito. These sirens stretched out taut across the clear blue sky over downtown Dallas, and they stayed there, not letting go. Maybe she thought the Russians were about to bomb us silly or something. People were always talking about stuff like that.

"And wouldn't this be the day to do it?" some people were saying out in the hall that morning. "Bomb us silly the day Jackie comes to town?"

"Well, I don't know about that," my mother had said, "but I'm not going anywhere today. Traffic's gonna be a nightmare, and I don't even know if they're running my bus."

Debbie and I decided to stay home too. Mother didn't mind either way.

"So long as you be quiet," she told us. "And keep Alan quiet."

She didn't get many days off, and she wanted to enjoy this one, lying on her bed reading stories in the *National Enquirer* about Judy Garland's drug habit and mutant hillbilly children and recent movie star divorces.

But then there were those sirens.

"Oh, no," my mother said in a flat sort of voice. And then the lady who was dusting nothing wasn't dusting anymore. A *CBS News* thing flashed up, and you couldn't see his face, but Walter Cronkite said something about Dallas, and that made Mother kneel down in front of the set.

"Oh, no. Oh, no."

That voice again. Only scarier, because it was cut with tears, and Mother wasn't one to show emotion. They went to a commercial for Nescafé, and she lunged forward to change the channel, but when you did it too quick, the TV died. This wasn't the most mechanically great functioning TV in the world. I kept trying to tell people not to change the channel too quick. And pounding on top of the set like she was doing wouldn't help.

"*Linda!* Linda, do that—that thing you do. *Get it back on!*"

She ran to get a radio. Outside the Marvelettes weren't singing anymore. I went to the set and rubbed my palms together like a safecracker. I was the only one who had mastered The Ritual. Jiggle the knob gently, blow in the vent slots, toggle the on/off switch, then, tapping briskly on the right side of the set, rotate the channel selector one click over, one click back, count to seven, toggle "on." Walter Cronkite appeared. His face folded back and forth like a paper doll, flipped upward a few times, then settled into a snowy but steady image. He played with his glasses, mentioned Dallas again. He said President Kennedy was dead. He didn't say if it was Russians who did it. Later they showed a crowd lurching around the bad guy, and the bad guy sinking into the whirlpool of dark suits.

In the foggy landscape of my childhood memories, Dallas's darkest day isn't all that much darker than the rest of my growing up. Events are disjointed and violent, jumbled together with grainy television images. Grassy knolls, tall buildings, twisted faces. Blood-spattered stockings, my mother crying. She tries to scramble over the back of the car, but my father comes after her. He raises a board over his shoulder, and she begs him not to hit her again. *Hush,* I tell my little sister. We're hiding in a closet. She has Alan tight in her arms. I have a hot iron ready in case our father opens the door. It's hard to separate reality from newsreel. For so many years I tried to forget.

Seems like the TV stayed on for days. A bunch of different men talking in the same deflated tone, except when they played plodding church music and hung a sign in front of the camera: PLEASE DO NOT ADJUST YOUR SET. THANK YOU. Debbie and I lay in bed at night, and the drone of it drifted under our door, along with a shifting, watery glow from the screen.

"Did the Russians kill Jackie too?" Debbie whispered.

"No," I told her. "But they said her beautiful dress and her legs were all covered in blood."

I was usually the one who told the ghost stories in this room and at Granny's house, when we stayed over sometimes with our cousin Susan. Somebody's legs all covered in blood seemed like a good start for a ghost story, but even as a grade school child, I felt the huge, sad inappropriateness of anything other than silence. I wished they'd all just shut up about it. I didn't like the way the announcers kept saying *dallastexas,* as if it was one word—and a bad word at that. As if it was our town's fault instead of crazy Lee Hearty Oz Wall, who was—I was pretty sure—from Cuba, which was practically the same thing as being from Russia, Granny said.

"What'll happen to John-John and Caroline?" Debbie wondered.

"What do you mean?"

"They're like us now. They don't have a daddy."

"We have a daddy."

"He hasn't been around here for a long time," said Debbie. "Maybe he's dead."

"He is not." I rolled over and scrunched my knees up against the achy hollow in my stomach. "He's just drunk."

Two people were arguing down in the courtyard. One person was saying Kennedy deserved to get shot *'cause he was a nigger-lover and a commie-lover*. The other person was crying and saying, *Shut up! You just shut up, you hear?*

"Maybe John-John and Caroline will go live at their granny's house. Do you think they will?" asked Debbie, curving toward me. "Maybe it's better at their granny's house. Maybe they'll be happy there."

"Stay on your own side," I said harshly. I loved my little sister, but she'd been known to pee the bed. Each night, before we settled in, I drew a line down the middle of the coverlet with the side of my hand to show her she couldn't come any closer than that. In the living room the TV was back to some generic announcer, talking over droning funeral music.

The day the World Trade Center fell, someone wheeled a television into the conference room, and we sat in front of the very same talking heads. They were in color now, and we were the ones with the folded gray expressions. My stomach felt as achy and hollow as it did in third grade. I couldn't reach my son. I didn't know where he was. All I knew was when the sky is falling down and the whole world seems like it's on fire, you need to hold on hard to the people you love, and the one I loved most was far away. Somewhere. That thought was making it increasingly difficult for me to keep my brave face composed. Whenever anyone asked me about him, it was all I could do to stop myself from drawing a line down the conference table with the side of my hand. No closer than this, please. I wasn't one to talk about personal things at the office. Especially things that made me want to weep.

~

My mother kept telling everybody for years that Daddy knew Jack Ruby. That he used to go drinking in this place Jack Ruby owned, so he actually knew him. And then the person's eyes would get big and they would say, *Really?* and she would nod importantly and say, *That's right, he sure did. Knew him quite well.* This was as close as she got, I guess, to knowing somebody famous. Being divorced from but sometimes visited by a man who used to drink with someone who assassinated an assassin.

I, on the other hand, had lots of famous friends. Wally, Beaver, and Eddie Haskell, to name a few. (Though Eddie Haskell was more like an acquaintance, really. Not the sort of boy I wanted to be friends with.) Then there was Kitten, Princess, and Bud Anderson and their mother, played by Miss Jane Wyatt. And their father. He knew best. And of course I knew Lawrence Welk and the whole Champagne Music Family. You couldn't help but feel like part of the Champagne Music Family, they were all so kind and beautiful.

"Goodnight! Sleep tight! Until we meet again," we would sing. "Adios, for a bar, I'll be the same!"

"You mean '*auf Wiedersehen,*' " Granny said, but she didn't laugh at us. "It's German for 'good-bye.' Y'all oughta know that. You used to live in Germany, you know. Debbie, you were born there."

Our cousin Susan had the knack for remembering lyrics, so Debbie and I just went "la-la-da-da-dum" until the tag-end part, where we'd shout out, "Good night!"

"You girls watch too much TV," Granny told us. "You'll ruin your eyes."

I started wondering if maybe she was right, because I had to squint or ask to get moved up to see the chalkboard at school. My fourth-grade teacher said I probably needed glasses, but Mother said we weren't the kind to go running off to the doctor for no reason.

"We dealt with enough doctors when you were small," she said, rolling her hair on prickly curlers, stabbing them through with pink plastic picks.

"In Germany?"

"Uh-huh."

"On account of I was deathly sick? And you were so worried?"

"Yup."

"And I was so thin, I almost died of starvation."

"That's right. Legs like chicken bones."

I liked it when I could prod the whole story out of her. How Daddy was in the army after I was born in New Orleans, and the army stationed him in Baumholder. And they had to take me to the hospital on the brink of death, but a handsome young doctor came swooping to my rescue (at least, I imagined he was handsome, in a European version of Dr. Kildare swooping to the rescue kind of way) with his discovery that I was suffering from a rare and virulent food allergy. I liked imagining my parents, clinging to each other, crying over my frail, failing body, pledging to God they would do *anything, anything, anything, only let our baby live!* because they loved me so much.

"I thought I told you to get those clothes hung out," Mother said, stabbing another curler through the heart.

Daddy told it better anyway. He had a slow, round way of pronouncing *N'awlins* that made it sound like a wonderful place to have been born. And instead of bluntly mentioning "diarrhea," he'd say, "You were awful sick on your stomach," which sounded a little more genteel. And then at the end he would look at me with admiration and say, "But you showed 'em, didntcha? You showed 'em how tough you were, huh, little one?"

When Mother told the story, it was usually by way of explanation as to why I had to eat a slice of bologna between two leaves of lettuce instead of having a normal sandwich like most kids. She had a way of making it sound more like her misfortune, even though I was the one who had to put up with the teasing when it came time to crack open my lunch box at school.

"Of course, nowadays they know it as celiac disease," she told Mrs. Pitts, the upstairs neighbor lady. "It's a gluten allergy. Couldn't eat any wheat products at all. But I guess she's finally outgrowing it. Starting to get a little meat on her bones."

I must have looked pretty hearty, because Mrs. Pitts invited me to babysit.

"I've been trying to find someone to come down and stay with Ronnie and Sis and the baby on Saturdays," she said. "Just while I get my hair done. And my nails."

Mrs. Pitts had to look nice for work. She was the secretary to the president at a bank. She said she would pay me ten dollars for babysitting. I could scarcely breathe at the very thought of such wealth.

Arriving at her door the following Saturday morning, I felt very grown-up—which I was, I would have been the first one to tell you. I was almost ten. Almost more than you could count on both your hands. That was something. I knocked boldly, and Mrs. Pitts opened the door.

"Y'all be good for the babysitter, you hear?" she called on her way down the hall.

The smell of burned toast, beer, and dank dishcloth clung like an oily moss throughout the apartment. The living room carpet was stained and reeked of urine. Toys and dirty socks and newspapers littered the couch, coffee table, and floor. Sis was playing with a ratty-haired Barbie on a naked mattress in the room she shared with Ronnie, who sat on an upturned milk crate in the living room. The baby stood in a playpen nearby, nose running, mouth wide open to full howl.

"Hey, there," I said. "How are you today?"

"Baby needs a new diaper," Ronnie said, without glancing up from the TV.

It had been quite a while since Alan was in diapers, but I thought I could remember how to do it. And if I couldn't remember, I could figure it out. Lots of people not as smart as me could change a baby's diaper, I assured myself. No reason why I couldn't do it. So I did it. And then I started cleaning. Not because I felt like I was supposed to, or because I liked Mrs. Pitts so much I wanted to do her a favor, or even because it would be a nice thing to do—for her children, if not for her. No. I did it because I couldn't bear the thought of spending the next several hours in that mess. It made me nervous. I was scared to sit down.

I just never liked things messy. It's something I passed on to my son without even thinking about it. He's not a neat freak. He loved to go out and get grubby as much as any kid, but he didn't want to stay that way once he got home. I had to laugh when he called me from California, complaining that one of his teammates had made some banana bread or something and left the gloppy bowl on the counter.

"How do people live like that?" he harrumphed.

"I don't know," I honestly answered. Truly, I never could stand it. Chaos. That everything-out-of-place feeling—it so pervaded my world when I was a child, I tried to bring order to whatever small spaces I could. My father went to AA after my son was born, and he learned that little prayer of theirs about "the serenity to accept the things I cannot change; the courage to change the things I can; and the wisdom to know the difference." It took me a while to master that accepting thing, and I'm still working on the wisdom, but I can't remember a time when I wasn't hammering away at changing the things I could. I wouldn't have been able to put it into words, but I understood that whenever we improve the world for someone else, we're creating a better world for ourselves. What it comes down to is this: sometimes you find yourself in a mess. It doesn't matter if the mess was made by you yourself or somebody else. You have the same two options either way—sit there feeling bad about the mess or get to work cleaning it up.

What are we gonna do—sit here and throw a pity party? I'd say to myself whenever things were falling apart. I knew I'd be a rusty old skeleton on the side of the road if I waited around for someone else to show up and rescue me.

"Well, look at you!" cried Mrs. Pitts when she walked in that evening. She wandered through the clean galley kitchen to the freshly vacuumed living room and looked in at the bedroom where Sis and Ronnie lay sleeping on clean sheets. "Just look at what you did today. My goodness, angel!" But then her eyes narrowed. "All you're gettin' is the ten dollars, like I said."

"I don't mind," I nodded.

"All right then," she shrugged, snapping open her purse. "I ain't gonna look a gift horse in the mouth."

"Thank you." I accepted the wrinkled ten, smoothed it between my hands, and tucked it in the pocket of my pedal pushers. "Should I come back next Saturday?"

"Oh, I hope to shout!" Mrs. Pitts exclaimed.

Mrs. Pitts understandably felt pretty good about the whole deal. She made it a habit to let her dirty dishes collect around the sink over the course of the entire week, and on Saturday, while the laundry was drying on the line, I stood there and washed and dried them all.

"You're crazy," Debbie bluntly informed me. "Why on earth would you volunteer to do her stinkin' dishes?" But we were both a little impressed with the idea that a person could have so many dishes they wouldn't have to wash and dry them after every meal.

Mrs. Pitts was sad when we moved five or six months later. But that's the way we did things. Mother would get another job, and we had to move closer to where the job was because she didn't do well driving. Packing up was easy enough, because the furniture belonged to the apartment and we just kept our clothes in boxes. Even if we had had dressers, there didn't seem to be much sense in settling in too much. The new apartment never was any better really, and I don't know if the job was any better or not. It was just something else, somewhere other than here.

"So you never lived in a house?" says my hippie girlfriend.

"Nope." And it doesn't take a licensed therapist to figure out that's why it was so important to me that my son live in one.

I do remember one nice place. Brand-new government housing that had just been built. Debbie and Alan and I rolled on the clean carpet and marveled at the pristine white walls, the virgin toilet that gleamed like a Tidy Bowl commercial, the countertops with no rusty water stains or cigarette burns. There was an actual shower above the bathtub, we were thrilled to report to our mother, who was busy putting away pots and pans in kitchen cabinets that still had a wonderfully clean sawdusty smell.

She chased us outside, and we explored the complex. The swimming pool, the little laundry house—even the fresh, undented Dumpster was like something you'd see on a TV show. We inspected the tall bank of mailboxes, unscratched by keys, unmarked by graffiti. Next to each shiny lock was a little nameplate with a neatly typed card tucked in, and we read the names aloud, making up stories about our new neighbors and wondering which apartments had kids our age living in them.

"And we saw another box with Mooneyham on it," Alan told Mother at supper that night.

"What?" She was looking at him funny. As if her food suddenly tasted bad.

"It said 'Mooneyham,' " Debbie said. "Just like us. Do you think they're relations? Do you think they might be our cousins or something? 'Cause if they are, I bet we could get together for picnics . . . or something. . . ." She tapered off when she realized Mother didn't seem too excited by that prospect.

Mother left the table, pulled a sweater on, and walked out the door. When she came back, she told us to pack up our things, which we did wordlessly. It didn't take long. The next morning we moved into an aging tenement a few blocks away. We didn't roll around on the carpet there. It was crusty in places and smelled like cat box. A patched area on the hollow-core door told the ghost story of the anger and brokenness of previous tenants. The pool in the courtyard was half empty, and autumn leaves littered the surface of the green water, which gave me a creepy feeling there was something unthinkable lurking below. All this was easier for Mother to abide than the thought of living a few doors down from that other Mooneyham woman. Turns out the other Mooneyham children were our age, but they were our half-siblings, not our cousins.

At the time I hated my mother for making such an incomprehensible choice. But looking back on it now, having made the unexpected journey that I've made, I understand the oddly crystallized moment when you just say, *This is beyond my limit to endure. If I accept this, I accept the death of my dignity. And if I do that, I'll die.*

At the time my father was still coming around, knocking on our door every once in a while, and Mother would invite him in, remembering, maybe, what it was they once loved about each other. After a while they'd go into Mother's room and shut the door. I'd sit down in front of the TV and turn it up real loud, knowing that when I woke up the next morning my father would be gone and my mother would be sitting there alone, one trembling hand cradling a coffee cup, the other gingerly pressing an ice pack to a split lip or a black eye. I guess the thought of looking out her window and seeing him stumble up the steps of another woman's home was just a little more than her battered pride could bear. Looking back on all the times she crumpled in front of him, I have to admire her for making that small stand. My father probably never knew or cared, but that didn't matter. She did it for herself. And that took guts, because of course everyone else thought she was a fool for turning her back on such a good thing.

~

"And so," I whispered under a blanket tent in Granny's spare room, "the spirit of the slain cheerleader wandered the earth for seven long years. And when she passed by people's houses, a chill went down their spines, because they could hear a faint voice far off in the distance . . ."

Debbie and Alan huddled together. Their eyes widened when my voice went all hushed and spooky.

"Raaaah raaaah sis boom baaaaaaaaaaaaah."

Our cousin Susan wriggled closer, trying to pretend like she wasn't scared.

"And then . . . one night . . . she came out of the woods near the house of a kindly old woman whose four grandchildren lay sleeping in the back bedroom. The ghost of the slain cheerleader wandered across the yard. . . ." I flipped the flashlight on under my chin to make my face look like a jack-o'-lantern. ". . . *Raaaaaah raaaaaaah sis boom baaaaaaaaaah."*

Alan whimpered a little. Debbie tucked him under her wing, always his mother hen.

"She came to the bedroom window . . . *raaaaaaah raaaaaaah sis boom baaaaaaaaaah*. And do you know what she saw?"

They shook their heads, too terrified to blink.

"YOU!"

I lunged forward, and my brother and sister about jumped out of their skin. Susan let out a shriek, and then we all buried our noses in our pillows to stifle the giggling.

"Y'all don't make me walk down that hall!" Granny called from her big recliner in the living room. She was tired from a long day of sewing ladies' dresses, and her size alone made the trip such an effort, we knew she'd be serious if she had to struggle out of that chair and undertake it.

"Yes, ma'am," Susan called, and we scooched close together so we could keep our voices down. "Linda, tell 'The Man with the Golden Arm.' Or how about that one where the young couple is at Lovers' Lane and they hear *scritch-scratch-scritch-scratch* from the trunk of the car?"

"No," said Debbie, "that one's too scary for Alan. Let's do something else. Let's play dress-up."

"No," Susan said sharply. "Y'all aren't allowed to touch my things."

She and Aunt Peggy lived with Granny, and in addition to the special amenities of Granny's house—the pretty towels, the talcum powder—Susan had a double bed that was big enough for all four of us to sleep in, a closet filled with beautiful dresses, and a vanity with a lift-up mirror inside the lid. We could only speculate on the treasures that lay within. From the way she defended it, you'd have thought it was the Ark of the Covenant.

"Weren't you insanely jealous?" asks my hippie girlfriend.

"Oh, no," I tell her. "We loved Susan. And to have a lot of things—that was just foreign to us. It didn't even occur to us that we were entitled. We were just like *shopping*? What's *that* all about?"

Granny made Debbie and me one dress each at Christmas or Easter, and we'd get a pair of shoes at the beginning of the school year. Black canvas tennies, which we wore without socks. After a while those shoes would get so ripe, we didn't dare take them off for PE or anything. In order to wash them, you had to go without shoes for the day, so it was hard to nail down an opportunity to do that. One time I was hanging mine out with the rest of the laundry, and I cut my bare foot on a rusty cable that had fallen from a telephone pole. Had to go get a tetanus shot. It occurs to me now, of course, that a second pair of shoes would have been cheaper than the doctor visit, but that simply wasn't set forth as an option at the time.

Another time Debbie (who was pretty athletic in her day) kicked a kickball and busted out the whole side of her sneaker. She was beside herself. It was barely springtime, and she knew there wouldn't be another pair of sneakers on her feet until school started in the fall. Luckily, Mrs. Rossi, my current babysitting employer, saw what happened.

She was generous enough to get Debbie a new pair of shoes and kind-hearted enough to make her think it was just serendipity.

"Oh, do you know how silly I am?" she said, casually handing them to me. "I bought these on clearance, so they can't be returned, and fiddle if they're not a size and a half too small! I was thinking maybe they would fit your little sister?"

Good, good woman, Mrs. Rossi. One of those great Dallas ladies. She was a shopper. And a smoker—which wasn't thought to be such a bad thing back then. We were used to seeing Lucy light up when she was a full nine months blooming with little Ricky, and he didn't seem stunted in the least by his mother's classy-looking habit.

I kept wondering what I would look like smoking a cigarette. Standing in Mrs. Rossi's freshly scrubbed bathroom, I dropped my eyelids to half-mast and held a ballpoint pen between my fingers, but that really didn't do me justice. I tiptoed to Mrs. Rossi's room, ever so quietly eased the dresser drawer open, glanced over my shoulder at the little girls soundly napping on her bed. I held my breath and nicked a pack of cigarettes out of her drawer, dashing back to the bathroom, my heart pounding in my ears. I watched myself in the mirror, tapping the pack against the side of my hand, just like I'd seen a beautiful colored girl do at the bus stop. I put a cigarette between my lips and Vogued to see which was my better side. I did look kind of like Lucy in that one magazine ad.

"Chesterfields are completely satisfying," I told all my fans. "They're milder. Much milder. They're my cigarette."

There was a little box of matches in a glass bowl on the shelf. I took one out and struck it on the side of the box, listening for any noise from the bedroom before I touched it to the tip of the cigarette. I took a shallow drag and smiled mysteriously. I took another drag and coughed out a little smoke puff, but maintained my classy stance for another moment before I realized how very truly bad it tasted. There was a charred feeling at the back of my nose and flecks of something dry and bitter on my tongue. I stubbed the cigarette out in the glass bowl and immediately regretted that. I threw the cigarette in the toilet and flushed, then scrubbed the glass bowl clean, dried it with toilet paper, and set it back on the shelf. But when I went to toss the toilet paper in to flush it, much to my horror, there floated the almost whole cigarette. It was soggy and bent, and the paper was turning a brownish yellow. I flushed again. It made a few swirling turns and ducked out of sight for half a second, but staunchly refused to disappear.

"Oh . . . oh, *fiddle*!"

I jiggled the handle and flushed again, with similar results. I tossed in the toilet paper and flushed again, hoping the cigarette would be swept along, but it bobbed back up with shreds of Charmin clinging to it. I must have flushed fifty times. That thing would not go down. I caught a glimpse of myself in the bathroom mirror. I didn't look like a voluptuous red-haired sitcom bombshell anymore. I was a stick-thin eleven-year-old with a mouse-brown ponytail, crimson cheeks, and a frantic, guilty face. Not too classy.

Mrs. Rossi's little girls stirred in the bedroom across the hall. There was nothing for it but to fish the heinous object out with my bare hand and—and what? I had no idea. Wrap it in a Kleenex and put it in my pocket? Jam it through the tiny hole at the side of the window screen and hope it landed in the bushes?

I don't even recall what I ended up doing. But I remember learning something at that moment. The things you do in secret don't always want to stay secret. There seems to be some kind of karmic magnet that pulls hidden deeds out into the open. Once choices get made, they don't like to get unmade. They like to hang around and hold you accountable.

~

I made my very first shopping trip to Levine's Department Store. Mother decided it was time for me to have a bra, and I about died of embarrassment, but it was pretty cool to step into this magnificent paradise of retail potential I'd previously been completely unaware of. It didn't take me long to realize that babysitting money could be better spent here than at the 7-Eleven candy counter. It also didn't take me long to figure out that babysitting wasn't quite as lucrative as it might be.

By the time I got into fifth grade, I had expenses. I'd started wearing panty hose on special occasions, and there were only just so many times you could stop a run with clear nail polish before you had to throw them away and buy a new pair. Then there was red nail polish, polish remover, cosmetics, feminine items, the occasional trip to Lonestar Donut with my best friend, Keri Darnell, and of course, Alan's Vitalis. He'd been known to refuse to go to school if he was out of Vitalis. These were necessities. The mother of invention, as they say.

Ambition is a healthy thing. Not the same as greed at all. The love of money is only the root of all evil if you couple it with an unwillingness to work. Honestly, I think wanting—no, *needing*—to earn money set an unquenchable fire in my belly that drove me to be organized, energized, and almost impossible to say no to. I learned to be thrifty. And I was grateful for opportunities to work. There's a part of me that mourns the silly, twittering adolescent I never was, but I know for a fact my future was defined by that drive, that fire. And for that, I'm glad.

Life in general wasn't like the happy black-and-white families I watched on TV—the Donna Reed mother, the father who knew best. But I don't look back with sadness. We colorize and edit our memories as needed—sometimes for excuses, sometimes for strength. And I choose the latter. From every negative, I am determined to extract a positive. I look for the diamond in the Dumpster, the blessing in the bummer. It's my coping mechanism of choice. I can't just squeeze lemonade from whatever lemons come my way; I have to plant the seeds, grow my own tree, start a meringue pie business, and use what's left over to mix myself a Tom Collins.

In Mrs. Pitt's filthy apartment, for example—well, right there's the origin of my firm belief that I can change my world if I'm willing to work hard enough. I consider that a gift. So there's no call for me to look back and judge this woman who was probably doing the best she knew how. Poverty taught me to create my own opportunities. Moving around taught me that change is nothing to fear.

Then there's my mother. She and I are about as much alike as silk and sandpaper, but with motherhood and grandmotherhood in common, we finally began to understand each other. After decades spent suspiciously eyeing each other across a Grand Canyon of hurt and resentment, we've come to a place that's quiet, if not exactly peaceful. She gave me my life, and she gave me the gift of survivorship. I passed that gift on to my son, and as it turns out, my son needed it.

Lance always has a big "carpe diem" celebration on the anniversary of his cancer diagnosis, and that phrase has become a sort of battle cry in his life. *Carpe diem! Seize the day!* Just think about that for a minute. It's not about sitting back and saying, "Well, how nice. Everything turned out peachy keen." No! It's an aggressive act! As angry as it is joyful. It makes me think of the grim determination my mother displayed every single morning just by getting out of bed. Life beat her down and her man beat her up, but by God she was on her way to work Monday through Friday without fail, doing whatever she had to do to seize a day's worth of living for herself and her children.

Lance was riding his bike after his chemo, but he was not winning. He was not joyful. He was being my mother's grandson: getting up every morning and doing something—*anything*—that felt like the opposite of lying down, defeated. The opposite of dying. Because at the heart of grim determination is hope.

I don't know what sort of statute of limitations applies to parental war crimes. I hope it's not too lengthy, because I stumbled and fell many times. Parenthood is humbling that way. At the end of the day I love my mother and daddy. I am who I am because they are who they are. In those moments when I *like* who I am, I'm able to be grateful. And in those other moments, I trust God to forgive us all.

THREE

NOW THAT I CAN DANCE

My hippie girlfriend sits at the edge of the pool, absently kicking her feet in the water. Her legs are heavy and very white. She's not like most of the women I know in Dallas. Most Dallas women are very conscientious about not letting themselves go. We're bona-fide show ponies. We fix up, from grade school to the grave. Won't so much as go to the corner store without lipstick and dangly earrings. My hippie girlfriend never wears makeup, though she does have some pretty big earrings. Today she wears four different kinds of silver dangles that don't match her African-print sundress or each other.

"Do you ever go in Dressing Gawdy?" I ask her.

"Hmm?"

"Dressing Gawdy. That store over on Park Street."

"No, but it sounds great."

"It is," I assure her. "And they have this jacket that's like—oh, sister—this is *the* best jacket in the world. Royal blue suede with a fluffy Sammy dog fur collar."

"Oh, my gosh," she says. "You need to have that."

"You think? I mean, at first I was thinking it would be perfect for that fund-raiser in Calgary. It's a huge deal for cancer research, and Lance is their speaker, and they asked me to introduce him, which gives me a chance to see him, and it's hard to pass up on that. So I thought maybe this jacket with those black pants, which are fitted but not too tight. And then I have these great boots. Black. High heels. But then

I thought . . . well, is this really what people would expect Lance's mother to be wearing?"

"Maybe not, but are you obligated to dress up in the Lance's Mother costume every time you walk out the door? Go get it! You'll be fabulous."

"Oh, I wish I could. I would love to wear stuff like that, but—I don't know. I guess all those years of Corporate Conservative sort of conditioned the Gawdy out of me."

"No way. That's heartbreaking."

"Yup. I couldn't even do casual Fridays. It just wasn't in me."

She splashes over to my floaty chaise.

"Promise me," she says in all seriousness, "that when you exit this pool, you will wrap a towel around yourself and proceed directly to Dressing Gawdy."

~

My mother had a red cloth coat with three big buttons. I thought that was the most beautiful coat ever, and my mother looked beautiful in it. When she wore it, her bold red lipstick was even bolder, and the reddish color of her hair seemed a little less faded. That red coat was so vibrant, so stylish and alive. She must have been feeling pretty flashy the day she bought it. She must have looked at herself in the mirror and felt that flashy shopping trophy feeling. That feeling of *Yes! I found it! It's mine! It was right there waiting just for me.* The day she bought it, she must have had hope. You don't go out and buy a red coat like that unless you feel something good about your life. Years of hanging in the closet hadn't diminished the bright rose blush of the fabric. Not much anyway. It still wrapped its power around her when she put it on, and when she walked out wearing it, she almost looked happy.

Mother worked downtown and knew the importance of presenting herself well. She had a few smart suits, homemade with Granny's help, and a worn pair of dark brown pumps that didn't perfectly match or drastically clash with any of them. Mother didn't specifically teach Debbie and me about putting ourselves together, but we couldn't help but have it rub off on us. She knew the tidiness of a woman's appearance and the properness of her behavior and speech made the difference between working seated at a desk or down on hands and knees. The corporate world hadn't exactly thrown its arms open to embrace women back then, especially uneducated single mothers. If you worked in an office downtown, you were either the secretary or the cleaning lady. It was worth the effort of teasing your hair up like a hot-air balloon, plucking your eyebrows down to nothing, and carefully applying a perfect face every morning in order to remain upright, hands dry, back straight. And no lady I know would have considered this an imposition anyway. Even if you were going nowhere other than the grocery store and post office, why would you *not* want to make the best of yourself? *It doesn't cost anything to have some personal pride,* they would have said. *You present yourself the way you see yourself.* And none of these ladies saw themselves in Business Casual.

Really, when I look back, I see this host of lovely Dallas ladies who so graciously demonstrated to me what a lady should be. Keri's mother, Mrs. Darnell, was divorced, which was a little scandalous, and she was hip enough to provide Keri with the latest records and up-to-date fashions, but still, she was reserved and well spoken and impeccably well groomed. Same with Carol Fagerquist's mom, whose husband drew pictures of beautiful homes being featured in the *Dallas Morning News* real estate pages. Carol was Debbie's best friend, and even though Mrs. Fagerquist was heavyset and a tad on the frumpy side fashion-wise, her manners were genteel, and she was generous about making Debbie feel welcome in their home. There were teachers who were kind and beautiful, mothers who volunteered to teach vacation Bible school at Granny's church every summer, neighbor ladies who hired me to babysit, even women walking down the street. Wherever I went, I noticed, I observed. I learned their gracious ways, their soft speech, charm school carriage, and *McCall's* fashion sense. I absorbed their southern civility. Politeness, grace, dignity. Even most of the poor women I knew afforded themselves the little luxuries like nail polish, lipstick, and earrings that dangled like wind chimes. After all, that's what made a woman of good quality: even if she couldn't afford the best things in the store, she always took full ownership of the best things in herself.

My greatest inspiration—my guiding light, as it were—was none other than the great Gussie Nell Davis—queen mother of all drill teams, founder of the practically world-famous Kilgore Rangerettes, and innovator of their trademark High Kick. Don't laugh. The High Kick was tantamount to doing vertical splits. One had to be limber enough and dedicated enough and consistently well conditioned enough to actually extend the foot directly above the head while keeping knees and ankles hard, legs true to form, perfectly turned out thirty-five degrees from accurately aligned hips. And of course, all this had to be done with a smile so dazzling it could be seen for three counties.

Gussie Nell Davis had a mission in this world: she lived to whip each new gaggle of unruly little girls into a finely honed cadre of precision performers, young women of posture, poise, and self-confidence.

"It won't be easy," Miss Spencer told my mother, "but I think our Linda is up to the task."

Seated stiffly beside her on the cheaply made sofa that came with the furnished apartment, my mother gazed toward the window. She didn't seem put out or anything, just not particularly engaged in the conversation. I pulled a chair over from the kitchen and sat on the edge of the frayed aqua vinyl seat, wishing fervently I'd known Miss Spencer was coming. I'd have used some of my babysitting money to buy Cokes and some little cookies. When my mother opened the door and saw my teacher standing there, she didn't even offer to make coffee.

"I've been so impressed with Linda's dedication to the drill team this year," Miss Spencer went on. "In all the years I've served as adviser, I can't say I've ever seen any girl with more drive and determination."

"Thank you," I murmured, and my mother glanced over at me with an expression I couldn't even guess the meaning of. She wasn't scared of Miss Spencer, that's for sure, and that was a comment on what a formidable woman my mother is. Miss Spencer was tall and athletic with close-cropped hair and dark, hedged eyebrows that matched her severe tone of voice. She was the stereotypical girls' PE teacher who never married, devoting her life instead to the proper maintenance and motivation of young girls' minds and muscles. She wore sharply pressed white blouses and hard-ironed slacks with narrow vinyl belts and creases as sharp as hatchets.

"Now, as I've explained to your daughter, the opportunity to attend Gussie Nell Davis's summer drill team school—well, it's a privilege," Miss Spencer continued. "A privilege and an honor. And it is a prerequisite for serving as drill team captain." She paused to see if anyone had anything to say about that, and when no one did, she continued. "Of course, it wouldn't be appropriate for me to favor one girl over another, but Linda has worked very hard this year. And I have to say, she stands an excellent chance of being captain next year. But as I said—about the drill team school?—it is a prerequisite. So . . . I would need a firm commitment prior to tryouts in April if Linda hopes to be considered for the captain position."

She paused again, but no one else seemed eager to push the conversation forward in the direction it was headed.

"I would need full payment is what I mean," she said. "Prior to April."

"How much is it?" I asked when Mother didn't.

"The tuition is $125," said Miss Spencer. "And then you'd be responsible for your uniform, of course—for the big final performance. And the hat and boots. That's another $95.50. Plus your individual team costume for competition. And you'll need a little something extra for snacks or treats and souvenirs and any personal needs."

There was a long moment of silence. The enormous number seemed to have sucked up most of the air in the room.

"I don't need any snacks or treats," I said. "Or souvenirs either."

A horsefly battered between a box fan and the window screen.

"And maybe . . . well, could I make my own costume?" I asked, trying not to sound like I was begging.

"Hmm." Miss Spencer's hedgey eyebrows scrunched together on her forehead. "I don't think so. It would have to be a perfect match to the other girls. And you'd still have to buy your boots and hat."

"Oh. Okay . . . but what if . . . well, I know some of the other girls don't have much money. Maybe we could agree to wear black shorts and white blouses instead of store-bought uniforms for the individual team competition."

"Yes! Absolutely," Miss Spencer said. "That's an excellent idea. Very thrifty."

We both looked expectantly to Mother, who didn't seem to grasp what we were fishing for.

"Well, I don't mind if she goes or not," she finally shrugged.

"Oh . . . all right. Wonderful. And then what about the, um, commitment?" Miss Spencer prompted gently.

Mother shrugged again.

"If she earns the money, she can do whatever she wants with it."

"I see." Miss Spencer nodded and gathered her purse and car keys from her lap. "Well, Linda, I'm afraid—"

"*No!*" I didn't mean to interrupt, but I wasn't about to let her leave it at that. "I can earn the money, Miss Spencer. I will. I promise."

Miss Spencer started to suggest something about a scholarship, but my mother headed her off at the pass.

"We don't take charity," she sharply reminded me.

When I walked Miss Spencer to the door, I stepped out into the hall and grasped her hand.

"I have almost eight weeks," I told her earnestly. "I can do it. Please keep a place open for me."

She nodded, and for a second I thought she was going to cry.

"A scholarship's not charity, you know. It's something you earned," she whispered stiffly. She cleared her throat and nervously sorted through her keys. "Well. This has been a very nice talk. A $25 scholarship is available in case—well, it's available."

I lay in bed that night, formulating my two-prong earn-and-conserve approach to conquering this Mount Everest of a financial dilemma, trying not to be distracted from immediate concerns by the shimmer of that white captain's hat suspended just above my head. Just out of reach. First, I broke the dollar amount into weekly earning goals and dissected my costs down to the last shoelace and spool of thread.

Then I calculated what I could do without (weekly Coke and doughnut, magazines, cafeteria lunch) and what I couldn't (bus fare, tampons, mascara). Babysitting was not going to cut it. Babysitting and house-cleaning left me at the mercy of people just as poor as we were. I needed a real job. I made a mental journey down Jefferson Street, trying to recall where I'd seen HELP WANTED signs.

Before I fell asleep, I made up my mind to secure employment at a nearby Kentucky Fried Chicken. You had to be fifteen to work there, and I was only thirteen and a half, but a lot of people might actually say "going on fourteen," which I felt placed me within shouting distance of the requirement. Close enough. Besides, I *felt* fifteen, and I knew I could do the job just as well as anybody else.

"That's what really matters, isn't it?" I asked Keri.

"No," she answered me flat out. "There are child labor laws, Linda. There are social security numbers and taxes and things when you have a real job. And have you even thought about what all that greasy steam is gonna do to your complexion? Linda, your pores are gonna open up like—like—well, they're gonna open up! And I read in *Young Miss*, you do *not* want that."

It didn't matter. Whatever it took, it was worth it. I've always been one of those people who'd rather ask forgiveness later than permission up front. Besides which, you can't put a price on your saving grace, and that's exactly what drill team was for me. Drill team channeled all my anger and want and hurt and love and restless, hormone-rife energy into self-discipline and sweat. I came to understand the spiritual tonic of physical movement and came to life inside my skin. I discovered a steel magnolia strength that was somehow different from the simple ability to work hard. We didn't sweat; we glistened. We didn't smile; we beamed. We shined, we gloried, we sparkled.

Isn't it the most uplifting thing to be part of something bigger than yourself? To join together with those of a like mind and strive together toward the common goal? Rusk Junior High School was in the early stages of integration, and there was a palpable contentiousness coming from both sides of the wall separating the races, even as we did our best to tear that wall down. But at drill team, we were equals, allies, and eventually friends. At a moment in time when it seemed like the whole world was all about fighting, drill team was all about unity.

~

The Kentucky Fried manager was either extremely nearsighted or flat-out desperate. He hired me on the spot. I started the following day after school and for the next two months spent my evenings and weekends frying chicken, loading mashed potatoes into little Styrofoam containers, and dragging enormous bags of trash out to the alley, where I could usually sneak a leftover wing or two to the stray cats. At $1.15 an hour, I was in the chips, plus I got to eat a free Drumstick Box dinner every day that I worked. And on days I didn't work I was babysitting and cleaning house for anyone who fit into my new schedule.

It panned out so well, I took it into my head that I was going to get Debbie a job there too. She was taller than me, and we figured we could style her long blond hair in a mature up-do. With full makeup, including a dash of Mom's bold red lipstick, we were confident my boss would believe she was at least sixteen.

"This here's your older sister?" he said skeptically.

"She was born in Germany," I nodded brightly, nudging Debbie forward.

"Is that so?"

"Yes, sir," Debbie said meekly.

I thought about tossing in a peppy *"auf Wiedersehen!"* but decided that might be a bit much.

"Uh-huh." My boss folded his arms across his grease-spattered belly. "Well then, I'm thinkin' y'all musta been in Germany pretty damn recent, 'cause she don't look like she's a day over twelve. So if this here's your older sister—"

"Oh! No—I mean—did I say *older*?" The moment I got a whiff that it wasn't going to fly, it was every man for himself. I started backpedaling. "No, no—she's—I meant to say—you know, I'm *her* older sister actually. Yeah, because—well, I'm just . . . you know . . . obviously I'm much older. I'm just . . . petite."

It's funny how when you've been lying, even the truth feels dishonest. Falsehood is one of those things that blurs the line between what you do and who you are. I have never been a good liar. I'd rather accept the consequences of truth than live with the stress of pretending. Anyway, I'd been going to church with Granny since I could remember. I'd been dropped off every summer for vacation Bible school. I knew it was wrong to tell a lie. But I couldn't figure out what good purpose was served by this stupid rule that shut me out of a job I desperately needed. And they needed me too. I was a hard worker who didn't dare complain about anything. Everybody was happy, despite the fact that all that greasy steam had in fact opened my pores as wide as church windows, just as Keri predicted.

It wasn't Debbie's fault. Bless her heart, she did a nice interview, even though she was trembling like a leaf. And I didn't blame the manager for firing me. He commanded us to sit in a booth, and we cowered there, not knowing if he was back in his office calling the FBI or just getting himself a bucket of chicken. I hoped he wasn't calling my mother. I'd rather face the FBI. He eventually returned and handed me my final paycheck.

$57.62.

I closed my eyes and held it to my heart. It was a fortune, a sweepstakes, a shower of blessings. In combination with the $174.47 I'd already saved, it was a week at drill team school, a pair of white boots, and maybe—just maybe—the white captain's hat. Up till now, I never saw beyond the small folded bill handed to me by a babysitting customer. It was money, delicious and distracting for its own sake. But this was different. I learned that it's what you're working for that makes you want to do a job you don't necessarily love.

"That's right," Granny told me. "That is the truth for sure." She was talking in her sideways way, with a half-dozen straight pins held between her lips. She lifted my arms out straight so she could fit the darts on my new white blouse. "Just like ol' Jacob worked for the woman he loved. Seven years he worked for his uncle Laban so he could marry his daughter Rachel. But on the wedding day his uncle gave him his daughter Leah instead. Poor ol' Jacob had to work another seven years for

Rachel. But it didn't seem like a day to him. He had his eyes on the prize, like the song says."

~

Sometimes it's not what we learn that changes us so much as what we *un*learn. Gussie Nell Davis inspired me to pursue my first seemingly impossible goal and *un*taught me all those self-defeating lessons a girl child picks up in the proverbial school of hard knocks.

"It's not going to be easy," she told us the first day, striding back and forth like a Baptist minister in front of the bleachers, where we all waited breathlessly for her words of wisdom. "But nothing worth anything is easy. If something is important to you, you don't mind working for it. You're glad to do whatever the task demands, because the goal is there in front of you. On competition day, your team may not win the trophy, but if you've done your personal best, you'll personally be a winner! You might not be better than somebody else, but you'll be better than you were when you started. And maybe someday down the road you will be the best of the best!" She stepped back and made a sweeping motion with her arm. "The Kilgore Rangerettes!"

We were instantly on our feet, screaming with the sheer thrill of the idea. The gymnasium erupted in a cascade of applause, cheers, and chanting as the Rangerettes filed in proudly, their captain barking out orders.

At first, all I could see was what I thought I loved about them: sequined hats and fringed boots, frothy confections of big hair, perfectly drawn eyebrows, tapered waistlines, and sculpted bosoms, lifted and separated with technical precision. The idea of being a show pony had always been enough for me. But now somehow—maybe because of how hard I'd worked to get here—I could see for the first time what it takes to be that beautiful. It wasn't a blessing. It was an endeavor. Gussie Nell's kind of pretty couldn't be painted on. It flowed outward from an inner core of pure energy. Before the fifteen minutes it took to put their faces on, there were endless sit-ups and push-ups and chin-ups and laps. There were endless hours of practicing, pulled muscles, dislocations, and sprains. There was the self-discipline Gussie Nell spoke of—the determination, devotion, and teamwork. All that was filling them up to the brim. Makeup was no more the substance of their beauty than frilly curtains are the substance of a good home. But having put in the kind of effort they had to invest in order to be as good as they were at what they did—well, you better believe they wanted people to notice them doing it, and for that you need some mascara.

The Rangerettes moved like a machine. They were choreographed like clockwork and rehearsed to the point that they hummed like an engine. To be one of them was to have your place in a perfectly balanced, three-and-a-half-minute universe—a body set in motion around a rhythmic center of gravity, orbiting, spinning, cartwheeling across time and space. For the length of one John Philip Sousa march, you belonged exactly where you were. I wanted that. With my eyes wide open to what it was going to take to get there, I promised myself I'd have it.

~

Go to any town in Texas, big or small, and you'll see—it's all about the football. A high school football coach can earn more than a college math professor. On any given Friday night you'll find more people in one high school football stadium than in all the theaters combined. And who has the power to bring order to the pandemonium there? Who conducts the noise like an orchestra?

"Why, the drill team, of course!" I told my girls. From the moment Miss Spencer awarded me the captain position, motivation was my mission. "The drill team girls are the most important people on the field. Well, except players, I suppose, but what do you suppose would happen to them if they're supposed to be going for a touchdown and the whole crowd is yelling, '*Defense! Defense!*' on account of, God forbid, we failed to lead them in the proper cheer at the appropriate moment? With that kind of confusion going on, somebody could get seriously injured. Paralyzed from the neck down!"

I let them absorb that for a moment while I settled my sequined captain's hat, feeling the weight of awesome responsibility right down to my made-for-walkin' boots. I was a strict taskmaster, but a kind one. I expected total devotion from the entire Rusk Junior High Drill Team, but I was sympathetic and motherly when someone sprained her ankle or jammed her thumb or had cramps due to her monthly visit from Aunt Flo. I'd give her an ice pack along with a Gussie Nell–style motivational talk about why we were here and what it meant to be part of something greater than yourself.

"We're not in it for ourselves," I reminded them. "We're here to support the Rusk Rams to victory! To inspire loyalty and school spirit in the hearts of our fellow students!" I lifted my silver whistle to my lips and shrilled them to their starting positions. The girls straightened their ranks and raised their chins. "Step! Step!" I called. "Left, right, left!"

The last day of camp, there had been a huge competition. The Rusk Rams drill team marched out in white blouses and black shorts. So what if the other teams had spangled costumes? What we lacked in dazzle we'd make up for with razzle.

"We've worked as hard or harder than anyone," I told my girls. "We deserve to win!"

Waiting for our music to begin, I searched the stands for my family. Squinting into the afternoon sun, I saw Debbie sitting with some friends, but Mother wasn't anywhere near her. I saw Miss Spencer, giving us a signal that meant "Smile!" I saw the parents of all my friends who were on the team.

Our music started, and we gave it our heart and soul. I remember feeling elated about the performance, but I don't recall what the final results were. Seems to me we won. Or placed, at least, because I remember marching out on the field again for the presentation of the awards. Miss Spencer came and joined us. There was a tidal wave of applause and cheering from the bleachers. I searched the stands again, but my mother wasn't there.

Funny, isn't it, how a whole grandstand full of applause can't drown out the silence of one empty chair. You can glitter and shine all over the place, but sooner or later your heart has to go home.

~

Having my own money made me bold. I liked feeling like I was in control of my own destiny. No one could tell me what I could have or not have. If I was willing to work hard enough, I could get anything I wanted. And what I wanted more than anything was freedom. My mother and I fought over everything. We fought over who had to do the dishes. We fought over anything I said that sounded fresh. We fought over the length of my skirts and which channel was on TV. But most of all, we fought about Fernando.

Of course, as drill team captain, it made sense for me to be dating the captain of the football team, and completely independent of that social mandate, Fernando Garcia was the love of my life. He was handsome and sweet, raised in a large, boisterous Catholic family. His mother didn't speak English, but that didn't stop her from having animated conversations with me. She'd taught Fernando to be such a lovely gentleman. More than anything I wanted to marry him and be the mother of a big, boisterous Catholic family.

I don't remember exactly what Mother had against him. I've done my best to check those specifics along with the rest of my emotional baggage. Whatever reasons she may have given at the time are lost among all the other negative, suspicious recriminations she screamed at me and all the dramatic, adolescent recriminations I screamed back at her. Seems like every fight ended with her voice on the other side of a slammed door.

"You're going to get yourself in trouble, Linda Gayle Mooneyham!"

But she never really went into detail about what sort of trouble "trouble" was, how to avoid it, or what one could do to remedy "trouble" if one actually did get herself into it.

Fernando and I talked on the phone every day. We walked hand in hand to and from the cafeteria. We didn't have the wherewithal to actually date much, but one night his big brother took us to a James Brown concert.

That was my kind of energy. *Git up offa that thang!* energy. The whole place went crazy. Toward the end of the show Fernando stood behind me and put his arms around my waist. I leaned back against him and swayed to a slow but intense rendition of "It's a man's man's man's man's woild."

Fernando saw me to the door, kissed me chastely, and went down the stairs to his brother's car. I jiggled my key in the lock and opened the door. There were boxes stacked on the kitchen table and floor.

"No . . . we cannot be moving," I said. "Mother, no! We are not moving!"

She didn't look up from her box of pots and pans.

"*Why,* Mother? Why do we have to move? I just got captain! I'll be letting Miss Spencer and everybody down. I have my babysitting job and friends and—"

"And what? That *boy*? I told you I wasn't going to stand for that anymore! I don't want you seeing him. I don't want you at the same school as him. I know what you're doing, Linda Gayle Mooneyham, and I'm not going to stand idly by while you go out and *get yourself in trouble*."

There was nothing I could say. I could have said, "I hate you," and meant it as much as any fourteen-year-old ever has, but I knew better than to open my mouth. I would have started crying, and no way was I going to let her see me cry. I just stood there, silently declaring my independence over and over and hoping she could see it blazing in my eyes. I stalked to my room with my head held high and my goal clear as Mount Rushmore in front of me. Someday she wouldn't be able to tell me what to do. I was going to have a car and not take the bus. I was going to have my own house and never move again. I was going to plant trees and watch them grow tall enough for tire swings, plant gardens and stay long enough to see the roses. I was going to have beautiful children and build them a solid brick house, instead of giving them a cardboard-box life that didn't feel like life at all—only bleak, wandering existence.

I was going to be rich and beautiful and strong and free. I was going to be a *Kilgore Rangerette*!

~

Adolescents get a bad rap, if you ask me. Think about the formula jokes that crop up when you say you're the parent of a teenager. "Oh, whoa—better lock them in their rooms till they're thirty," and da-da-da. I hate that. What's so terrible about not wanting someone else to control your life? And what's so terrifying about letting your child steer his or her own course to a certain extent? Frankly, if you can't trust the kid when he's sixteen and wants to borrow the car, then you haven't done a very good job fostering a trusting relationship before that day. Seems like we're always yelling at them, "Control yourself!" but all the while we're working so hard at controlling them, they hardly get the chance.

I suppose I could have exercised a little more control over my son, and I'm sure there were people—from the high school principal to the local police—who wished I would, but I remembered how I reacted when people tried to control me. It didn't go well.

However, I also remembered how the structure of drill team—the goal-setting and the physical exertion of it—kept me on an even keel. I wanted to help my son inhabit his body that same way. Remembering how I searched the stands, hoping to see my mother at that drill team competition, I sat in the stands at every swim meet—and strong-armed other parents into staying there with me so Lance, who was always in the very last event, would have a cheering section.

We try to reparent ourselves sometimes, don't we? What was missing from our own childhood, we're determined to create in the life of our child. Sometimes it's the simplest little things. A hot breakfast. A familiar face in the crowd. But a happy childhood is the sum of all those small moments. All those little things that add up to love.

FOUR

PAPA WAS A ROLLING STONE

Okay, I take it back.

Eddie Haskell *was* the sort of boy with whom I could be friends.

More than friends. Because, let's face it—Eddie Haskell was cool. He was edgy. He was a rebel, a walk on the wild side. He was funny and dangerous and didn't care what anybody in authority thought he should or shouldn't do with his life and times. The Eddie Haskells of this world are usually handsome in the most devilish sort of way. And they always drive hot cars, which they stand around discussing on street corners with other devilishly handsome boys and a stringer of female admirers.

Best of all, Eddie Haskell was the exact sort of boy my mother did not want me to become involved with, which enhanced him with the delicious perk of driving her crazy. He was the sort of boy who had the potential to get a girl "in trouble," no matter what sort of shady definitions you assigned that term. And maybe—looking back on how it broke my heart to leave Fernando behind—maybe he was the sort of boy I knew I wouldn't mind losing. Maybe I figured that if love was always a prelude to pain, it would be less painful if I felt less love.

When we moved into the second-floor apartment on Zang Street, I felt like I'd descended into hell. The building was in serious need of an exterminator, and the windows had been painted shut, which turned the rooms into ovens late in the afternoon. Our apartment was built like a Motel 6. Four buildings set in a square with a courtyard in the middle. Each building was two stories high. Your door would open to a breezeway that went across and led to a stairway that took you down to the parking lot.

On the other side of the courtyard, Eddie Haskell lived in an apartment with his mother and an older sister, who was a student at Baylor. He had another big sister who was married with two tiny boys, and when she came to visit, it was like a movie star was coming to the neighborhood. Just like in the gossip magazines when the paparazzi hide in the hedges and photograph the perfectly put-together actress who's just become a mother, and the baby is dressed in starchy ruffled twosies and glowing with chubby Buddha smiles and the actress's fresh blouse is protected by a perfectly white receiving blanket over her shoulder. She wears sunglasses and has a bobbing ponytail, and everyone comes out to meet her; they coo at the baby and tell her how beautiful she looks, how it's taken her no time to get her figure back, and how she looks so rested—the baby must be sleeping like an angel. Everyone makes a fuss, showing her to a chair by the pool, arguing over who gets to hold the baby, and even someone like Eddie Haskell is suddenly reduced to *ga-gas* and *boo-boos* and sweet babblings, tweakings, and extraordinary gentleness.

I probably wouldn't have even noticed Eddie except Alan and I were coming home with groceries one day and saw the building manager and two policemen yelling at him and his friends for starting a fire out behind the Dumpster. He always seemed to arrive at the pool shortly after I did in the evening, and then he'd be goofing around, doing cannonballs and pretending to fall off the diving board and floating facedown like a dead man for as long as he could stand it just to see if anyone would care enough to check and find out if he was actually dead, which no one ever did.

School started shortly after we moved in, and everyone at the new school hated me. I wasn't part of the established crowd. I couldn't find a job, so I didn't have money for decent school clothes to start my sophomore year, and I know every high school girl in America will stand behind me when I say that is a much bigger deal than you think it is. It was *demoralizing*. Did you ever think about that word? It's like an attack on your ability to even *hope*.

I'd taken a harsh step down from my secure position in the social pecking order, which is tough territory to carve out and defend. Talking to Keri on the phone just made it harder. She was still with her perfect boyfriend, and her dad was going to buy her a car for her sweet-sixteen birthday, and everyone at drill team said to say, *"Hey!"* and homecoming court had just been announced, and *if only you'd still been there, Linda!* Keri was certain I would have been royalty. I'd hang up the phone, and if my mother said so much as one word to me about anything, I'd go in the bathroom and lock the door. I couldn't stand the sound of her voice. The stench of her home perms. The rattle of pages as she lay in bed, reading the *National Enquirer,* and the rattle of her breathing after she fell asleep.

Seems like I never had this much trouble making friends before. I was always just naturally friendly, and that tends to come back to you with happy returns, but the cool kids were completely uninterested in my attempts to chat them up. I did manage to start a conversation with a stoned-out girl in the cafeteria one day, and she invited me to a party, which, as it turned out, would be my whole experience with the psychedelic sixties. Black lights, strobe lights, Grateful Dead posters, pot. I thought it would be a fine way to show my mother what's what, but the truth is, that druggy stuff always scared the fool out of me.

"Y'all!" I exclaimed. "This is *illegal*! The cops could come and take us to jail!"

They all got a big hoot out of that, I'm sure.

~

My father went off to Vietnam, and like the song says: "All he left us was alone." It was a relief, honestly. The jungle he went to was no more tangled than the love–hate relationships he'd forged here at home. He wasn't around much anymore, and when he was I was just holding my breath, praying he'd go away again. He said things that made us uncomfortable, used the *n*-word freely, and told me in common language that the reason he and Mother got divorced was because she wasn't enthusiastic about doing her conjugal duties. (I guess it hadn't crossed his mind that his beating her, abandoning us, and getting another woman pregnant may have had something to do with it.) It was easier for me to love him when he was far away, in a place that only existed on television. Like Brigadoon, it became real only once a day, during the six o'clock news, then vanished back into a dream world. Once he crossed over to that side of the glass, I could imagine anything I wanted to imagine about his life offscreen. With no real-life daddy to come around and mess things up, I could create a Vietnam daddy, filling in the blanks with acts of heroism and wistful longing for the children he loved.

I wrote to him every week, telling him about my boyfriends and babysitting customers, what I bought at Levine's Crazy Days sale, where I was going on Friday night.

Dear Daddy,

How are things at the war? Things are fine here. I have set a goal for myself. I am going to get on the JC Penney Teen Board. You get to wear the newest JC Penney fashions right the minute they come in. You get to have your picture in the paper too. Also you can get a job at JC Penney if you want to and I do. Well, take care of yourself, Daddy. I love you.

Love, your daughter Linda

I never heard back from him, but he did send Alan a photograph. One of those old black-and-white squares with the scalloped edges. I still have it tucked in a photo album, though I don't remember when I swiped it from my brother. In the photo, my father stands in a clearing, looking very handsome and heroic. Even in the humid tropical environment, he has his suavely swept-back Daddy hairdo. "To Alan: Congratulations on a good report card" it says on the back. Peering through this little window into my father's dark jungle world—well, I missed him. I didn't see him any less than when he was living just a few blocks away, but this was a different kind of gone.

Autumn turned cool. The only coat I had was my drill team jacket from junior high, and wearing it was apparently some kind of capital crime. Once the scent of that blood was in the water, the sharks were circling the moment I got on the bus every day. After a while I decided it would be easier to get up early and walk.

I was just turning the corner at the top of the stairs one morning when I heard a voice over my shoulder.

"Look out! It's that Mooneyham girl!" Eddie Haskell called, and punctuated this with some kind of caterwauling howl.

When I saw who it was, I rolled my eyes and kept walking.

"Hey, Linda," said Eddie, falling into step beside me. "How are you today?"

"Fine, thanks. Good-bye."

"Can I carry those books for you?"

"No thanks. B'bye now!"

"You know, I been thinking—in view of the fuel crisis confronting our nation, I think it's our civic duty to carpool whenever possible, so"—he made a broad-armed gesture that was more goofy than gallant—"I'd like to offer you a ride in my luxury automobile to the destination of your choice."

"No thanks."

"We could blow off first period and go over to Norma's," he said. "I'll buy you some breakfast. Doughnuts and coffee. What d'you say?"

"I say *no.* Thanks."

"Suit yourself!" Eddie shrugged.

He swung his leg over the rail, slid down to the sidewalk, and took off toward the parking lot. I came around the bottom of the stairwell just in time to see him screech a Y turn out into the open. And I know I'm terrible, but . . . well . . . he had a *really* nice car. I'd seen him and his friends tinkering with it on my way to and from babysitting jobs, but never once did it occur to me that it actually belonged to him.

I stepped off the boulevard, so he could coast alongside me as I walked.

"Sure you won't reconsider the ride?" he called.

"I don't know. Maybe."

"Like my car?"

"I don't know. Maybe."

"Nineteen sixty-eight Pontiac GTO." He proudly revved the engine. "Tight 400 V-8 with YS code engine, his-and-hers shifter, hideaway headlamps, factory stereo eight-track plus a CB to keep track of ol' Smoky, rally II wheels, dual exhaust with chrome tips (as you can see there), PB, PS, rally clock, G77 x 14 wheels on the ground, and look here—that's a factory-installed edge guard, which is rare!"

"Oh . . . cool." I nodded as if I actually understood or cared about any of that.

"And! Look. Look at this here." He reached over to the passenger seat and reeled the seat belt in and out. "Always with your safety in mind, madam."

"Good to know," I smiled.

"Yup," he smiled back. And he had a great smile.

"You have a very nice car."

"Nice? *Aaagh!*" He clutched his chest as if he'd been tomahawked through the heart. "*Nice*, she says. Like I bought it off a little old lady who only drove it to church on Sundays."

"Yeah, I think that was my granny," I said. "She decided she needed something with a little more get-up-and-go."

"Oooh! Okay now, girl, that's unnecessary roughness! That's what that is."

For some reason it made me feel delicious when he laughed. It had been quite a while since I'd had a conversation in which participants actually laughed. Leaning toward the window, I looked him in the eye to make sure he wasn't stoned on drugs or crazy or anything. He had great eyes too.

"Hop in," he said. "I'll take you wherever you want to go."

I glanced back to the apartment building to see if my mother was looking out the window, hoping in a less than gracious corner of my heart that she would be.

"Straight to school," I said. "I'm not going anywhere else with you."

"Straight to school. Scout's honor."

"Oh, you're a Boy Scout, are you?"

"Be prepared! That's my motto," he grinned and held up an eight-track tape. "*Voilà!* Brand-new Aretha Franklin tape here. And I know you love Aretha, 'cause I was watching you dance while you hung up the wash the other day."

"So you were spying on me, huh?"

"Yeah, I was," he said seriously. "You're pretty easy to look at, you know."

I stepped back from the window and shifted the weight of my books in my arms. Eddie hopped out, slid across the hood, and had the passenger door open for me by the time I got there.

"Your chariot awaits, m'lady," he said with an expansive coachman's gesture.

What is it about the Eddie Haskells of this world? Every woman I know has at least one she keeps tucked between the pages of her memory. Our ability to think of them without cringing hinges on our willingness to keep the moments when we loved them and let go of the times they made us cry.

~

Having a steady boyfriend with a fast car didn't hurt my standing in the caste system of W. H. Adamson High School. Eddie wasn't one of the in-crowd by any means, but that's what was so perfect about him. He was this off-the-wall guy none of the cheerleaders or drill team members would have dated in a thousand years—a mysterious outsider with just enough hair to be hip and just enough cool to be socially acceptable.

I started working at JC Penney after school and made good on my ambition to get on the JC Penney Teen Board. By the end of second semester I was wearing the newest clothes in the catalog and even had my picture in the paper. By the time drill team tryouts came around at the end of the school year, I was in full-on Rangerette mode: bright, perky, impeccably well groomed, and ready to mow down anyone who stood between me and a pair of white fringed go-go boots.

Eddie didn't feel like celebrating when I told him I made drill team.

He was preoccupied with end-of-semester exams and his search for a summer job that would provide enough money for gas and Jack-in-the-Box and still leave him plenty of time to party. But Eddie's mother threw her arms around me.

"Congratulations, Linda! I'm so proud of you!" She beamed. "You deserve this. I know how hard you worked."

"Thank you, Miss Mamie," I beamed right back.

Eddie's mother, it turned out, was one of his best qualities. I loved sitting at her neatly set dinner table, which always had candles or flowers or a seasonal centerpiece. I loved hearing her talk with Eddie's sisters, asking them about their day, laughing at their stories, enjoying their little victories and commiserating over their little woes; she listened to them in a way that seemed like she was completely interested in every little thing. I loved having her treat me the same way she treated them. Special. Worth caring about.

That summer Eddie and I did a lot of riding around. Cruising the downtown Dallas drag until the dizzy edge of curfew, we let the hot wind and loud music blow through the GTO's wide-open windows. It felt so good. It felt so free. I hardly recognized myself without that tight feeling across the top of my forehead. Is it any wonder that along about August we started thinking we were in love?

Sometimes when my hippie girlfriend talks about sex, she calls it "human comfort." I like that image. And I so very much understand that need. To be held, to be known. Comforted. Transplant that childlike need into an almost adult body; add hormones and stir; bake in the dry heat of a Texas summer night. If that's not a recipe for disaster, I don't know what is.

~

The trouble with being crowned homecoming princess is the way they jab the bobby pins in to make the tiara stay on. It's been known to draw blood. But I didn't mind that one little bit. No pain, no reign. Besides, it took my mind off the blisters on my heels from the incredibly uncomfortable shoes I'd gotten off the clearance rack at Levine's. I climbed into the back of a convertible alongside the captain of the football team, cupped my hand in a princess wave, and smiled, smiled, smiled—just soaking up that stadium full of applause.

The only fleeting shadow on my dazzling moment in the sun was the fact that I had no date for the homecoming dance. Eddie had been suspended a week or so before.

"*What?*" I choked when he told me. "What for?"

"For exercising my constitutional rights as a citizen of the supposedly free country of the United States of America, man! For protesting the unjust killing of millions of innocent people and babies in Vietnam!"

He went on about that sort of thing for a bit and finally came to the point that he had joined up with some people from his English class and put together an impromptu peace rally—as if any of them could have found Vietnam on a map—and it had ultimately gotten horribly out of hand.

"So we're all sitting there in the hall," he told a group of slack-jawed hangers-out who were gathered around his car that afternoon. "And we're like, 'Power to the people! Down with the war pigs!' And Patty's playing guitar and singing 'Blowin' in the Wind,' and this one guy comes flying down the stairs with the flag from Mr. Bayless's room, and Bayless the Phallus—oh, man!—we can hear him yelling from the third floor, and he's trying to run after this guy, but he's so fat—he's like *wuf-wuf-wuf!*" Eddie demonstrated the lumbering gait complete with puffed-out cheeks and crossed eyes. "And he looks like he's about to have a heart attack, right? He's like hanging on the railing in the stairwell, yelling, 'You're gonna see detention for this, ya hoods!' and, 'If you think this isn't going on your permanent record, you better think again!' And the one guy shoves the flag in the trash can, and one of the girls whips out a can of hairspray and like sprays all over it, and I take my lighter—"

"Eddie, you did not!" I wasn't laughing with the rest of the crowd.

"Oh, I did, girl! And—and *whoosh!* It goes up like a—a—I don't know, man! It was just like *ka-whoosh!* And there's smoke all goin' up the stairs, and Patty and Sherry Anne are tryin' to sing, but we're all chokin' our lungs out, and finally Bayless wallows down the stairs and he pulls it out of the can and throws it on the floor, and it's totally flaming now—I mean the thing is *engulfed* in flame—and it's making this huge black spot on the floor, and he's cussin' and goin' nuts, because he wants to stamp out the flames, right? But he can't stomp on the flag of the United States of America, right? So he's—he's—"

This was just so funny that Eddie couldn't even speak to tell us the end of the story, which was that he would not be welcome to return to classes until after Christmas. He slumped onto the hood of the car beside me and just laughed himself breathless, along with everybody else, including Patty, who was wearing a bleached muslin peasant blouse that left very little to the imagination, as the fabric was really too sheer to be worn without proper undergarments.

I disengaged Eddie's arm from my shoulder and turned to face him.

"You are no kind of American," I stated icily. "You are no better than a Communist or—or a hippie or a—a I don't know what! And I have never been so ashamed for anybody in my life!"

"Oh, c'mon, Linda," he grinned up at me with his souped-up GTO grin. "Think of it as a pep rally—only for Southeast Asia." He got a big laugh with that.

"Well, pardon me, Eddie, but I just don't find that very amusing. My father is in Vietnam defending that very flag at grave risk to his own health, safety, and personal appearance this very moment. And he's not doin' it so a bunch of lazy, ungrateful tick hounds with no school spirit whatsoever can burn it and disgrace our nation. He is over there safeguarding *your* freedom, Eddie Haskell! Your *freedom!*"

"You're right," said Eddie. "So I guess I better not waste it." He took my hand and tugged me toward the curb. "C'mon. Let's go for a ride."

"In addition to which, homecoming is a week from tomorrow, and there is a strong likelihood that I could be crowned princess. I've already been nominated to the royal court, and I happen to know that virtually everybody in marching band is voting for me. And now I don't even have a date, because my boyfriend is suspended for burning our nation's flag? How does *that* look, do you suppose?"

"I don't give a flyin' f——. I mean, *geez*—you know I can't stand that rah-rah shit."

"Fine," I said, gathering my things to go. I turned on my heel and made what I thought was an effective exit.

"Fine! Be that way!" he called. "Walk home! See if I care."

"Fine!"

"Don't expect me to come after you!"

"Don't!"

I didn't even have to look over my shoulder to know he was already ambling across the lawn.

"Linda, wait!"

When he caught up to me, he took the books and jacket from my hands and put his arms around me.

"C'mon now. Don't be mad," he whispered. "I'm sorry I screwed up your big night. But I know you're gonna be crowned princess anyway, 'cause everybody knows you're the most beautiful girl in Dallas, Texas. Those other heifers are fifty miles of bad road compared to you."

"Be nice," I giggled. "They're my friends."

"I'll be nice," he promised very softly right behind my ear. "I'll be nice to you, and you'll be nice to me . . . and we'll cruise over to 7-Eleven, get ourselves some Cokes, and we'll just have our Cokes and drive around for a while, and then . . . who knows? Maybe we'll find someplace to pull over for a while and enjoy a little life, liberty, and pursuit of happiness."

We were dancing to the slow music of the easy autumn breeze. Somehow I hadn't even noticed when he started to sway me.

"C'mon, Linda," Eddie whispered against my neck. "You know what they say: Make love, not war."

~

After my coronation lap around the field, I got into my drill team uniform for the game. Out on the sidelines, I was greeted with that particular timbre of squeal that only comes from the throats of teenage debutantes. I'd cultivated a perfect posse for myself. The drill team girls were the prettiest, most popular girls in school, and none of us took that lightly. We felt it was our responsibility to set a good example for those with less social savvy. Being on drill team was almost, if not definitely, just as important as being on the JC Penney Teen Board. It was up to us to provide leadership and fashion trends, not to mention decorations and themes for all the dances, including the homecoming dance, which I was now going to be attending *stag*, if you can imagine.

"Linda Gayle Mooneyham!" Missy and Pru embraced me, blinking back tears of joy. "We just *knew* you were going to be crowned princess!"

"Oh, no," I replied in all modesty. "I just *knew* it was going to be Brenda Carnahan!"

"Brenda? Hardly!" sniffed Ray Jean. "Didn't you hear? She got expelled last week."

"Expelled? What for?" I asked warily. "Did it have anything to do with a . . . a demonstration?"

"Oh, God, no," said Pru. "She wouldn't be caught dead with those roaches. No, she was, um . . ."

She glanced over her shoulder, then drew the letters P-G in the air with a manicured index finger. The other girls let out a shrill giggle and clapped their hands over their mouths.

"I don't know who she thought she was fooling with those bulky sweaters," Missy said. "For goodness' sake, it was almost a hundred degrees outside. Then she threw up at Lou Ann's slumber party the morning after Halloween and tried to pretend it was just on account of drinking too much the night before."

"Anyway, I heard she was going to go to some special school over in San Antonio. Some church school for wayward girls where they help you get your GED and find a nice church family to adopt the baby."

"You know what I heard," Ray Jean said darkly. "Charlene told me Liz said Wanda overheard Brenda in the girls' bathroom telling Patty she intended to—well, you know."

"*Get rid of it,*" Pru whispered.

"I could never do that," I said, and I wasn't lying. This was 1970, remember. Abortion wasn't safe or legal or even sanitary, and the very thought of it made me feel sick inside. Having heard only a few hushed horror stories about the barbaric procedure involved, I was positive such a thing would forever separate a person from God and humanity. I'd heard about a girl who bled to death in the bathtub and another girl who went insane and had to go to the nuthouse afterward, which made the first girl seem lucky. How could a girl live, after all, without feeling forever alienated from her own body and her own soul and any future she might have imagined for herself? That vague term "in trouble" took on every sort of horror in my imagination, bolstered by urban legends and cafeteria mythology but very little actual information.

Ignorant is not the same thing as stupid, you know. I was a smart kid. And I've had a lifelong habit of collecting information and putting it into action. But I had no information when it came to adult behavior and relationships. No information was made available to me. I was too shy to ask questions—even if I'd known what questions to ask—and no one was volunteering any explanations. Except Eddie. And it turns out there were a few vital elements he'd left out.

Later on, frantically doing the math over and over in my head, I tried to figure some way to keep my secret. December, January, February, March, April—maybe I wouldn't be showing that bad by the end of the school year. I made a mental note to stay away from bulky sweaters. The JC Penney spring catalog was full of smock dresses, peasant blouses, and empire waistlines. That helped. And Debbie had all those baby-doll tops with the poofy sleeves, shirred bodices, and billowy embroidered fronts. Those were good for obscuring any trace of a waistline. Maybe people would just think I was fat. If I could make it to the end of the school year without being expelled, maybe no one would notice when I didn't come back in the fall. They'd think I just moved away again. They'd think I was still a princess somewhere else.

~

Rumors started flying right around Valentine's Day. Juicy stories about the homecoming princess were passed around the springtime parties with the stuffed tomatillos and Frito pie. By March my sugar-cookie-perfect circle of friends had crumbled, and I was ostracized. A scarlet woman.

Eddie's mother was generous and supportive. My mother was . . . not.

I put off telling her as long as I could, and when I did tell her, my heart was pounding in my throat. She just sat on a chair in front of the vanity table, wearily dragging rollers from her hair, and for a long time she didn't say anything. The mirror needed resilvering at the edges. The scratchy patches faded into the gray of her complexion, leaving very little of the reflection I used to watch with such fascination as she applied her lipstick and eyeliner.

"Did you hear what I said?" I finally asked her.

She dragged the last roller away from her forehead, leaving a stiff tube of hair that would become a teased-up froth of bangs when she was done.

"Mom, I said I'm gonna have a baby."

"No," she said quietly. "No, you're not."

"I went to the doctor, Mom. He said I am."

She just shook her head.

"No."

"He said I'm almost three months—"

"*No.*" She pushed back from her vanity table and walked toward me. "No, no, *no, you're not!* Do you hear me? *You are not having a baby.*"

"I *am*, Mom. There's nothing you can do about it!"

Debbie sat on the floor in the hallway with her knees hugged up to her chest. I heard her make a small sound when my mother came toward me.

"Well, there's something you can do about it, Linda, and I suggest you go on out and get it done or you can find yourself someplace else to live."

"Mom, you don't mean that. . . ."

"I told you this would happen! I *told* you not to let—" She shook her head, her mouth clenched and thin at the edges. "I knew you'd end up in *trouble.*"

She opened the closet and took out her brown suit. I thought I saw her hand linger for just a moment by the old red coat, but then she pushed it aside. This wasn't the sort of weather for it.

I stood there, listening to the even clicking of her footsteps down the hall, and each step sounded like *No*.

No.

No.

That tiny word, I've come to realize, is what makes up the enormous difference between my mother and me. By the time we stood facing each other in the narrow hallway of the shabby apartment on Zang Street, she'd had all the *yes* beaten out of her, all the hope and possibility starved from her heart. I don't think she really thought about what she was telling me to do. I'm not sure she had any concrete idea about how it would actually happen. I think she was just overwhelmed at the idea of another mouth of feed. And that didn't leave any room for what *could* happen. All she could see was what couldn't, shouldn't, mustn't.

But I could feel a whole new world growing inside me, and the potential for joy eclipsed any inkling of the potential pain or hardship. Given the choice—to undo the possibility of this life or leave home—I decided to leave.

~

I also decided Eddie was going to marry me. We *had* to get married. Isn't that the meaning of the expression "had to get married," after all? You *have* to, because—well, you just do! Miss Mamie backed me up, and Eddie didn't resist. He'd been wearing the same stunned expression for several days. Seems like all he could do was nod grimly whenever I tried to enlighten him with another wonderful aspect of my developing plan for our new life together.

The vacant apartment right across the courtyard from his mom's place. The HELP WANTED sign at the Kroger store. The half-price crib I was going to put on layaway for just three dollars a week.

"I'm gonna have a girl," I told Debbie as we stood in front of Levine's, looking at a display of little fairy princess Easter dresses.

"How do you know?" she asked.

"Oh, I just know," I told her with a womanly sort of confidence. "She's going to be a perfect baby. And she'll grow up to be a lady—but nobody's fool. And I'm gonna name her Erica. Like Erica Kane on *All My Children*."

"But Erica's horrible!" Debbie exclaimed. "She's mean!"

"She's not either," I argued. "She just does what she has to do. She overcomes all obstacles! She knows what she wants, and she's not afraid to go after it. Sometimes people just don't understand her. She's very complex."

"She's mean to Tara, and she's always wearing shirts that show her cleavage," Debbie said. "All the guys on the show drool over her all the time."

"You can't knock her for that! She can't help it if she's naturally well endowed. And don't call her mean in front of the baby," I added, placing my hands protectively over my midsection. "I don't want Erica exposed to any negative thinking."

~

Being discovered meant being expelled, so I was determined to keep my secret—officially, at least—until the end of my junior year. I did my best to look like myself, but I hardly recognized my reflection anymore. Shrouded in Debbie's clothes that were way too big for me in the bosom but nicely draped my growing midsection, I'd be rosy in the face and sweating by the time I got to class at the top of the stairs. Everything about my body was changing in ways I had no way to understand and no one to explain. Not just the swelling of my stomach—my skin and my hair seemed to have a different texture. My face looked different. Wiser. I had this secret. A buried treasure. My eyes were a deeper blue and quick to well up with tears over just about anything. There was a heightened sense of everything—emotion, perception, awareness. I knew nothing about what was going on inside me, but I wasn't afraid. I was entirely happy and optimistic. I was having a baby!

There were a few people who were happy for me. Sadly, Eddie

wasn't one of them. After we got married, we rented a little apartment in the same complex where both our mothers lived. I didn't see much of my mom, but Debbie came to visit me, and Miss Mamie helped me set up housekeeping and prepare for the arrival of the baby. We salvaged a twin bed from somewhere and transformed it into sort of a sofa thing by tucking a ribbed green throw blanket over the mattress and some pillows set against the wall. We also came up with a little table and two wooden chairs and some good, sturdy boxes for a makeshift coffee table and bookshelf.

Aunt Peggy, Granny, and the rest of us all hogged onto every S&H Green Stamp that crossed our path. It didn't take too long before I had a baby swing *and* a plastic changing table with little pullout drawers for diapers, plus bumpers and sheets for the old crib Aunt Peggy gave me, and I had enough left over to get the sweetest little mobile with a windup music box on top and little bear cubs and puppy dogs dangling down.

Eddie graduated at the end of May, and we celebrated with his family. He had a job throwing papers at night, and we decided it would go a lot faster if I helped. While Eddie cruised the GTO slowly around the route, I sat in the backseat, rolling each paper, stretching a rubber band around it, handing it to Eddie. He'd fling it out the car window into the subscriber's yard and pull forward, while I rolled another one. My hands were raw and cramped by the end of the night, but I didn't mind. Every paper that flew out the window meant fifteen cents in the Haskell family coffers. *Cha-ching!*

"Porch."

Eddie stopped the car, and I scrambled out. Some subscribers required their paper neatly set on the porch instead of just flung up there in the yard. After a while it got hard for me to lumber out of the backseat, though, and Eddie had to put the car in park and get out and porch the papers himself.

"You know," he told me, "it'd be easier if you could drive."

"I was gonna take driver's ed in school next year," I answered, leaving the rest unsaid.

"Well, I could teach you. You're seventeen now. You could get a hardship license without taking driver's ed if you just tell 'em about your . . . you know."

I won't say Eddie Haskell never gave me anything. Of course, there's my son, the greatest gift possible, but even before that, Eddie put wings on me by teaching me to drive. Speeding down Central Expressway made me feel grown-up and free, and it still does today. I'm a woman who loves her wheels.

On the Fourth of July we went over to Miss Mamie's place for seven-layer salad and sloppy Joes. We sat on the couch and held hands and watched the parade on TV, and I fell asleep with my head on my husband's shoulder, feeling like family. That night, surrounded by a sea of papers in the back of the slow-cruising GTO, I snapped a band on a paper and handed it to Eddie, thinking about Miss Dallas in the back of a powder blue convertible, waving the princess wave, surrounded by a sea of white crinolines. Believe it or not, I thought I was the lucky one.

~

Eddie was out a lot. It was hard for him to stay home. All his friends were out on the street, doing things friends do on a summer afternoon. They were partying on the weekends, and the revving of their engines outside was a siren song Eddie was powerless to resist. I was working at JC Penney during the day, throwing the papers at night, and in between I wanted to cook dinner and sit talking about the baby. I wanted to listen to music on the stereo Eddie got as a graduation present. I wanted to walk to the 7-Eleven and get an ice cream sandwich and stand right there on the corner and eat it while it melted in my hand. I wanted us to be a family.

Eddie wanted to be . . . out.

When he came in, he kicked the door closed and threw his keys on the counter.

"Lucy, I'm home," he called wearily.

"Hi!" I came out of the kitchen and gave him a hug, which he stiffly returned. "How was your day?"

"Peachy. I just had to sit in the friggin' gas line for an hour in the ten-thousand-degree heat is all."

"Oh." I stepped back and laced my fingers together in front of me. "Umm. You didn't fill it up, did you?"

"Yeah, I filled it up! Or else I get to sit there again three days from now."

"*Eddie!* I told you to only put in five dollars. We needed the rest for groceries."

"Stop trying to tell me how much friggin' gas I can put in my own friggin' car, all right? I said I'd figure something out, and I will."

"When?"

"*When you shut up for five seconds!*" The sound of his own voice seemed to scare him a little. He shoved his hands in his pockets, and kicked at the edge of the braided rag rug. "Look, I'm sorry. Okay? I'm sorry I yelled. It's just—this is all getting kind of . . . heavy."

"I know," I said, and I truly did.

"I mean . . . man . . . oh, man, I look at you and you're . . . geez," he breathed unsteadily. "Man. Geez. It's really starting to get big. And I just don't know if I can handle it."

"It's okay. Let's not fight."

"I'm not fighting, Linda, but I just—I can't think about all this crap anymore. I just want to go and—and just be—I don't know. *Happy.* Just for a while." He put his arms around me and kissed the top of my head. "C'mon, Linda. Can we just be *happy* for a little while?"

"I'm happy!" I said. "I am! Like today when I was on the bus, I felt Erica kicking and—oh, Eddie, you can't believe what that feels like! You can't believe how amazingly, amazingly cool it is."

I took his hand and tried to place it on my middle, but he pulled away.

"No, I mean—look, I told some people I'd meet them for a couple beers. C'mon with us."

"Eddie, we don't have any money for that. And I have to sleep for a while before we go out on the paper route, because I have to go to work as soon as we get home. And besides—I'm making soup. Just like your mom's. She showed me how."

"Oh. Yummy."

"Why don't we just stay in tonight?"

"No, why don't *you* stay in, Linda? Because you're the one who wants to play house, not me."

"I'm not *playing*, Eddie." I felt the Donna Reed draining right out of my bloodstream, replaced by someone weary and impatient and a whole lot less magnanimous. "Because, you see, I don't get to *play* anymore. It doesn't really matter if I want to go out and *play* or not. I have this baby growing inside me, and she's going to need a home. She's going to need a roof over her head and food in her stomach. She's going to need a mother and a daddy who isn't so selfish and childish that he—"

"I know!" Eddie bellowed. "You don't have to tell me all the time! You don't have to keep twisting the knife in my gut! I already know I'm a stupid fuck-up who got you pregnant, and I'm trying to do the right thing, but *no*!" He seized my shoulders and pinned me up against the wall. "Nothing I do is ever gonna be right enough for you, is it, Linda? *Is it?* It's *never—gonna—be—enough!"* Each word reverberated through my shoulder blades as he slammed me against the paneling. "You're not gonna be happy until you've got me pussy-whipped into some kind of goddamn pipe-smoking, sleepwalking—*goddamn it!"* He pounded his fist into the wall next to my head. "*Why*, Linda? Why'd you have to go and—you ruined everything! Everything was great, until you—you just had to . . . *Jesus friggin' Christ*! I can't friggin' *breathe*."

He slumped sideways in the rocker and covered his face with his arm. I didn't move or make a sound. I just tried to occupy as little space in the room as possible. Tried to take an internal inventory, wondering if my baby felt my fear through the umbilical cord or just a sudden rocking, the same way it did when I ran to catch the bus or jumped to avoid the broken step out on the front walk. I tried to speak to her inside my head. *It's okay, baby, it's okay*.

When Eddie finally spoke again, his voice was shadowed and hoarse, the words almost too quiet to make out.

"I'm gonna go meet those people," he said. "Are you coming with me?"

I shook my head.

"Fine," he shrugged. "Great. I guess it won't cost as much money then."

He went in the bedroom and changed his shirt. When he came out, I was sitting on the edge of the bed-couch-sofa thing, tipping back and forth only the smallest bit.

"Eddie . . ."

"I'll be back at three to throw the papers. Make sure you're ready to go."

~

The JC Penney ladies were always up for a good baby shower. Wedding shower games were never quite as much fun. To my horror, Debbie offered to host. She was working at JC Penney now too, so she knew all the ladies, but I was nervous about her history of less than meticulous housecleaning, and I had no idea what she was planning to do with Mother during the event. But I should have trusted her. Everything was neat as a pin when I arrived, and Debbie looked like Doris Day. Mom lay on her bed reading until the ladies started to arrive. Then she came out and sat on the couch, eating the little sandwiches Debbie had made. She had curlers in her hair—like she wanted me to see there was something else going on in her life that was worth curling her hair for, even if my baby shower wasn't.

We played Toss the Clothes Pin in the Diaper Pail and Baby Name Bingo, and then I opened presents from ladies at the store and a few of my old babysitting customers. While Mrs. Hillary carefully placed small squares of cake on the pink-and-blue paper plates, Debbie pulled me into the bathroom. She pushed up the puffy sleeve on the baby-doll shirt that used to be hers, turned me toward the mirror, and pointed to the deep blue-purple fingerprints on my upper arm.

"What's this?"

"I don't know. It's—it's not anything."

"Well, it sure looks like something to me. In fact, it looks like your eye did last week."

"I bumped it is all!"

"On what? Eddie's fist?"

I turned on the water to make sure no one could hear us in the next room.

"I told you, it's not anything," I hissed. "Now, c'mon. Let's get back."

"Linda, all you are these days is black and blue."

"It's none of your business, Debbie."

"Linda . . ." Debbie struggled to come up with something to say, but we'd never been much for saying things in our family. She hadn't had much practice. "Are you sure you know what you're doing?"

"No. But I'm trying to do what's right."

"Okay," Debbie said softly. "Let's go have some cake."

Poor Debbie, I thought. *She must be wild with jealousy.* She had to trudge on off to school in the morning and sit there for English and algebra, and I got to have *Baby Erica*. She had to stay here and be a helpless kid and live with *Her,* and I got to be Mrs. Eddie Haskell, a wife with a pretty home and my own refrigerator and a handsome husband, who drives a very cool car, and a darling baby daughter to dress up in pretty clothes. And if Eddie was having a little trouble adjusting—well, he'd get over that as soon as he saw his little girl all bundled up in the pink flannel receiving blankets I'd just gotten as gifts from two ladies who worked at the JC Penney glove and watch counter. He'd count her perfect baby toes and smell her wonderful baby powder smell and be smitten, despite all his blustering about wanting a boy. And someday he'd come home from work in his business suit and tell me he'd been promoted to—oh, I don't know—vice president of something! And we'd move to the good part of Dallas, and I would join Junior League, and Erica would be captain of the junior high drill team.

Yeah, I actually thought that. And I love it that I believed that daydream. It's a wonderful thing to be that full of hope. Looking back, I don't feel silly at all. Looking back, I see a girl who always believed in a better day. So I'm an eternal optimist! What of it? It strikes me as a lot more productive being hopeful instead of jaded. Being hopeful pulls you into the promise of the future; being jaded chains you to disappointments of the past. That faith never hurt me a bit. Sometimes denial is the best you can do for the moment.

I tugged my sleeve down over the bruise, relieved that Debbie hadn't brushed my hair aside to see where he had grabbed the back of my neck, and I went back into the living room to open the rest of my gaily wrapped gifts. I almost hated to tear the paper. Such care had been taken to make the packages pretty, and somehow the contents I imagined were always better than what was actually inside.

"Eddie! Come and see all the new baby stuff!" I called when I got back to the tiny apartment.

Eddie stood in the doorway with his hands in his pockets.

"Are you still mad at me?" he asked.

"No, of course not! Come and see."

"Just a minute. I wanna show you something first."

He took my hand and led me to the bedroom we were all going to sleep in. The whole family. There in the middle of the floor on a spread-out sheet of newspaper was a rocking chair. Eddie had painted the rails red and white, and the seat was blue with white stars.

"It's supposed to be like a flag," he said.

"Oh, wow . . . it's great, Eddie. I love it."

"You can sit in it." He stuck out his foot and pushed the chair toward me with the toe of his shabby high-top sneaker. "It's pretty much dry, I think."

I sat down and rocked a little. I wanted to tell Eddie something, but I didn't have a handle on what it was exactly. I didn't understand what I felt any more than I understood what was going on inside my body. It was all a wonderful mystery. Something about this huge love that was bubbling up inside me like a freshwater spring in the bottom of a lake. You can't quite tell where it's coming from, but you can feel that cold water as you swim by. I knew we weren't going to be able to give Erica everything she wanted. But the wellspring feeling made me believe that she would never know what it felt like to be unloved.

A little girl could be happy with that, I wanted to tell him. That could be enough. So there was nothing to be afraid of.

~

Flash-forward sixteen years. I discovered a stash of condoms when I was cleaning my son's room. (Yes, I cleaned his room! Not because I was the housekeeper, but because I was a professional woman with a lot going on, and this was the one sure way I could keep tabs on what was going on in there.) We never had that closed-door thing going on. I didn't have time for that. I didn't have the luxury of eavesdropping or hovering. I had to collect information and take action. Only, in this case, I truly didn't know what action to take. Mack-truck-flattened by the realization that this person I regarded as an extension of my own life had a life that was utterly unknown to me, I held those little Frisbees of impending Lord-knows-what in my hand, wanting to cry, wanting to talk to him, wanting to pretend I'd never seen them.

But then I thought about Eddie.

How fatherhood barreled down the road toward him, while he stood there, blinking dumbly in the headlights. Accountability. He hadn't yet learned the meaning of the word.

For years I despised the guy. He made me believe in love, then he left me. He opened my soul to the profound joy of physical intimacy, then shut my heart with the profound humiliation of physical abuse. For a long time, though God told me to forgive, I could force no forgiveness for him, because I truly believed he'd walked away from it all unscathed. For all those years I basically stamped the universal NO symbol on any thought of him. Just drew a big red circle around that part of my life and slashed a big fat line through it.

"Didn't Lance ever ask about him?" wonders my hippie girlfriend.

She has a hard time understanding that if you've never had a thing, you never miss it. A boy born color-blind doesn't spend his life mourning the loss of purple. He finds a purple joy in texture or depth, where someone else might never notice.

"But if he had asked—what would you have told him?"

"That would depend on when he asked me, I guess."

If Lance had come to me when he was five and asked, "Where's my daddy?" I would have told him, "I don't know and I don't care. He was a jerk."

If Lance had come to me when he was ten and asked, "Who is my father?" I would have told him the man's name and said, "He wasn't a very good person."

But if Lance had come to me that day in his room, as I sat there, stunned, staring at those condoms, if he'd sat down beside me and said, "What happened?" I would have said, "Son, there was this boy I loved. And he loved me. But he was a boy trying to live a man's life, and he couldn't do it."

And each one of those answers would have been true. Because truth—and love too, I guess—rides like a tire swing. However far you sail to one side, that's how far life takes you back the other way, and eventually you come to rest at the center. That's where I am with Eddie Haskell.

I don't know the man, but I can look back and forgive the boy. All he saw was what he couldn't do. All he felt was the thrashing panic that comes just before you drown. He just couldn't unclench his fists long enough to scoop up the great handfuls of blessings that wanted to come to him. But being a screwup when you're seventeen doesn't make you a screwup forever—and thank the Lord for that! Think of the pickle of a situation we'd all be in.

Sometimes we're so busy telling our kids what not to do and threatening them with what will happen if they do it anyway, we forget to teach them that accountability is not just consequences. It's an opportunity for redemption. It's funny how I never really had to explain the concept of responsibility to Lance. He seemed to know—whether from years of watching me work or from all those nights he rode around inside me, throwing papers—that responsibility equals freedom, and freedom is worth it.

Given the same set of circumstances, Eddie retreated into the life that had been shown him, not because it felt right, but because it felt familiar; I envisioned a different life and began to work toward it, not because it felt safe, but because it felt right. He saw himself trapped and struggled to escape. I knew I'd been liberated and readily shook off the defeated ideas that kept so many people I knew boxed in all their lives.

My son was my salvation. Binding myself to him set me free. Raising him uplifted me. His father chose a different road. I hope with all my heart it took him home.

FIVE

BABY LOVE

That August was as hot and heartbreaking as a Texas summer gets. Eddie was seriously chafing under the pressure of impending fatherhood. I was the logical focus for all his frustration, and somehow neither his cowboy gallantry nor his peace-protesting hippie ideals ruled out beating me up when it all got too much for him.

We scraped and skimmed to afford the obstetrician payments. The first time I went to the office, they explained to me how much I'd have to pay at my checkup every month in order to have the delivery paid for in advance. The obstetrician was a middle-aged man—tall, gaunt, and bony-fingered. He had little to say during the appointments. I didn't even know what questions to ask, and he volunteered zilch in terms of information or compassion.

"I'm getting so big," I told Debbie. "I don't know if it's normal. Because . . . I mean, how does the baby—you know—if . . . if it's that big, do you think . . ."

Debbie just shook her head, wide-eyed.

I was a tiny thing, so by the time I was nine months along, I could hardly struggle through the day. I couldn't take a bath, because I couldn't get out of the bathtub. Eddie convinced me to go with him to a party one night, and the people had a waterbed on the floor, which I made the drastic mistake of sitting on. It was so comforting while I sat there. I closed my eyes and let it cradle me the same way I was cradling my baby with my body. But then it came time to go, and I couldn't get up. Somebody had to go get Eddie to pull me up. That may have been the last time I saw him laugh.

~

By mid-September my appointments were once a week, and Eddie had to sell some things so we could make our final payment to the hospital. Walking back and forth at the bus stop, I double-checked my purse to make sure I had it. It was hot out, and I couldn't sit down. My dress was short, and I wasn't sure I'd be able to get up without embarrassing myself. There weren't too many people on the bus, however, so I decided to risk it. I went to a seat that had a pole nearby, so I could use it to pull myself up when the time came. The bus was like an oven. I rested my head against the pole and closed my eyes.

When I arrived at the doctor's office, the receptionist took one look at me and rang for the nurse, who scurried out and bundled me to a back room.

"Lordy, sugar, you are red as a cherry," she said, laying a cool, wet towel across my face. "Now I'm gonna have you lie here nice and quiet for a little bit. You just set here and cool off, sugar, while I tell Doctor you're here."

She squeezed my hand before she stood up and turned off the light. I lay there in the dark, comforted by the breeze from the ceiling fan and the lingering sensation of her gentle touch on my forehead—so, so grateful for that small act of mercy. People don't realize, I think, how much their small kindnesses mean. In that moment, when I was so young and so alone and so scared, a cool, damp cloth and a kind word meant the world to me. Even now—after all these years—every time I think about it I feel a little golden bloom of thankfulness for that woman. Just imagine if you went through your life planting seeds of kindness and collecting those marigold moments of gratitude like she did. How they'd all come back to you as blessings beyond number. I think that's what they mean by "karma."

When the doctor came in, he prodded and measured me without saying anything, until I gathered my courage together enough to ask some questions I'd been collecting in my head.

"I was wondering," I began timidly, "since I never had a baby before . . ."

"Well," he huffed, "you're pretty young to be having this one."

"So I wanted to ask you," I continued, undaunted, "is the baby . . . well, is she *normal*? I mean, it seems awful big."

"You're a little girl," he said curtly. "Baby's normal enough. Probably around six pounds." He stretched a tape measure over my belly. "Maybe seven."

"Oh," I said. "Okay. Well, I was also wondering—do you think it's time yet?"

"No, not yet. I'm not gonna do a vaginal exam today. We'll check you next week."

"It's gonna be another week?" I said, my heart sinking.

"Oh, at least."

I couldn't speak for trying not to cry, and he left without saying anything else. I went to the bus stop and leaned on the back of the bench, pushing my fists against my aching back. By the time I got home, I was crying and couldn't stop. Eddie didn't know what to make of it.

"I can't—I can't—not another week!" I sobbed deep wracking sobs.

"C'mon, Linda . . . geez . . . it's okay." He tried to pat my back without getting too close. "Hey, why don't you stay home tonight. Okay? Linda? You just stay here and lay down, and I'll go do the papers, and you'll be okay. Okay?"

Honestly, I think he was relieved to escape out the door without me. I sat in the rocking chair, crying and fanning myself with a magazine. My back hurt, and my belly felt cramped and hard. I was too uncomfortable to go to bed, to walk, to breathe, to sit, to stand. I got up to go to the bathroom, and there was a rush of wetness between my legs. Nobody had told me about the idea of water breaking. I thought I'd peed, but then I got to feeling worse and worse, and I wondered if maybe that water meant there was something terribly wrong. I prodded at the baby, then held my breath until she pushed back with a tiny foot or little fist. It got on toward morning. Eddie wasn't back yet. I was exhausted and scared, and though I couldn't believe it, didn't want to admit it—more than anything else in the world I just needed . . . I just wanted . . .

"Mother?"

She'd picked up the phone but was too sleepy to say hello.

"Mother!"

"Hmm."

"Mom, it's me."

She didn't say anything for a long moment.

"It's . . . it's me," I repeated.

"Yes," she said. "Yes, baby."

She said yes.

~

At the hospital Eddie bounced his heels on the tile, doing the sewing machine thing with his knees and anxiously drumming his knuckles on the arms of his chair.

"Would you please stop that?" I asked, when I could breathe for a moment between contractions.

"Oh. Sorry," he said, and switched to pattering his palms on his thighs.

"Get him out of here," I begged the nurse. "Get him out of here, or I'll go crazy."

Having absolutely no idea what to expect, I was horrified when they came to prep me for the delivery.

"Pull your knees up, sugar."

A nurse whisked the sheet up off me. She had a bowl of water and a razor. Somebody else came with some kind of tools and examined me all over.

"Let's take her in," the doctor said, and suddenly everything was moving. The ceiling sailed by over my head, like thunderheads do when you lie on the ground and watch them right before a storm. There were faces above me and lights. In the delivery room they were telling me to push. My legs were lifted apart, and I felt cold metal behind my knees and under my feet.

"Push," the nurses kept telling me. "Push harder, Linda. Come on, sugar, you gotta get this baby out. I can see the top of the baby's head, sugar. Push!"

I tried to put my hand down there to see if I could feel anything, but they brushed it away. The doctor said something I couldn't understand, and a nurse took a plastic bottle from a metal table. She squirted something red across my thighs, making a high wide arc with her arm.

"Turn your head, sugar," someone said.

She tipped my face to the side and, before I could ask why, clamped a surgical mask over my nose and mouth. One breath of an acrid metallic taste, and I was gone.

~

"Lindaaaaaaa . . ."

Debbie was calling to me from across the field. My sequined captain's hat flashed at the corner of my eye. I tried to walk toward her, but my white boots seemed stuck in the mud or something.

"Linda?"

The sun was blazing. Too hot for a football game. Maybe that's why the stands were empty.

"Linda?" It wasn't Debbie after all. It was Eddie's big sister, Belva.

"Uh-huh."

"You have a baby boy," Belva said.

"Hmm?"

"Linda, can you hear me?"

"I have . . . a baby . . . boy?"

"That's right, honey. A beautiful baby boy."

"I have a baby boy."

Of course, I thought. *Of course, my baby is a boy! A baby boy is perfect for me! How could I have ever thought I wanted a girl?* Pure happiness poured over me like a bucket of cool water.

"There's something wrong with his head, but he's gonna be okay."

"Wh— . . . what?"

"Oh, that's nothing," said Miss Mamie. "It's just a little pointy. What do you expect with such a big boy coming out of her tiny little body? Just hush up about that, Belva. Linda, don't you worry a bit. It'll go normal after a day or so."

"Oh . . . okay."

My voice sounded dry and distant. My lips felt brittle as rice paper, but I smiled.

"He's a beautiful, beautiful child," Miss Mamie said, and then she made a little hiccup sort of sound, but my eyelids were so heavy, I couldn't look up to see if it was laughing or crying. "Most beautiful thing I've ever seen—just like all my grandbabies. And I'll tell you what else. He's the biggest baby in the nursery! Ten pounds! You oughta hear him down there, raising a ruckus, telling those little pipsqueaks what's what!"

"I want to hold him. I want to see him now."

"They said not until your fever goes down."

No, now! I want him now! The words were lost somewhere in my head and wouldn't come out. Miss Mamie reached over and pulled a little chain to turn off the rectangular light, and a hot, spiderwebby sleep settled over my forehead. She squeezed my hand, and I wanted to tell her how thirsty I was, but I couldn't even form the words in my mind. I was trying so hard to hold on to the only thing I needed to know.

I have a baby boy.

~

Two days went by.

"When can I see my baby?" I kept asking and asking, while nurses and doctors came and went, doing this and that, making me drink stuff, taking blood. They said they thought I might be diabetic or something, but frankly I was like *whatever—just let me see my son!* I couldn't tell how much time had gone by. Every once in a while I managed to open my eyes, but the darkness and light didn't make any sense.

When a nurse finally brought my son in on the third day, she took one look at me and said, "Oh, honeychild! This can't be *your* baby! I better double-check and make sure I got the right room." I was so tiny, and he was the biggest baby in the nursery. She couldn't believe it.

"The biggest one!" cried Aunt Peggy. "Oh, my stars."

"And he's the most beautiful," I said. "And he's not leaving my sight ever again."

Once I finally got to hold him, I knew I'd die if I ever let him go.

"Well, I guess you're not gonna name him Erica," Debbie said. "Maybe Eric?"

"No," I told her. "I'm gonna name him Lance. After Lance Rentzel, wide receiver for the Dallas Cowboys."

(Yes, I know, I know—Rentzel came to a bad end. But back then he was about to start another great season, with his wife, Joey Heatherton, dressed in pink hot pants, cheering like crazy over on the sidelines.)

"What's his middle name?" asked Eddie's mother.

"Edward," I told her, but I added, "*after my father*." Just to clarify.

I don't know if becoming a grandfather had anything to do with my dad getting sober, but he was the only one who was truly happy for me when I announced I was bringing this new creature into the world. Most people reacted to my pregnancy with something in the range between stark disapproval and mortified pity. Even Granny pressed her hand to her bosom for a long moment before she nodded and said, "Well, I think you're doing the right thing." But Daddy seemed genuinely excited.

"Aw, Linda," he'd said when I first told him, "that's good news. That's—that's something, I'll tell you what."

My radar was always pretty sharp. From the time I was seven or eight, I could tell immediately how drunk he was, and I'd instantly be braced for all hell to break loose. But when he showed up at the hospital, he was completely sober for the first time in my living memory. It took him a couple months to climb solidly on the wagon after Lance was born, but by November he was a regular at the AA meetings in the basement of the First Christian Church. Sunday mornings he was upstairs in the same building, like someone on a day pass from purgatory. He embraced the faith Granny had always tried to tell him he could cling to should he ever need a lifeboat, and he didn't just talk the talk. He went to people and apologized and asked to be held accountable. He made and kept promises. He walked taller and seemed to be more at home in his skin than I'd ever seen him. Even his eyes were more alive. They had always looked sort of watered-down and sad, but now they were clear and sharp, filled with a spirit I didn't recognize.

"God grant me the serenity to accept the things I cannot change, the courage to change the things I can, and the wisdom to know the difference."

This was Daddy's new mantra. But whenever he got his arms around Lance, all that twelve-step gravitas gave way to an innate silliness possessed by all granddaddies on some level. I'd hear him talking baby talk to Lance when I was getting ready to go or look up from ironing my hair to catch him studying the baby's feet. This was the first long sober stretch of his adult life, and with it came the weighty realization of all he'd missed while his own children were small.

He'd lost his driver's license just before he sobered up, so I was driving him around on his job, which was taking medical histories from veterans and helping them fill out their insurance forms. I'd wait in the car, just singing along with the radio and snuggling my baby in my arms. Sometimes I'd get scared because it was dark, and some of the veterans lived in pretty rough neighborhoods. If I heard or saw something suspicious, I'd take Lance and huddle on the floor by the backseat until Daddy came out.

Once a week I went to the laundromat while Daddy was seeing people. I'd cuddle my son in the basket on top of the towels, which were warm from the dryer. Seems like the place was usually full of older people—elderly couples who pulled little red wagons down from the apartment complexes to do their wash in the evening when it wasn't so hot. But one night after everyone else left, I came out to the car, and there was a guy in the parking lot. At first I thought he was just urinating against the back wall of the building, but then I realized he was drunk and doing something unspeakable over there. I got so scared, I couldn't go back, so Daddy bought me a mini-sized washer and dryer of my very own.

Seems like while we were doing all that driving around together, I was able to open up to him or something. You know how you can talk to someone you truly love, or you can talk to a perfect stranger in the right situation. This was like a combination of the two. We didn't have the years of expectation and discipline and baggage that mutes a lot of father–daughter relationships. We really didn't know each other at all, but we so very dearly wanted to, and because we were both trying to get started in a brand-new life, we were willing to let bygones be bygones.

He wasn't the only one who noticed that my arms and neck were almost always tattooed with bruises, but he was the only one who called me on it when I tried to dismiss it or explain it away.

"Oh, I tripped over the cat," I'd tell Granny and Debbie. "I bumped my cheek on the kitchen cupboard when I was fixing Lance's bottle."

But Daddy knew I was lying. He knew what those marks were, because he'd made them on someone else, and he was no longer affording himself the luxury of looking away.

I tried to explain to Daddy—tried to understand for myself—how it always got started. Basically, I wanted to be home with the baby in the evenings, and Eddie couldn't stand to be trapped in the house. I wanted to save up money for a stroller, and he couldn't even stand to think about what it would take to buy the next can of formula. He wanted to hold the baby, but I didn't like the way he did it, and I couldn't help it—I had to tell him over and over, "Support his little head!" and after a while all these arguments ran together. There was really no way to tell where one ended and the next began, because we seemed to live in this swamp of resentment and struggle—just the two of us screaming the same things at each other over and over until the hitting and clawing began. Then there was usually some twisting, some shoving, a glimpse of ceiling, a taste of floor.

He always wanted to make up later. He was very apologetic. Genuinely sorry. I wanted to believe he could change, and I was quick to forgive him and tell him everything would be all right. "Make love, not war," he always liked to say, but it didn't take long before even the lovemaking felt embattled.

"If it's getting too bad, you know," Daddy said one night as we drove away from his last appointment, "you and the baby can come stay at my place."

"Daddy," I breathed, "could we?"

"Sure, little one. That would be fine."

"It would just be for a little while, I promise. Until I can afford my own place. And I'm getting on as Christmas help over at the post office. It won't take long for me to save the money for a security deposit."

"It's up to you, of course, but I think you should," he said, and I grabbed on to that lifeline.

He and Debbie came the next day to help me move out. I packed up the crib and changing table, the diaper pail and my clothes. That was basically everything I owned. At first, Eddie tried to coax me to stay.

"Linda, c'mon! I love you, girl. And you love me. I know you do. Don't try to tell me you don't. I'm sorry if I haven't been a good enough husband, but I promise . . ." And he went on to promise all the same promises he'd already promised, but they were frayed and worn through like the knees on his old blue jeans. I no longer had any hope for them. He started getting mad. Yelling at me. Telling me the husband gets to tell the wife what to do, and he was telling me to by God sit myself down in that chair and shut the hell up.

His mother had gotten three little outfits for Lance at Sears, and I put those in a paper grocery bag with five clean diapers, two receiving blankets, a bib, and a little canister of baby powder I'd gotten free with a coupon. That was pretty much all we had.

Eddie threw a beer bottle at Daddy's back as Daddy and I made our way down the stairs with Lance's crib mattress and bumper pads.

"You're not taking her away from me, you friggin' wino!" Eddie howled. "So just get your fat drunk ass outta my house!"

Daddy didn't say anything. He didn't raise his eyes from the sidewalk. As we drove away I held Lance against the butterfly beating of my heart. I didn't know how to tell my daddy how much this moment meant to me. For the first time in my life, I felt *rescued*. It didn't erase a whole childhood of being scared and wanting. It didn't undo the damage that was already done. But a precious drink of cold water means a lot more to you when you've been wandering the desert than when you've been sitting by a swimming pool.

"Daddy," I said, trying to keep my voice from crumpling into tears. "Daddy . . ."

But I couldn't put any words together beyond that. Even if I'd grown up in a family that said things to each other, I'm not sure I would have known what to say right then.

"I've been thinking about something," he said after a while. "This thing somebody said at one of them meetings the other day. This one guy, he says, 'Today is the first day of the rest of your life,' he says. And I says, yup, you got that right."

He pulled into the parking lot outside his apartment and sat for a moment. I could feel him turning the words over in his mind.

"Today is the first day of the rest of your life," he repeated. "Ain't that right, little one?"

"It sure is, Daddy."

That night, as Marvin Gaye and Tammi Terrell sang a soft duet on the radio, I slow-danced my baby around the tiny living room.

"Heaven musta sent you from above," I sang in his sleepy little ear. "Heaven musta sent your precious love . . ."

Daddy smiled and set to putting Lance's crib together in the corner, running his hand along the bar to make sure there were no splinters, tightening all the bolts as sturdy as he could.

"You gave me a reason for living . . . taught me the meaning of giving . . ."

~

My father did the hardest thing a human being can do. He changed. And for that, he will always be my hero. Twelve steps, one step at a time. Somehow his grandson (did I mention he was the biggest baby in the nursery?) opened the man's eyes, mind, and heart. Suddenly, Daddy looked around at his life, saw the wreckage he'd caused, and somehow found the strength to own up to it. Eddie's mother, as loving and concerned as she was when she saw my bruises, couldn't see how they got there. She needed to believe her son could never be like that. But my father had been like that himself. It wasn't possible for him to close his eyes. Not if he wanted to make this day the first day of the rest of his life.

He was the last person I would have expected to come to my rescue, which just goes to show: the potential for good, the possibility of growth—it's there in every single human being.

Including me.

Including you.

We choose every moment who we want to be, and every new day is an opportunity to turn it all around.

SIX

THAT'S WHAT I WANT

Daddy and I mounted a mutual rescue operation. I drove him on his rounds in the evening; he took care of Lance during the day while I went out job-hunting. After I found a temporary position as holiday help at the post office, I helped Daddy study for the postal exam so he could get a job there too. The baby and I slept on Daddy's old sofa, snuggled close, breathing easy for the first time since Lance was born, and I'm certain our presence helped Daddy stay on the wagon during those first difficult months. I guess all three of us were starting out on a whole new life, each of us in our own way.

After Christmas I got to stay on in the dead-letter office. I liked the job, sorting through all those lost souls and thinking about the stories behind them, the same way Alan and Debbie and I once made up the people behind the mailbox nameplates. I saved every dime I made, and after a month or so I had enough to put down the security deposit and rent on a one-bedroom apartment. It wasn't easy finding a babysitter I could afford and who didn't insist on grilling me with a bunch of questions about how old I was and why I wasn't staying home with my child like a proper mommy should, but I finally found a woman in the apartment complex who was taking in children for five dollars a day.

"Here's his diaper bag," I told her when I dropped Lance off the first morning. "And here's his schedule. He just had breakfast at 6:45, so he'll need four ounces of formula at 9:15. And when you burp him right after, you'll get two little ones before the really good one. He gets half this jar of strained peas mixed with two teaspoons of rice cereal for lunch at 11:00 and half this jar of strained peaches for an afternoon snack when he wakes up from his nap. Oh! I almost forgot. He takes his morning nap from 9:30 till 10:15 and then goes down right after lunch for about an hour and a half."

She stared at me with a kind of blank, expressionless gaze that made me think of a cow in a pasture.

"I know it's a lot to remember," I smiled, handing her a little chart I'd made. "Here. This'll help."

I'd done my homework and learned everything there was to know about how to be a good mother. I was proud of that fact. And you'd think this person would have had a little appreciation for how hard I was trying, but when I returned that afternoon, I found Lance still in the crib where I'd left him. He was soaking wet, screaming, and covered in spit-up.

I went ballistic. I don't remember what all I said, but I know I said a lot, and there was no mistaking how I felt about a so-called babysitter who'd apparently been sitting around on her big bovine ass all day.

"Just you watch your mouth, little girl!" she finally broke in. "What do you know about takin' care of kids? You don't know squat! Look at you! You're a kid your own self! Don't you try to tell me how to handle a baby. You ain't any more specialer than anybody else, and that little brat of yours ain't any different from a hundred babies I've took care of. A little puke ain't gonna kill 'im. You'll spoil him, treating him like some kind of little prince or something!"

The visceral, animal biology of motherhood rose up inside me, a fierce protective impulse that blacked out any notion of politeness or even reason.

Let's just say there was a confrontation and leave it at that.

My insides were still trembling half an hour later as I bathed my baby in the kitchen sink. I took him out and wrapped him in a towel I'd warmed up in the little dryer Daddy gave me. I hated that fat cow on the other side of the complex, and I had no idea what I was going to do for child care the next day, but beneath all that there was a strange sort of exhilaration. *This is what it means to be a mother*, I realized. It had nothing to do with being old enough or knowing everything or keeping to a strict schedule. It had to do with loving someone with a love so huge, the rest of the world became insignificant by comparison. No fear I felt would ever amount to anything compared to what I felt for my child. No task would ever be too hard for me. No one would ever be able to make me feel small. I was The Mama. You don't get any bigger than that.

I wasn't raised to be particularly assertive. I was raised to be nice. So I'm glad for that incident, wretched as it was. It bolstered me for other battles to come—hassles with the high school principal; a lawsuit with an intractable trucker who ran Lance off the road and stomped his bike to smithereens; countless hassles with teachers and neighbors and even the police. There's only one thing strong enough to overcome the strict civility of a southern lady: the raw devotion of a barracuda mommy, who's not afraid to bare her teeth at the world once in a while.

~

I worked hard, and sometimes the baby kept me up at night, but, oh, did we have fun. Lance loved to boogie with me. I set his feet on top of my feet and held his hands up for the numbers that really rocked. For the slow dances, I got down on my knees, and he wrapped his arms around my neck, nuzzling against my chin with his soft little head that always smelled like Johnson's baby shampoo. I loved taking him out for walks in the sunshine and dips in the pool. When we were feeling particularly extravagant, we'd stroll on down to the 7-Eleven and share a Slurpy. He started walking at nine months. Crawling just wasn't fast enough. He had places to go. At first, he'd grip my fingers and walk toward me in great big, tottering steps, his eyes bright with the thrill of this great new discovery: *locomotion!* One day he stood up all by himself and made a solo voyage across the living room. Seems like I was chasing after him from that moment on, and there were days when it wore me smooth out.

As time went by Daddy was actually doing well enough to rent a little house a few blocks away. Alan and Debbie were having a tough time at Mother's, so they moved in with him, and they all came by on Saturday afternoons to sit with me and the baby next to the little swimming pool in my apartment complex. Alan just couldn't get enough of playing with that baby. While Debbie and I worked on our tans, Lance would scooch off my lap, toddle across the pavement, and leap out into the water where Alan waited to catch him.

It gave Granny a lot of comfort to see her son sobered up and working, living the responsible Christian life she'd always hoped for him. And she loved Lance. She was having some trouble getting around, so I made a point to drive down to her house in Terrell every week to scrub the bathroom and the kitchen and clean up around the place. Granny's house had always been a haven for me. An oasis of order and comfort in the midst of my messy childhood. I couldn't bear for her to sit there in the gathering dust and growing mildew just because her body could no longer keep up with the housekeeping standards she'd set for herself as a young mother. While I was busy, she held Lance on her lap, and they cooed and smiled at each other.

"Granny, I decided to remodel your bathroom today," I told her, nestling Lance in her arms with a bottle of milk and a stuffed bear.

"Remodel! My!" She wasn't really listening, already lost in baby talk.

"I got a gallon of periwinkle blue paint that was left over from Daddy's house. And look what I got on clearance at Sears—café curtains with matching hand towels. And these little soaps. Look at these. They're shaped like little birds. Aren't they the cutest thing?"

Granny reached out and squeezed my hand.

"What a blessing!" she declared.

Whether she was talking about the little birds or my little boy or her boy or the bathroom I don't know, but I could see in her eyes that she meant it with her whole heart.

When I got the call from Daddy a few days later, I didn't break down crying or make any noise. That would have scared the baby. I just sat by my window and cradled my son, thinking, *What a blessing, what a blessing.* She'd lived to see her son redeem himself, and she'd gotten to hold her great-grandson one last time. Hazel Nan Mooneyham came into the world by way of East Texas, found a hard life, infused it with love, and died with her feet up in her favorite chair. That was my Granny.

"You were blessed to have known her," Eddie's mom said. "Everybody should have a grandma who loves them."

I knew it was breaking her heart that Eddie and I were officially divorced now, and any hope of working things out had been killed by the way he'd acted after I left. At first, it was just a lot of phone calls and knocking on my father's door at all hours. Then he started following me to work, offering me a ride, yelling at me when I wouldn't get in the car. I guess he thought I would have to get in if I didn't have another way to get to work, so he dumped sugar in my gas tank and slashed my tires. Needless to say, this didn't go a long way toward winning my heart. To me, love means never having to say "restraining order."

But Miss Mamie was a generous, loving person. She wanted nothing more than to be Lance's grandma, to just love him up and spoil him and rock him to sleep. She looked after him during Eddie's court-ordered visitation time every Saturday afternoon from one to five and kept him as often as she could in the evenings, which helped me a lot, since my scant budget only allowed for babysitting during the day. If I worked overtime or helped Daddy with his route, I had to take Lance with me or find someone who wanted to watch him just for love.

Anyway, I loved Miss Mamie. Maybe that's why they thought bad news was better coming from her.

"Eddie's afraid you'll be mad at him," she said, trying to find a politic way to open the conversation. "There was a little accident, and—"

"*Accident?*" I didn't get mad. I went directly to full-blown panic. "*Where's Lance? Where's my son?*"

"Now, sugar, stay calm. We took him over to the hospital, and—"

"*What? What for?*"

"He didn't mean to hurt him. He just wanted to take him for a little ride. His first ride on the bicycle, you know? That's all he was tryin' to do. And he thought he had hold of him. He thought Lance was holding on, and he told him—I heard him tell the child—he said, 'Hang on,

Lance, okay? We're goin' for a bike ride, so hang on.' I swear, he thought he was hanging on, Linda. Don't be upset."

I couldn't breathe. I couldn't think. I was supposed to be his mama, and now he was hurt and he was crying somewhere and I wasn't there.

"He's needed a few stitches," said Miss Mamie, "but he's fine. He's just a little sleepy, so I thought I'd keep him tonight."

"*No!* No, I want him home. I want him with me! *Now!*"

"Linda, calm down! Honey—"

By the time she realized I'd hung up, I was down the stairs and halfway to her place, but when I pounded on her door, no one answered. Eddie's car was gone. I guess maybe they were still at the hospital, but my mind wasn't processing things that clearly. Somehow I felt like they were taking him away from me. They were never going to give him back and I would never see him again and I would die because he was the precious, precious bone marrow and heartbeat and soul of me. I pounded on the door until my fist felt bruised and swollen. I paced back and forth, crying, then ran all the way home, called her number, and let it ring forever without being answered. I went back and pounded on her door again, then went home and called the police. They were familiar with Eddie and trudged on over to his mother's place, while I waited by the phone, then trudged back over to my apartment and tried to settle the matter.

"Calm yourself down, missy," the potbellied officer told me. "You're not helping things by gettin' all upset. Now, they're over there to the hospital, tellin' me that fella's the baby's daddy, and that means he has every right in the world to take him. And his mama's over to her place tellin' me the baby's fine and she's takin' care of him for tonight. And that's all there is to it. Y'all can sort things out in the morning."

"No! No, they can't have him overnight." I tried to swallow, so I wouldn't feel like screaming and crying and coming apart at the seams. "They can have him till five. That's all. At five, he comes home. The judge said! *In court!*"

"Well, I don't know nothin' about that, and we don't wanna get involved in no domestic situation between husband and wife."

"He's not my husband! We're officially divorced. He gets to take the baby one day a week to his mother's house. That's the agreement! So you go on over there and bring my baby back!"

"Now, I told you to calm down, didn't I?" The officer tucked his thumbs into the holster at his hips, fanning his arms open like a peacock fans his tail. "Didn't I tell you to control yourself there?"

"Yes, sir," I said meekly. "But *please* . . ."

"Your husband's mama probably got the baby all tucked in by now. She's only tryin' to help. You're dang lucky to have a good woman like that to help out. Now, I'm tellin' you to go on in and get to bed, and you better listen up, missy. You better listen to your elders and take some advice instead of runnin' around gettin' yourself in trouble in the first place."

After they left, I paced and cried for a while. Then I called and pleaded with Eddie's mother until we were both crying, and then I paced and cried some more, and then I called her again, begging for my life, seems like, and then I paced and cried until the next morning, when she brought Lance home.

"Linda, I hope you understand I was just trying—"

"Give him to me! Give me my son."

I pulled him into my arms and tried to stop shaking so I could hold him.

"Now, I know you're upset, but—"

"I'm not upset. Just go away now. Everything's fine. Just go away, and tell Eddie to just—just go away."

"Linda, next Saturday . . . maybe I should come and pick him up next Saturday?"

"No," I said stiffly. "I don't think that's a good idea."

"Please, sugar, don't say that!" She was crying now too and trying to tuck Lance's blanket around him, but I pulled away. "I'm just trying to help, sweetie. You kids are so young to be trying to take care of a baby. It's no wonder—"

"Well, I don't need help! From now on, I'm taking care of my baby all by myself."

"Linda, don't say that. Who's going to look after him when—"

"I'll get a babysitter," I told her. "I'll work harder and earn the money."

"Linda, there's no way you can give him everything he needs all by yourself."

"Yes, there is. Because all he needs is his mama! He doesn't need a mixed-up, broken-up, messed-up family. So you just tell Eddie to leave us alone from now on. He's no kind of daddy for my son, and he never will be!"

"Sweetheart, just be patient with him, can't you? Y'all two are so young. He's just a boy and he's learning to—to be . . ." She shook her head, not knowing what words to use. "Please, can't you give him another chance?"

I gripped my son in my arms. He was mine. Like a diamond. You don't just go sharing that around. You hold on to it and protect it.

"Eddie Haskell had a million chances," I said, and this might be the first time I heard a truly hard edge on my voice. "All he had to do was love us, and he blew it. He's not getting another chance to hurt us ever again. I don't want your son in our life anymore, Miss Mamie. And I'm sorry, but that means we can't be in yours either. I think it's best for everybody if we all just do our own thing and get on with it."

After a long moment, she hugged her arms across the front of her and nodded tightly.

"Maybe," she whispered. "Maybe it is for the best."

"It is. It's for the best," I repeated as firmly as I could, when what I really wanted to do was throw my arms around her and beg her not to go.

"I know," she said, brushing the back of her hand across her cheek. "I do know that. But . . . it's just that . . ."

She couldn't say any more, and she didn't have to. I didn't doubt how much she loved her grandbaby. It was hard for her to let go of him, and it was hard for me to let go of her. It was breaking both our hearts. But we each had to do what we thought was best for our own boy.

~

"Wow," says my hippie girlfriend. I can tell she's searching for words, just like Miss Mamie did that day. "Don't you think . . . maybe you, um, overreacted just a tad?"

"Totally!" I exclaim. "Oh, I totally overreacted. I came down like a ton of bricks. And you know why? 'Cause I'm a hard-ass."

"Oh, Linda!" She laughs. "You are not either. You're a cream puff."

But I know my own heart, and I can make it like flint when I need to.

Twenty-five years after Miss Mamie and I said good-bye, our baby boy had cancer. He was so very, very sick, he could hardly come up with the strength to turn his head to vomit. I've never been so terrified in my life. Sitting in the waiting room, waiting for him to come back from some test or procedure, I tried to put thoughts together, tried to pray, but I was too cold. My whole body felt hollow except for the slow searing core of grief in my chest.

"How ya doin', little one?" asked my father. I just shook my head. He sat down beside me and took hold of my frozen hand. "Little one, I've been meaning to tell you . . . I was over to the store one day last week, and you won't ever guess who I ran into."

I don't think I even looked up.

"It was Eddie," he volunteered when I didn't ask.

"Eddie who?"

"You know . . . *Eddie,*" he said. "Haskell."

I pressed my fingertips against my temple. Hollow, hollow, hollow. So what could be causing it to ache like this?

"He was asking about Lance," Daddy continued, and then he went on and said something about him doing fine . . . nice family . . . thought of Lance as their brother . . . seen about Lance on the TV . . . was wondering if maybe . . .

"What?" I suddenly started listening. "He said what?"

"He said he saw on TV—how Lance is real sick. He said he'd like to come by, little one. Said he'd like to see him."

"*Now?*"

"Well, yeah, I guess so."

"No."

"Linda . . ."

"No," I repeated. "Nobody's gonna lay anything else on Lance right now. He's had enough. Every day it seems like something worse. I'm not letting anyone—because—*why?* Why should Eddie want to see him now anyway? Because he's famous? Because he's rich?"

"No, little one, I think it's because—"

"Because he thinks Lance is dying? Well, he's not!" I took a deep breath, hoping to bring down the shrill tone of my voice. "He's not," I repeated. "And if you see Eddie again, tell him he signed away his parental rights twenty years ago. That dog's been walked."

Daddy didn't push it. He just sat there beside me, resting a Bible back and forth between his leathery hands, and I just sat there feeling the utter dryness of my eyes.

Hard-, hard-, hard-ass. Go ahead and say it. I have every right to be. I've developed my self-defense mechanisms, and I'm stickin' to 'em. Besides, some cigarettes just don't flush, you know? That's accountability. That's consequences. You can be as sorry as you please, but it doesn't unwalk that dog. I can accept that the man has changed. I can even truthfully say I forgive him. But I didn't forget. I earned a thick skin and learned how to hide inside it. The only thing that manages to sneak through and soften me up once in a while is the memory of Miss Mamie.

I do think of her from time to time, and I hope her life is as good as I imagine it. She's one of those great Texas ladies I love, and when I inventory the little parts of myself that were given to me by those great ladies, I see that she's the one who showed me how to put someone else's welfare above my own. She could have made this whole thing very difficult, but as much as she wanted to be with Lance, she understood that her son did not. And she genuinely wanted what was best for both of them.

I wonder if behind every Eddie Haskell in this world there is a Miss Mamie, running interference, making apologies. Cleaning up spilled milk and trying not to cry over it. Lord knows I ran interference for my son a time or two . . . or dozen. I tried to protect him from everyone, including himself. That's what mamas do. And Miss Mamie was a good mama.

She never had big grandiose plans to set the world on fire, but she wasn't just a get-by kind of person. She worked hard and cared deeply.

I suspect she went on to hammer out a happy life for her family, and now she's one of those beautiful little old ladies, surrounded by her own friends and activities, but still very available to her children and grandchildren. She deserves to be content. I truly hope she is.

~

We were dead broke, me and my son. But like Granny used to say, "This ain't no pity party goin' on!" I didn't have time for any of that. I had a responsibility to this child. I was going to find him someplace safe and clean and pleasant for day care, and then I was going to get a better job so I could get him out of this dump we were living in, and then I was going to keep my eyes open for a nice man who would love us and take care of us and we would make a real home for ourselves. We'd work hard and save until we could buy an actual house. Instead of a dumpy little one-bedroom apartment in Oak Cliff, my son would grow up in a pretty house on a pretty street in Plano or Richardson or one of the other nice Dallas suburbs.

Grace Temple Baptist Church had a lovely little preschool, but you had to be potty-trained. Lance was only eighteen months old, so I hadn't even begun to contemplate what all was involved in that. But they said they'd help me. I guess it was sort of a specialty with them. They had a whole row of little potty chairs lined up against one wall, and within a week or so Lance joined a half-dozen other toddlers seated there looking at Little Golden Books and going about their business.

It was the policy at Grace Temple that you couldn't bring your child if he had a temperature, so whenever Lance had a cold or an ear infection, we had to stay home. And it seems like Lance had one ear infection after another. I never had much trouble finding a job, because I was always polite and professional, a hard worker, and a quick typist. But I had trouble keeping jobs, because the working world hadn't quite caught up to the idea of working mothers yet. When Lance was little enough to need day care, there were very few options available.

"Now, you're not planning on having any more children, are you, darlin'?" one prospective employer asked me during an interview. "Because we don't intend to waste our time training you if you're just gonna turn up pregnant and quit."

Another fine gentleman at a place where I'd been working as a typist told me it was no problem if I missed a few days, as long as I'd have sex with him the following week. He told me I should plan on it and even mentioned some particularly distasteful specifics. I left the office so scared and upset I couldn't even face going back there to collect my last paycheck.

"Why don't you let me pick him up when you're working late?" asked my mother. "We'll stop off for a Slurpy and wait for you by the pool."

"Oh," I said. "That would really be . . ." I stopped myself before I said anything that might sound gushy. We just weren't like that. So I just said, "Thank you."

I started looking forward to the days when Mother got Lance. She seemed like she kind of liked it too. He made her laugh, working on his Slurpy with this gigantic smile on his face. And later, when I got home, we'd sit by the pool, soaking up the late-afternoon sun and talking about things like two women. Not like mother and daughter, but like friends. She never said so, but I'd like to think I won her respect by rising to the occasion. I certainly had a new respect for her, having discovered what it meant for her to support us all those years.

Making my rent and keeping Lance at Grace Temple took up more than three-quarters of what I earned. But I managed. I managed to put fish sticks and corn on the table for dinner. I managed to buy a little plastic three-wheeler—seems to me it was called the Green Machine—for Lance's second birthday. It sat low to the ground, with a wide seat, butterfly handlebars, and a big front wheel with pedals on the sides. Mother and I couldn't stop laughing as we watched him make the miraculous discovery that pushing his little feet on the pedals could turn that wheel around and that meant *go power*! Then it dawned on him that the faster he pumped those pedals, the faster he could tear around the parking lot, which was a powerful incentive for someone whose feet were just never fast enough for him. He wanted to ride that thing from morning to night. That Green Machine.

Who would have thought?

Something to keep in mind next time you see some rowdy little kid doing whatever it is he's wild about doing. You just never know.

~

I lost another job when Lance got sick with the croup and ended up in the hospital. For three days they kept him in an oxygen tent, struggling to breathe. I stayed there, holding his hand, rubbing his back, pacing, and praying, while he barked and wheezed all night. There was nowhere for me to lie down, but I could sit on a chair next to the bed and rest my head next to his. By the time he was finally well enough to go home, I was trembling with emotional and physical exhaustion.

"Who's your insurance company?" asked the lady at the front desk when I was filling out the forms to check him out.

"I don't have any," I said. "I'm sorry."

"Well, how in God's name do you think you're going to pay for this?" she asked, folding her hands on top of her desk. I glanced nervously at the line of people behind me, the waiting room full of upright citizens between me and the door. Lance whimpered and pushed his warm, damp forehead against my neck.

"I suppose you're gonna file for public assistance to pay for it," the lady said.

"No, ma'am," I said, because I'd been raised on the belief that you don't take charity. "I'll make payments."

"Oh, you'll make *payments*, will you? How wonderful. I am sure that will come as a great comfort to the taxpaying citizens of Dallas County. Because girls who are foolish enough to go out and get theirselves a baby without any husband can always be trusted to make their *payments*, can't they?"

I didn't know how to respond, which was okay, because she was on a roll, her voice echoing off the marble floors and up the elevator shaft so everybody plus God could hear her.

"I know exactly what you are, missy. You are one of them welfare mothers who lives off of charity from the government outta pure laziness! You're no better than a nigger. You just wanna sit around all day, eatin' popcorn and watchin' movies and collecting that welfare check off of the good working people of Texas."

There was a whole lot more, but you get the idea. She went on like that, while I stood there, trying to fill out the forms with one hand, balancing my sleepy, sick child with the other. She wound down to a conclusion—something about how I wouldn't even get a bill and the good working people of Texas were getting the bill every single day—then turned her back on me. I practically crawled out of there, feeling like I was an ant on the floor.

But you know, I got home, and I started thinking about it, and I resolved two things in my mind. First, for the rest of my life, in all my dealings with other people, I was going to be kind and respectful, no matter which side of the desk I was sitting on. And second, I was never going to let someone give me a ration of crap like that again. I don't like conflict. Avoid it whenever I can. But when it becomes unavoidable, sister, you better believe I'm not gonna be the one who ends up feeling like a greasy spot of you-know-what on the bottom of somebody's army boot.

~

My son and I became brave and self-reliant. I was twenty. Not a teenager anymore. And Lance was three, feeling the full power of his big-boy status. We both took great pride in doing for ourselves. He always wanted to get his own shoes on and take charge of his belongings as we headed out the door. If he was on antibiotics, he wanted to take the bottle to school in a brown bag and hand it to his teacher.

"I carry it myself, Mama!" he sternly informed me, and I didn't care to argue. I was packing his lunch one morning when I heard it smash on the floor.

"Oh, Lance!" I said, hurrying over to pull his hand away from the broken glass. "That medicine was ten dollars, Lance. *Ten dollars!*"

"Oh." He studied the thick pink liquid oozing from the bag, then looked up at me with huge eyes. "I'm sorry, Mama."

"It's okay. Let's clean it up and get to school."

I spent the morning trying to figure out what to cut from the food budget so I could replace the medicine. *Looks like lots of mac-and-cheese this week,* I sighed to myself, standing in line at the pharmacy over my lunch hour.

The next morning, as I put the bottle in a brown bag, I felt Lance tug at my skirt.

"I carry it myself, Mama! I carry it myself," he sternly informed me.

It seems small. Silly even. But mothering happens in moments like this. You have a precious glass bottle in your hand, and a precious boy child tugging at your skirt. He reaches up, determined to do for himself, believing he is completely capable. Do you hand him the bottle and risk losing it? Or do you hang on to the bottle and risk the loss of that child's faith in himself?

"Be careful, son."

I handed Lance the brown paper bag, and he smiled his big goofy smile.

"Say, you," I said, "where did you get those beautiful blue eyes?"

"Jesus gave them to me," he said matter-of-factly and headed for the door.

I never had any baby-talky names for him. I always called him "Lance," or I'd say "son" because I loved the way it felt to say that and have it be real. "Son" is such a simple yet enormous word, the perfect word for the center of your universe. He wasn't the kissy-poo type anyway. Neither one of us had the option of being mollycoddled. It simply wasn't in the emotional budget. When he came to me with his first wiggly tooth, I unceremoniously popped it out and handed it to him. He was pretty astonished, but I was like, "Oh my, look at that. There ya go." Seems like stuff like that gets surrounded by a lot of unnecessary drama, and I simply didn't have time for that. My no-frills mothering style was born of necessity, based on common sense, and firmly grounded in the reality that self-indulgence and histrionics were among the luxuries we couldn't afford. This seemed to suit Lance fine, thank God. *What in the world,* I've wondered on occasion, *would I ever have done with some fussy little Erica?*

When I watch Lance now, pounding up the Alps or grinding through a time trial, pumping so hard it leaves his eyes bloodshot and burning with resolution, I think back on the treadmill quality of our life during his early years, and I see the birth of his ability to endure—to thrive, in fact—when the terrain is at its most rugged. When things are tough, you develop this dog-with-a-bone determination to push on forward toward something better and squeeze out every ounce of *fun* you can latch on to along the way. Simple joys become so precious. Tough as times were, I loved those baby and preschool years. We loved to make each other laugh. He brought out an utterly silly side of me I never even knew I had; he unleashed the kid in me and taught me how to play. We couldn't afford movies or anything like that, so we entertained each other with games and songs and goofing around.

"Leg-wrestle me, Mom!" he'd say when I was finishing up the dishes and was finally about to sit down in the evening. I'd look at the couch, feeling in my bones the long day of work and chores. Then I'd look at Lance, bouncing back and forth on the balls of his bare feet, dancing like the butterfly side of Ali.

"C'mon, Mom! C'mon!"

"Oh, you think you can take me? Do ya? Do ya? C'mere, you!"

We'd growl and glare and square off like professional wrestlers, then lie down on the floor, link our legs, and try to flip each other until we were laughing too hard to continue.

When my son was little, I worried about all the things I wasn't able to give him. Now I know what mattered most in the long run was what I was able to show him. There were certain realities in our life that couldn't be changed. We could sit around and cry about it, or we could find our way around the roadblocks. Our answer to every setback, sorrow, and upheaval has always been to push back, try harder, be smarter. We weren't afraid of failing—only of stopping, of giving up. Losing is worthwhile if you learn something from it, but quitting is the defeat of hope.

Stumbling and getting up again—that's a journey.

Stumbling and ceasing to try—that's a destination.

I'll tell you what, though. I was getting real tired of stumbling.

SEVEN

HEARD IT THROUGH THE GRAPEVINE

When I try to remember how I met the Salesman, the event crumples into the folded hands and crossed ankles of a thousand other job interviews. You see, the entire focus of my life during those days was to acquire whatever my son needed to survive, and I know I'm terrible, but if I were to be entirely honest, Sales fit into that category. According to conventional wisdom, my son needed a father, and Lord knows I was desperate for someone to share both the burdens and the joy. So when a pleasant, churchgoing man reached out his hand and offered to do that, it was easy for me to call it love. After going it alone for so long, it felt good to be on a team again.

I believe in love. I believe in the chemistry of man and woman together. Companionship is no less a human need than water, work, or vitamin C. Sales was a charming man, and I was long overdue to be charmed. He didn't put any big masher moves on me. True to the art of the sell, he simply revealed to me that we shared a common vision. Marriage. Family. A little house in the suburbs. Picket fence, freshly mown yard, station wagon, church on Sunday. He couldn't have come up with anything more entrancing than that rosy picture. And if I do say so, I had the raw material to be plenty entrancing myself, when I wanted to be. We quickly and easily convinced ourselves that all this meant we were meant for each other.

I don't remember how or when he proposed. I can't even recall that much about our wedding or the reception in the church fellowship hall.

All I remember is crawling into bed with a living, breathing partner and thinking, *At last!*

Perhaps his mother sensed all that, and that's why she treated me and Lance like something Sales had picked up at the Goodwill store. I suppose this proper minister's wife had a certain vision of family, same as I did, only hers had something to do with a virgin bride and seven or eight grandbabies who all had her father's nose and her mother's talent for piano. I think it hurt her to see her son saddled with another man's child, especially as the years went by and no child of his own was born. I guess it would be impossible to keep those feelings to yourself. At least it was for her. When my father-in-law Reverend thundered that "cast the first stone" story from the pulpit, she always seemed to be looking right at me during the part about the fallen woman who was reviled by everyone in town except Jesus himself. I was not a girl she was proud to take to the mother-daughter tea at the country club. I wore Wal-Mart, not Neiman Marcus.

I suppose I was doing the reverse-snobbery thing on her, though. Poor people always want to believe that the wealthy are desperately unhappy and morally corrupt under all that expensive fashion. But I took great pride in my appearance, my work, my home, and most of all, my son. She'd sent Sales off to military school when he was little, while I got up every morning and actually *raised* my kid. So there.

The Reverend tried, I suppose, to love Lance in an ecclesiastic "spare the rod spoil the child" sort of way, but this didn't go over too well with a little boy who'd been raised to believe he was the center of the universe. The one time I sent him to stay with them for a few days, he was trembling with fear, anger, and exhaustion when I picked him up.

"I'm never going there again," he told me as we drove away.

"What? Why?" The tone of his voice was what concerned me most. It was hard at the edges. "Son, what happened?"

"I'm never going there again," he repeated. "Don't try to make me."

I promised him I wouldn't, and I kept my promise.

~

Lance got his first bicycle from my dad. It was a present for his fifth birthday. I baked a cake shaped like Cookie Monster, and somehow

Lance ended up inviting all girls to the party. Daddy got a charge out of that. Late that evening he and Lance were out in the garage, pumping up the tires and tightening the training wheels with a wrench from a little toolbox Daddy gave him to go with the bike. My husband was sleeping in front of the TV with his feet up on an ottoman. I was cleaning up the party mess in the kitchen as a harvest moon was coming up over the trees in the backyard, and I couldn't help but hum a little song from a Disney movie we'd recently seen.

Life was good. Cleaverism, at last, had been achieved.

Almost.

~

I have a love–hate relationship with filling out forms. On the one hand, there's a comforting neatness about them. Lines and boxes. A place for everything. But when you don't fit into the lines and boxes, you're suddenly in this offsides territory where you feel like you have to explain yourself, and the explanation always makes you sound much worse than you really are.

Marital status: Married? Divorced? I was both. And you aren't supposed to be both. And when you're as young as I was, you probably shouldn't be either one.

Last name: My last name was not the same as my son's last name unless I used the name of someone who didn't love me anymore instead of the name of someone to whom I'd pledged my undying devotion. And if I used the last name I was born with, we were suddenly three strangers lumped together in one house instead of a family, united under one banner, which could be held up to the outside world as proof that we had a happy home.

Mind you, all this was taking place well before the ground rules of modern love began shifting beneath our feet. Elsewhere in the world—Sesame Street or L.A. or wherever—definitions were being redefined, social structures were being deconstructed. Not in Dallas. In Dallas, Texas, a woman was still supposed to be home, homemaking—looking her best, cooking a nice dinner, and filling out forms with the same name as both her husband and her child. Obviously, it would take

Christ himself to forgive any woman who failed to fit in, and there was never a shortage of folks who felt free to cast the first stone.

Maybe I introduced the topic of adoption to Sales in order to gain that final stamp of approval. Or maybe he introduced the topic to me in order to deflect questions that always seemed to shadow his smooth explanations about stray florist receipts and odd hotel matchbooks. We were both masters at making the other person think they came up with an idea.

"It'll be great to be adopted," I told Lance as he and I hurried toward the bus stop. "You'll have the same name as me."

He dragged at my hand, scuffing his feet to slow us down.

"I don't wanna be named Linda!"

"Armstrong, silly."

"I know," he grumbled.

We reached the bus stop, where he picked up a stick and started poking at a fire ant hill at the bottom of the signpost.

"C'mon. You want to ride the bus, don't you?" I coaxed. "You're a great big boy of five, and I think it's about high time you had a bus experience. A person wouldn't want to go his whole life never having a bus experience."

He glared at me, unconvinced, but the idea grew on him as we waited. By the time the mammoth city bus rolled up, stopping just for us, hissing like a dragon, snapping its doors open like a salute, Lance was dancing with excitement. He hopped up the stairs, gleefully clanked his coins into the slot, hopped over to a seat, and made conversation with the driver all the way downtown.

"He had sunglasses and a hat and there was hair in his ears," my son happily reported to the social worker as she ushered us into a windowless meeting room.

"Well, this is a big day for you, isn't it!" She smiled.

"Uh-huh," Lance said, but something about her tone made him suspicious. His grin wilted a little at the edges. "Well . . . not *so* big. Just the bus."

"Do you know why you're here, Lance?"

I fervently wished she wouldn't use that solicitous sweetie-pie voice on him. Anytime a grown-up took that tone with Lance, he could just smell a TB shot or a dose of cough medicine or some other "this is for your own good" agenda in it. I started to say something, but she raised her hand slightly.

"Do you, Lance?"

"Getting 'dopted," he curtly informed her.

"And do you know what 'adopted' means?" she asked.

"Same name," he said.

"And how do you feel about being adopted today, Lance? Do you want to be adopted today? Are you happy about being adopted?"

I should have prepared him better, I realized. I'd been so focused on gathering the information and organizing the paperwork. First I had to save up the money, then I had to get a lawyer to serve Eddie with papers (which he apparently signed without incident) and help me get the applications and birth certificate so a new one could be issued. But I should have coached him on what people want a good little boy to be like. The more she plied him with questions, the further his bottom lip stuck out. I tried to pull him onto my lap, but he wasn't one for sitting still, especially with those windowless walls closing in around us. I knew it would be better for everyone if I let him explore whatever small space was available.

"Who's going to adopt you today, Lance? Do you know?"

Lance said my husband's name.

"And do you want him to be your daddy from now on?"

"C'mon, Mama," Lance said, tugging at my hand. "Let's go back on the bus now."

"Pretty soon," I said. "But first we have to talk for a little while."

The social worker picked up a pen and clicked it in and out a few times.

"What does your new daddy do, Lance?"

He stared at her for a long moment, then grudgingly offered, "Work."

"And what does he do when he's at work?" she asked.

"*Work,*" he enunciated, then looked at me and rolled his eyes.

"I see. Okay. And does he . . . does he play with you? Does your new daddy do any fun things with you? Hmm? Lance? What do you like to do with your new daddy?"

"My mom plays leg-wrestle with me," he told her.

"Leg-wrestle?" the social worker echoed.

"And she takes me on the bus."

"That's nice. And does your new daddy take you places?"

"Church."

"Oh, that's good! Church is a good place to go, isn't it?"

"No," said Lance.

"It isn't? What don't you like about church?"

"You have to be too quiet and sit there."

"Oh, right," she nodded sympathetically. "That's hard sometimes, isn't it? Sometimes people get mad at you when you're not quiet, don't they?"

"Did you ride the bus here?" Lance asked.

"No, I drove my car, but—Lance, does your new daddy ever get mad at you?"

"What kinda car?"

"Does he ever get mad or yell at you or spank you?"

"The bus pulls up like this," Lance told her, illustrating with bold gestures and loud sound effects. "Doors open! *Shoosh!* Get on and pay your money! Like this—*clink-clink!*" He put imaginary coins in a slot and clapped his hands together, laughing, because an imaginary bus was all it took to make him completely happy, regardless of whatever was going on around him, and he fully expected everyone in the room to ride along.

"Do you love your new daddy, Lance?" the social worker continued prodding. "Is your new daddy nice to you?"

"When is the bus coming back?" Lance asked me.

"Son," I said softly, "it isn't polite to ignore someone when they ask you a question."

"But not if they're stupid!"

"*Lance!*" I whispered. "*Be nice!*"

"Well," said the social worker. "Let's get to our paperwork. Maybe we won't feel quite so shy later on."

I scooched my chair a little closer to her desk and offered a manila folder with the carefully typed forms. Fiddling with the reading glasses that hung from a pearl string around her neck, she watched Lance construct a pile of paper clips and then bulldoze it with a little truck he'd pulled from his pocket.

"That's a very nice car you have there," she said, shuffling the papers into the proper order. Lance made a revving noise and drove up the wall by the door. "Lance, would you like to sit down with us?"

"No," he said, and then to my tremendous relief added, "thank you."

She put on her reading glasses and went through the forms. There was no sound for a while except a rattling from the air vent and a soft revving from Lance's imaginary motor.

"Well. All right then, Mrs. Armstrong. Everything seems to be in order," she finally said. "And I guess our interview portion has been satisfactory. So that's all we need."

"Okay," I smiled. "Great."

"It's a shame Mr. Armstrong couldn't be here today."

"He's out of town on business," I said. (I always thought saying "out of town on business" made it sound as if he was usually home.) "They told me it wasn't necessary for him to be here."

"That's right, but—it's just that some people—well, a lot of people make a big occasion of it, you know. It's a pretty big deal to most families."

"Oh, it is! Of course. Yes. We're . . . we're all just so excited we can't hardly stand it. We're planning a big celebration as soon as he gets home. *Huge* celebration. With all the family and everything."

"Ah. I see. That's wonderful," she said. "Won't that be wonderful, Lance?"

He looked up at her, startled to be suddenly included in the conversation.

"Truck," he said after a long moment.

The social worker's forehead crinkled. "How's that, sweetie?"

"It's a truck," he told her patiently, and he held it up to show her. "You said 'car' before."

Smiling tightly, she shuffled some papers back into the manila folder and showed us to the door. Lance Armstrong and I walked down the hall and out onto the hot sidewalk.

~

The wife is always the last to know, and you know why? Because she's the last one who wants to know. When the phone finally rang, I wasn't ready to answer it. From the first jangle, I had a gut feeling it was going to be one of those phone calls. Calls that almost always launch some kind of clichéd soap opera scenario. So inconvenient. So *not part of the plan*. Here I was, working very hard at constructing my new and improved, whiter, brighter, "golden drop of retzin" life, and here comes the plot twist.

My weary BS-o-meter was purposefully tuning out warning signs. I didn't want to know anything bad about my charming, handsome husband. I didn't want any wrinkles in my crisply ironed life. Having someone else pitch in with economics, warding off mashers with a wedding ring, fitting perfectly into the Wonder Bread marketing demographic—I was seduced, sedated, and you know what else? *Happy*. Ignorance is bliss, even if you have to work pretty hard to ignore some things. My powers of rationalization worked like the snooze button on an alarm clock. *I know, I know,* you lie there thinking, *but let me be peaceful and oblivious for just ten more minutes. Just five minutes more*. And before you know it, the minutes have taken away hours of your life. Or years.

The caller identified herself as the wife of the Salesman's boss, so I was in dinner party invitation mode, immediately thinking about whether I'd have time to make myself something new to wear. She was a well-groomed lady, who always wore Dinah Shore–style palazzo pants with matching pastel blazers and blue eye shadow with burgundy-colored lipstick. I attempted to do the small-talk thing, but she sounded strained and uncomfortable.

"Darlin'," she said, "the reason I'm calling . . . umm . . . I just wanted to—to discuss—well, not discuss really, because of course, it's really none of my business . . . but there's something you need to know. About your husband."

"Oh?" A cold electric residue trickled down my spine.

"Hon, he's not who you think he is."

You know, when you think about it, "burgundy" is just another word for "purple," really. I couldn't imagine anyone with any class wanting purple lips.

"Hon, sometimes when you care for someone, you—well, you want to trust them, of course—and not that that's a bad thing! Trust is a good thing. It is. But there's a time to trust and then there's . . . other times. Because a man has needs, you know. Men have those needs for—for manly . . . needs. And well, you're very young, sugar, you're—what are you, twenty years old? Maybe twenty-one? And of course, it's not my place to say, but with experience, a wife might learn to be a little more, umm . . . aware of . . . of keeping your eyes open for . . . you know. Telltale indications of anything . . . indicative."

Mrs. Garishly Purple Lips fumbled around for words and finally paused as if she had actually come to some sort of point to which I was expected to respond.

"Ah," I said blankly.

"I just thought you should know."

"Uh-huh."

I really must be going. Someone at the door! Oops, there's the oven timer! B'bye now! The words were plain as anything in my brain. I'm not sure why they refused to come out of my mouth.

"Look," said Mrs. Lips So Purple All They Can Do Is Spew Lies About Other Women's Husbands, "all I'm saying is, you need to keep your eyes open. Just pay attention is all I'm saying."

"Well . . . okay then! And thank you so much for calling," I told her politely. There's no excuse for being impolite.

"It's just that—you seem like a real nice girl. Real sweet."

"Well, thank you!" I said brightly. "And thanks again for calling!"

"And your little boy—he seems real . . . energetic."

"B'bye now!"

"Sugar, I'd just hate to see y'all get caught up in—"

"Uh-huh! Yes! Okay then! But I should really get going," I practically sang out. I didn't know what I was saying, but anything that made her shut up was good conversation to me. "Yeah, we were just saying the other day, you know . . . we've just *gotta* have y'all over for barbecue one of these weekends, and so . . . so I will get back to you about that real soon."

"Sweetie, I only—"

"B'bye now!"

"Hon—"

"B'bye!"

Maybe it doesn't count as hanging up on someone if you say "b'bye" first.

I don't think she was trying to be mean. Even at the time, I felt she was trying to help me, but from the perspective of an attractive young woman (if I do say so myself, and I've worked hard enough at it that I feel I can) who'd been married for just one year to a man who consistently said the sweetest things and offered the smoothest answers to even the most perplexing questions—well, it just didn't compute. There simply wasn't a word in my vocabulary for someone who would do me that way. (I have since come up with several, but most of them are not printable.) There wasn't a word in my vocabulary for what that made *me*.

My marriage to Sales lasted ten years, but it probably wouldn't have endured that long if the man had actually lived with us. Thing is, he worked for a meat company that supplied hot dogs and corn dogs and barbecue beef to school cafeterias and other consumers of industrial quantities of meat, and the job kept him on the road at least five days a week. He was a traveling salesman—as in "Have you heard the one about the traveling salesman?" and then the joke goes on to couple him with a farmer's daughter/storekeeper's wife/steno pool/bowlegged waitress . . . et cetera, et cetera. Make that a traveling wiener salesman, and the off-color tragicomic potential literally boggles the mind. Someone ought to do a doctoral thesis on the sexual mythology of the traveling salesman. I don't get it. All I wanted was a father for my son.

Of course, if I could go back in time and stand beside myself, I'd take the phone out of that girl's hand, shake her by the shoulders, and say one word: *run!* But I was on a quest, and a quest is always easier when you don't know it's impossible. I had this vague idea of what a happy little family was going to be. I had seen it on TV. And just like the happy little homes on those happy little TV shows, we lived on a carefully constructed set. Pretty wallpaper disguised the thin shell and empty flats that stood in place of solid walls. Thick makeup was quickly applied to the ugliest realities. Unbearable moments were quickly edited out and forgotten. Cardboard extras at church and work took the place of any real friends who might have been forthright enough to tell me what an idiot I was.

I wanted more than anything to live that seamless sitcom life. So calm and pleasant. Such small problems so easily solved. Everyone just happy, happy, happy at the end of each tidy episode. I felt I deserved that. I'd earned it. And I was willing to keep on working for it, but in order to have that life a certain format had to be followed. The cast had to include a perfect mommy, a charming daddy, and a beautiful little boy. There had to be a clean house on a shady street. Dinner had to be served, voices moderated, explanations accepted without question.

Truthfully, I *was* happy most of the time. The odd thing is, I don't remember my husband really being part of it. He was on the road all week, so we didn't see much of him. When he was home, he tended to be more and more withdrawn as the years went by. After a while he was more like a prop or part of the furniture. An overstuffed chair that's off to the side, occupying its defined space in front of the television. When it starts getting shabby, you slipcover it so you won't notice. And if you stub your toe or bark your shin on it—well, that's your own fault.

What was real and true and overwhelmingly happy about my life in those days was my son. Like most people who never had the opportunity to be a kid when they were a kid, I've never let go of the child inside me. I loved to play with Lance, and as he grew we settled into a leg-wrestling, bike-riding buddy rapport. He hated being cooped up at day care until I got off work, so I made my best attempt to wear him out when we got home. I saw a little thing in the paper about BMX bike racing in Dallas with events for kids as little as kindergarten.

"That sounds like fun, doesn't it?" I asked as I set dinner on the table.

"Sure!" That was Lance's standard response. He was up for anything that involved keeping his little body in motion.

I hadn't quite figured on the expenses involved. I went into Richardson Bike Mart with a certain dollar figure in mind for the purchase of a gently used bicycle, and I came out having spent three times that amount after learning there's a lot more equipment involved in BMX bike racing than just the vehicle—and there's no such thing as a gently used BMX bike. It's either new or it's trashed (illustrating the need for all that safety equipment).

"You spent three hundred dollars on a bike for a six-year-old?" Sales raged when he came home the following Friday. "You're spoiling that kid, Linda! He's gonna be a spoiled brat if you keep it up. A mama's boy, that's what he's gonna be."

Oh, I hope so, I thought, but out loud I just said, "Well, why don't you come on over here so I can spoil you a little bit?"

"And you hear the way he talks to me," Sales grumbled. "If I talked to my daddy like that, I knew what was coming, and I'll tell you what—it wasn't somethin' good."

"You're just tired," I said, rubbing his shoulders. "You've had a long day. I thought you'd be home a couple hours ago. What were you working on so late?"

"On the other hand," said Sales, "it's probably good for the boy to get involved in some activities. Healthy, you know. Good exercise."

"Really, honey? You sure you don't mind?" I said sweetly. "Because of course, you're the man of the house."

"Whatever you think is best, sugar."

"Oh, thank you, sweetheart."

That's the sort of dance we did. Sometimes I'd hear Lance mocking us from the other room. "Oh, honey sweetie sugar bear," he'd say in a high voice. It made me cringe a little. But I bleakly figured, hey, we're all getting what we want. Why mess with a good thing?

~

The toughest times motherhood has to offer are those letting-go moments. By the time Lance was in third grade, he didn't want to go to day care after school anymore, but he was such a live wire, I worried about leaving him home alone. He seemed to have a core of pure energy that threw off sparks when it wasn't being channeled in the right direction. He was staunchly proud, fiercely loyal, and exhaustingly creative when it came to manufacturing fun and mischief. He was not a big kid, but he didn't take any guff from anybody. When he got mad, it didn't matter if the other kid was twice his size, he would scrap like a little badger.

"Lance, why on earth would you fight with Ian?" I asked, wiping his knee with Mercurochrome so I could put a Band-Aid on it. "Ian is your friend. You guys are buddies."

He launched into an animated story about a heated conflict at the crosswalk that started with one of them calling the other "jerkball" and ended with both of them sitting in the principal's office.

"Oh, *Lance* . . ."

"I'm sorry, Mom." He was always so contrite. He didn't want to disappoint me or cause me any hassles.

"I know you are, son," I said, ruffling his sun-streaked hair.

"And he had it coming!"

"Well, be that as it may," I said, "you're not supposed to fight, and you know that. And you know there are consequences when you do stuff you're not supposed to do. Mrs. Washington says you can't ride the bus for the rest of the school year. That's the punishment for fighting in the bus line. There's still six weeks of school left, and I don't know how you're going to get there. Or get home. You know I have to be at work, son."

"It's okay," he told me. "I can ride my bike."

"I don't know about that," I hedged.

"I can!" he said earnestly. "I ride to pee-wee practice every day, don't I? And I ride to Ian's house and J.R.'s and the pool."

It was one of those letting-go moments you're never quite ready for, and frankly, working mothers are forced to face them a lot sooner than they'd like to. I don't know how else I would have gotten him to school. So he started riding, and once you start a thing, well, it's easy to continue. From then on, if he needed to be somewhere while I was at work, that's how he got there, and even though I usually showed up before practice was over, offering to put his bike in the trunk and drive him home, he preferred to ride. Helmets weren't generally available or encouraged back then, but I tried to remind him of basic safety rules.

"Your bike is your freedom," I told him, "and that's a big responsibility."

He nodded gravely. I knew he understood the meaning of the word and didn't take it lightly.

~

Lance went out for his first track meet in fifth grade. He was a little nervous that morning, but he told me in no uncertain terms: "I'm gonna be the champion."

"You can do it!" I told him without one shred of doubt. "I wish I could be there, son. But wait a sec. I'll be right back."

I went and got a silver dollar from my dresser drawer.

"What's this for?" he asked when I pressed it into his hand.

"For luck. I got it for change at the store a long time ago, and I noticed—look here. See? It's from the year you were born. So I saved it. I thought there might be an occasion sometime when you needed a little sprinkle of fairy dust."

"For luck," he nodded, sliding it into his sock. And boy howdy, was it ever.

I don't know what ever happened to that silver dollar—maybe he still has it—but it crossed a lot of finish lines with him over the next several years, and it didn't seem to be weighing him down one bit.

~

You know how it is when your kids get to that age. The years start spinning. I was working two jobs to make ends meet, but we still made time for BMX bike racing and other activities. There was always another birthday party to plan, another football game to cheer for, and another call from Mrs. Cravitz next door, complaining that Lance and his hooligan friends had made a bike ramp out of her trash can or stuck their fingers in a freshly cemented sidewalk or committed some other unpardonable act of boyishness.

"Mrs. Armstrong," she admonished, "I very nearly ran over your son this morning. He was tearing down the street as if he owned it."

Seems like she had something new to tell me at least three days a week.

"Mrs. Armstrong, your son was jumping over my rosebushes again, and I've told him several times not to climb my mimosa tree!"

Mrs. Armstrong, that boy of yours . . . dah-dah-dah . . . diving between the hedges . . . chasing squirrels with the garden hose . . . hooting and hollering with his friends . . . playing kick ball and tipping over the trash can . . .

You get the idea.

It got so I almost dreaded to pull into my own driveway, knowing she was just waiting for me to get home so she could waddle across the street and tell me what a holy terror my kid was and how remiss I was in not staying home from work to properly raise him. I guess I was supposed to seal him in a Tupperware container, while I went out back and plucked a few hundred dollars off our money tree. It's not that I'm an inconsiderate person, but I had to work. I wasn't about to corral him in front of the TV and stuff him with cookies every day after school. Trying to put a lid on Lance wasn't something I even wanted to attempt. The only way to keep him out of trouble was to enroll him in every activity imaginable. If I could wear him out by twilight and tuck him in before ten—mission accomplished.

Lance and I were blowin' and goin' every weekend, completely independent of his stepfather. Too much hanging around the house always led to some kind of falling-out between Lance and Sales, which led to a falling-out between me and Sales, which led to me trying to squash Lance into submission, which was an exercise in futility. Sales coached Lance's Little League team. He did do that. He gets some credit for effort there, but I'm not sure how much he enjoyed it. Lance wasn't the budding baseball star Sales would have liked him to be. Overall, it was better to either keep a healthy distance or engage everybody in some kind of activity that would leave us all too exhausted to argue.

Elementary school rolled into middle school.

Lance played football in grade school, but you've gotta understand the dynamic of little boys playing football in Texas. If it isn't readily apparent from the age of three that your kid is going to be seven-foot-ten and built like an oversize, side-by-side, ice-making refrigerator—well, then what's the point? Lance had fun, but he wasn't rabid enough or big enough to impress his coaches. He obviously didn't have what it took to lead his team to that glorious hometown victory. (And that's what children's sports is all about, isn't it? *Victory! Victory! Victory!* Why waste time teaching silly things like character, sportsmanship, and the joy of physical fitness, hmm?) When it stopped being fun, Lance stopped playing, but that's not to say he didn't care. I still have the eight-by-ten group photo from his last year on the team. On the back of it, he carefully cataloged the name of each player and kept a meticulous record of each game: who they played, who won, what the score was. I loved the way he respected the game, even though he wasn't fantastically good at it. And I loved it that when it wasn't a good fit for him to play anymore, he didn't see it as quitting or failing; he saw it as moving on.

"My friends are all on COPS anyway," he told me. "They said I should come to practice next week and join, Mom. Can I?"

I set a plate of pork chops on the table and handed him a box of kitchen matches so he could light our candles.

"What's COPS?"

"City of Plano Swimmers. They practice every morning at six, and then there's swim meets and races and stuff on the weekend."

"Where would you be going for practice?"

"Over at Los Rios Country Club."

"Ah. Great." Lance and I weren't exactly the country club types, but it wasn't too far for him to ride.

"So can I?"

"Sure," I said. "Sounds like fun." It also covered the rest of his unsupervised time. And I thought Lance had the makings of a terrific swimmer. Until I saw him swimming.

The day of team tryouts, we cruised over to the swanky side of Plano and located the sign-up table that had been set up at the Plano Aquatics

Center. Standing on the sidelines with the cream of the society crop, I felt like a fish out of water, and Lance was anything but a fish in it. He flopped into the pool and beat his arms and legs down the lane like a paddle barge. One of the swim instructors came over and gingerly informed me they would be starting Lance with the nine-year-olds.

"But he's in middle school," I pleaded. "He'll be humiliated!"

We both glanced over at my son, who was flailing his way toward us, thrashing half the water out of the pool. I recognized the little sister of one of his friends as she skimmed past him and hopped out before he'd made it three-quarters of the way back.

"Okay," I sighed. "I'll tell him."

When he got out of the pool, I went over, wrapped a towel around his shoulders, and briskly rubbed his back.

"Good try, son! Good job!"

"It wasn't either. I stink at this," he groaned as he stood shivering by the side of the pool. "Even the little kids are better than me."

"No way," I told him. "Nobody tried harder than you. And that's what counts. So what if those guys are better right now? They've been taking lessons since kindergarten, and you're just starting. Think how impressive it'll be when you can turn around and whoop their little behinds. Huh? Then you'll be glad you put in the time to start at the beginning and learned to do it right, won't you?"

Lance nodded. He never needed a whole lot of pep-talking. Usually just a reminder that it wasn't about what was going on with other people, about whether or not they were better than you. It was about what was going on inside yourself, about how you could be better than you were to start with. And it didn't take Lance long to get better at swimming. He was natural as a stingray, and he had a terrific coach, Chris MacCurdy, who genuinely cared about the kids and wanted to help every one of them succeed. Within a month or so Lance had joined his friends in the seventh-grade group, and a year later he took fourth in the 1,500-meter freestyle at the state competition.

Funny, isn't it, how a person dives into things in his life and the ripples that go out from that moment travel so much further than you imagine. If Lance had allowed himself to be discouraged that day, he wouldn't have gotten into the triathlons that really launched his career as an athlete. He would have been a very different boy living in a very different body.

Years later, when Lance was in high school, he was zipping down the street on his bicycle and got hit by a Jeep Cherokee. He flew over the handlebars, over the hood of the SUV, and landed headfirst on the cement. As I stood shaking in the hospital corridor, listening to the laundry list of injuries—concussion, gashes in his head and foot, sprung knee—I could hardly believe he'd managed to survive it. And I wasn't the only one amazed by the fact that he was still walking. Almost every single doctor and nurse who came through the emergency room felt compelled to tell me how easily he could have come away from this a quadriplegic. It was the swimmer's body that saved him. Had it not been for the beefed-up shoulders and powerful neck he'd developed during all those years of laps and practices—well, I'd be telling a very different story.

But of course, I didn't know all that back then, standing in the sunrise, waiting for Saturday morning swim meets to begin at subdivision pools in Plano or Dallas or Richardson. All I knew then was how much I loved to see that boy in motion. There were moments when there was no division between the rhythm of my heart and the cadence of his kick. Like watching pure sunlight cut through water. I don't even know how to explain the dance of it, the joy—this amazing combination of electricity and humanity and physics. It just filled me up to see him.

~

Time flew faster, and so did my son. He didn't seem to have but three gears—sleep, eat, and full speed ahead. During the week we had our routine. While he ate a good hot breakfast every morning, I cleaned house and organized myself for the day. I left for work early, and when it was time, Lance hopped on his bike and got himself to school. He always called me when he got home; then he'd fix himself a snack and go outside to mess around with his friends or go for a long bike ride if he was training. When I got home, I made dinner, and after dinner we'd go running or drive around a new bicycle course to get the exact measurement of it. By the time nine or ten rolled around, we were zonked out sleeping.

From Friday afternoon till Sunday night, we were always busy with housekeeping chores, yard work, and whatever sporting events the season presented. I'd get back to work on Monday morning, and people would be talking about some game they saw on TV or some ribs they'd barbecued or how they had dinner at the in-laws. Someone would ask me what I did over the weekend, and I'd say, "Well, Lance was competing in Waxahachie, so we drove over there." They about couldn't believe all the places we went and things we did.

When Lance came home one day and told me about this IronKids thing he'd seen advertised—a junior triathlon that involved swimming about a thousand laps, then bicycling about a thousand miles, and then running farther than most people walk in a year—well, I'm telling you, it didn't sound like a whole lot of fun. It sounded pretty grueling. And it sounded like a good way for a kid to get hurt. But he was so excited by the very idea of it, I had to say, "Sure! That sounds like a blast!" and then quickly set to work convincing myself that was exactly what it would be. How can you not encourage your kid when he comes to you with that look in his eyes? If it's activity and it's a challenge and it's outside, you're just plain crazy if you don't encourage that. That's a healthy thing no matter how you slice it. Over the years I saw a lot of Lance's friends start something enthusiastically but fizzle on it because their parents conveyed the message "No, that's too hard. Too much time. Too much effort." And then they turned around and moaned because their kids were sitting on the couch eating potato chips. They didn't understand how powerful that message was. I wanted to send the message that doing something—anything!—is worthwhile simply because it makes you a person who *does stuff* instead of a person who sits around.

Unfortunately, not everyone sees it that way. As my son's range of motion and mischief expanded, so did the neighbor lady's scolding.

"Mrs. Armstrong, that boy of yours runs wild! You just let him do whatever he wants to do!" (This would have been Lance's idea of heaven had it been true.)

I guess I was supposed to feel guilty or something. Here she was, this perfect wife and mother who was home taking care of her kids all day instead of abandoning them to go off to work. And here I was, this working woman who left a key under the mat for her feral child to let himself in after he made his way home from school, pedaling his little bike through rain or shine. Lance was a "latchkey kid" long before anyone came up with that term—before there were ideas and facilities and practical strategies for dealing with the reality that some families simply didn't function according to the *Father Knows Best* model. It was easy for people to put me down for that. But then the years went by, and while Lance was off tearing up the tracks, that neighbor's boy was hanging out with his stony friends and getting himself into a dozen kinds of trouble. Then I could look back on that day and say, "Yup, I pretty much let that boy of mine do whatever he wanted to do. Thank God!"

It just seems to me that when your kids come and tell you about something they want to *do*, it's different from when they come and tell about something they want to *have.* Instead of saying, "Buy me this!" they're saying, "I think I can do this! Do you?" Squashing their interest sends the message, "No, I don't think you can, and it isn't worth my time or trouble to help you." The problem is, it's so much easier to just buy them something. The money is nothing compared to the time and effort you have to invest in facilitating their activities—making sure they have the equipment they need, checking out the adults involved, driving them around, sewing little patches and logos and numbers on things, juggling schedules, attending their events, cheering them on.

Luckily, we were so broke, buying Lance off with toys and electronics was never an option. All I could afford to give him was my time and attention. We brainstormed about what was needed and who could provide it. I helped him set up a Rolodex with contact cards for possible sponsors, and when they generously came through, I sewed their logo patches on the back of Lance's shirt and made sure he wrote them nice thank-you notes. I got him a desk calendar and helped him organize his time and schedule. And I cheered him on. That I could do. I might have been a typist on the outside, but deep down I still had the heart and soul of a Rangerette.

~

My radar was rusty, but I could feel it again. Just there, at the back of my head. And that wound-up-spring feeling I'd had as a child was coming back to the pit of my stomach—the feeling of being poised, waiting for trouble to roll in like a thunderhead, voices escalating like a windstorm until hands and fists flashed out to strike. The older Lance got, the more he and Sales clashed. I ran interference as much as I could, because Lance had no fear of his stepfather anymore. When he was little, Sales could "paddle" him (and to this day I hate that euphemism—it's just a coy way to say "hit and keep on hitting"), but once Lance got to be twelve or so, he was too big for that. When Sales yelled, he yelled back, and on one occasion when Sales tried to take a swing at him, he swung back. They ended up in a scuffle, with me crying and pleading on the sidelines and Sales ultimately telling Lance, "You get the hell out of my house and you stay out until you learn some respect!"

But respect can't be learned. It has to be earned. By nightfall Lance still hadn't come back. The next day (Mother's Day, ironically enough—how's that for a lovely gift?) he was still gone, and I was pacing the floor, sobbing, calling everyone I could think of until I tracked him down at a friend's house. That night Sales was preparing to leave, and Lance came home. Nobody said anything. We just went to our separate corners. And it haunted me for a long time, knowing that the corner I should have been in was my son's.

I had a lousy health year when I was thirty-two. Nagging problems (which I won't go into, as a favor to both you and me) eventually led to a hysterectomy. As busy as Lance and I were, there was no way to schedule it when it didn't conflict with some event of his, so I persuaded Sales to take a couple of days off and take him to a triathlon in Houston.

"How'd it go?" I couldn't wait to ask when they got back.

"Lousy," Lance mumbled on his way to his room.

"Oh, no! What happened?"

"Mom, I totally bonked. We didn't have enough water bottles or the right food, and then when we were coming home . . ." He shook his head and turned away to unpack his duffel bag. "It just sucked, that's all."

"Why? What's wrong?"

"Never mind. It doesn't matter."

"Lance, tell me."

"No, it's just—I was worried about you. Are you okay?"

"It hurts some, but yeah, I'm okay. Are you okay?"

He just shrugged and shoved his racing clothes into the laundry hamper. I went out and closed his bedroom door. Later I discovered a hollowed-out book on his shelf, and in it were notes Sales had written to a woman he was seeing. He'd written them while he and Lance were on the triathlon trip, and Lance had found them in the trash. It killed me to know that's how Lance felt. Hollowed out with an ugly little secret inside. That was the impossible situation in which he'd been placed.

It wasn't the beginning of the end. It was the messy middle. The beginning of the end was probably the day Sales and I got married. And the end of the end was near. That wound-up spring in my stomach was about as tight as it could go.

~

I'm not a natural blonde, but I'm blond now, and even before I went for the gold, I knew how blondes must feel. When you're pretty, a lot of people automatically think you're stupid, and sometimes you let them think that, because it works to your advantage to be underestimated. Blondes make great detectives.

When I tracked her down, I was surprised to find that the girlfriend wasn't petite like me. She was tall. Statuesque, I guess you'd say, in a gawky, no-class, big-foot kind of way. She had long blond hair, a decent figure, a classic face. But I wouldn't say she was all that pretty. Not *irresistibly* pretty, certainly. Not someone you'd be talking to over corn dogs and suddenly be completely smitten with. She stood in the doorway smiling, maybe thinking I was the Avon Lady or canvassing for the Lady Bird Johnson Garden Fund or something.

"Are you Pamela?" I asked.

"Yes," she said. "Can I help you?"

"Hi. Um . . . my name is Linda." I had no idea where to go from here but directly forward. "I want you to stop dating my husband."

Her smile froze and faded like a little pink vinca hit by a hard frost.

"Excuse me?" she said.

"You heard me."

"Ma'am, I have no idea who you are or what you're talking about, and I want you to leave." She started to close the door, but I didn't step back.

Trying to sound as tall as possible, I said my husband's name, and her eyes opened wide.

"He bought a Steuben bowl," I said. "I have the receipt for the delivery, and I can see the bowl right over there on your hutch."

"My—that's—that was—" She looked over her shoulder at the hutch. She looked at me. Then pointed at the bowl. "Listen here! You are mistaken. D'you hear me? I received that bowl as a birthday present, and I resent you barging into my—"

"Yeah, well, I resent that money from my household is buying you birthday presents. I have a son to support. I have a mortgage and bills and responsibilities. What I *don't* have is a Steuben bowl, and I have no intention of paying for yours!"

"Look," she said, "he told me everything. I know what's going on with your divorce and the house and everything, and I'm not going to get dragged into the middle of it, okay? Now please leave!" She extended one giant finger and poked me in the shoulder, pushing me back from the doorway.

"No, it's *not* okay," I said, standing on tiptoes so I could poke her shoulder. "And don't you pick a fight with me, sister!"

"*You're* the one picking the fight!" Poke.

"And *you're* the one screwing someone else's husband!" Double poke.

"I told you—"

"And I told *you*—"

She shoved me. I shoved back. She slapped my hand away. I slapped hers. There was a flurry of sissy girl-fight moves, and we ended up gripping each other's wrists in kind of a struggling Watusi dance clench.

"Okay, *stop!*" I told her. "Let's just stop it right here."

"*You* stop!"

"*Let's both stop!* Okay?"

"Fine!"

"Fine!"

"Okay."

Dallas women are scrappy, but we're not about to chip a perfectly good manicure unless there's life or death at stake. We stopped and rearranged our rumpled blouses, then stood there in awkward silence, wearing the same weary expression. Eventually, she let out a long sigh, and one big tear slid down her cheek. Suddenly she didn't look so tall and young and classic anymore. A huge sadness aged her before my eyes.

"It occurs to me," I said, "that we're standing here fighting over nothing. If I'm mistaken, then I'm sorry. I apologize. But if I'm right—well, then I don't think this man is worth your time or mine."

It was empty bravado, considering the ten years I'd already invested, but the girl blinked hard and nodded slightly.

"He told me you were getting a divorce," she said after a moment. "He said your house was up for sale. He said all his stuff was packed up, ready to leave."

"Well, why don't you come on over to the house," I suggested. "See for yourself. Then we'll have some coffee and wait for him to get home and when he does . . . well, I guess that'll clear up any misunderstanding."

To this day I do not know why I said that. And I can't imagine why she followed me home. For all she knew I was an ax murderer. I guess she wanted to know the truth. And so did I, I realized. Finally, I really did want to know. I was ready to know. I had no idea what this thing was or what I would do with it, but I wanted to look it in the face.

You'd think Sales would have been mighty surprised to see the two of us sitting there when he opened the door. If he was surprised—or angry or scared or stricken with conscience—it didn't so much as ruffle the surface of his expression.

I stood up and tried to sound calm. "Do we need to talk?"

He smoothly explained away the receipts and circumstantials and basically made it out that he was being stalked by her. As he tried to wriggle out of his own tangled web, his lover stood there, drop-jawed;

she was utterly baffled and betrayed and crushed. I was having a hard time hating her as she blazed off down the street.

"Linda?" Sales was standing behind me with his arms around my waist before the dust settled on the driveway. "Sweetheart, I'm so sorry you had to go through that. And let me tell you, I'm glad you're too smart to be taken in by someone like her. Yeah, thank the Lord, you're smart enough to get how a misunderstanding like this can happen when a person is in sales. That is for sure one of the things I love about you, honey. This keen understanding you have about sales. 'Cause you understand how it is—that when a person is in sales—you know, a *salesperson* is required to be nice to people. You gotta catch those flies with honey, not vinegar. Am I right? It's our bread and butter at stake. How I can be that way with people—how I can bring them around to my way of thinking—well, that's how I make a living. For you and Lance. That's what puts food on your table and provides your son with everything he needs. And that's why it's so important to me, Linda. Because God gave me that boy to care for as a son, and I consider him a gift. I do. A gift from Jesus. And in order to take care of him and take care of you, I have to—to do what I have to do. And if someone misinterprets that—some obviously unstable person—or dangerous even! Who knows what they'll say or do? I don't think it was very smart of you to let her know where we live, you know? You really should've talked to me about it first, and then we could've avoided all this misinterpretation of the situation. I mean, think about it—she could've gone completely psycho on you. Am I right?"

What scared me most was how much I wanted to believe him. But as I stood there, up to my ankles in the utter ridiculousness of this great fable, all the equally lame stories I'd already swallowed over the years stirred in the pit of my stomach and then rose up in my throat to gag me. I had to cover my face with my hands. I was so damn mad, I couldn't stand the sight of him. It would have been less painful to have a fire ant in my eye.

"I'll tell you what, Linda, it's lucky for you I got home when I did," he went on. "Because who knows what sort of terrible things an unstable person like that might do to an itty-bitty thing like you."

He kept talking as I walked away, but I was busy imagining the terrible things an unstable person might do to a no-good wiener-schlepping, potbellied, pathologically deceptive rat bastard who apparently labored under the misconception that he was allowed to have his cheesecake and eat me too.

I went and did the only thing you can do when your house is slowly burning down around you. I cleaned the bathroom. Then I started folding laundry. After a while I heard the lawn mower start up out back. Then it stopped. Then started again a little while later. Why did he always mow the lawn in portions like that? I'll never understand. For cryin' out loud. If you start something, finish it.

Finish it, I kept telling myself, but six more weeks went by. I just didn't have it in me to step off that cliff.

The jangle of the telephone made my stomach jump. Lance picked up the phone in the kitchen before I had a chance to say anything.

"Hello?" he said.

"Hi!" said a young woman. "Is this . . . umm . . . who is this?"

"This is Lance."

"Oh. Okay. Well, I was looking for—"

"I've got it, Lance," I interrupted. "You can hang up."

"Who is this?" the young woman asked again.

"This is Linda. Who's calling?" The phone sounded hollow as a seashell against my ear. "Is this Pamela?"

"No. This is Jennifer, but—umm, I think I probably have the wrong number."

"No," I said. "You probably don't."

She was silent for a moment, then asked, "Is he there?"

"He'll have to call you back," I said. "He's busy packing."

I clapped the phone into the cradle. This undoubtedly did count as hanging up on someone. Tough shit.

"Mom?" Lance called from the kitchen. "I'm going over to Mandy's."

"Okay, son." I tried not to let my voice tremble or crack. "See ya later!"

As soon as I heard the front door close behind him, I headed toward the living room, where Sales was napping in front of the television. It was a rude awakening for all concerned.

~

Here's the thing about being a hard-ass. You're just as relentless about holding on to love as you are about holding on to a grudge. You think that if you grip something or someone with all your strength—well, sooner or later they're bound to grip you back and love you just as strong. I have always been willing to give a person chance after chance. But once that tree falls on my head, I'm done. I looked at this man with whom I'd tried so hard to build a life, this man to whom I'd been faithful and caring for ten years, and suddenly I saw . . . he was *paunchy*. And his hairline was receding. And you know what? When I met him, he was missing a front tooth. That smile he smiled when he was lying to me—I *paid* for that damn thing! That perfect white tooth was *mine*. And if he'd stayed in the house one more day, I swear, I would have repossessed it.

I didn't want my son to be around for the seriously unpleasant stuff, so I waited until my husband was gone, then called Lance at his girlfriend's house.

"I need you to come home," I told him.

"Mom? What's wrong? Are you okay?"

I checked, and at the foundation of me, I could say, *Yes I am,* for the first time in years. Closer to the surface, though, I was shivering. My stomach was a hornets' nest.

"He's gone. I threw him out."

"Mom, that's great," Lance said, and the relief in his voice made me think he understood more than I'd given him credit for. "It's about time."

"I know." I was trying to keep my voice steady, but it kept getting crinkled and ragged in my throat. "I'm sorry, Lance. I'm so sorry for everything that's happened. And I'm not sure how it'll all work out. The finances and everything. But I'll figure it out. We'll manage."

"It's okay, Mom. We'll be okay."

"We will. I promise."

"I'm on my way home," he said. "I'll be right there."

"Lance?"

"Yeah, Mom?"

"Son, I need you to just—*please*. Please, promise me you won't cause any trouble right now. I can't take it."

"I'll be right there," he repeated. "I love you, Mom."

~

"What's the sweetest thing ever said to you?" asks my hippie girlfriend.

I thought about all the flattery that's come my way from various persons with their various agendas. All those things you enjoy hearing but don't necessarily believe.

"My son says, 'I love you,' whenever we get off the phone," I tell her. "Even though I already know, and he knows I know—he still says it every time. That's the sweetest thing."

It's important. To say it, even when it's already been said. When it's already known and serves no agenda. And now, when I talk to my grandson on the phone, I hear my son in the background, coaching him.

"Tell Mimi you love her. Say, 'I love you, Mimi.' "

"Duv yo, Mimi!" Luke says dutifully.

"I love you too, Gogie," I tell him. And I promise to send him banana bread.

It seems to me that when two people agree to join their lives together, certain things should be understood. There will be no hitting. There will be no screwing around. There will be listening. There will be honesty, care, and—how would you even express it?—there will be *presence*. You're promising you'll be home even when you're away. No matter how many cases I see to the contrary, I'll keep believing it's possible.

On the other hand, what do I know? I'm the one who married a traveling wiener salesman.

~

Lance and I were officially on our own. A long way from Cleaver Street. But when the burden of keeping up that pretense was lifted, I started to see how cumbersome it truly had been. Maybe—just maybe—the entire world, from Ann Landers to the nosy neighbors, was full of BS, and the real definition of family was "two or more people who may or may not have the same name and might or might not have a perfect life, learning to muddle through together." *I am enough family for my son, and he is enough for me*, I decided, *no matter what* Better Homes and Gardens *has to say about it*. On a day-to-day reality basis, it wasn't all that different. Since Sales was only home on weekends, it was easy to ignore him (and I'm willing to admit that probably didn't encourage him to curb his philandering). But being married to him supplied me with the correct answers when I was filling out forms. Returning to no-man's-land after all this time—it scared me.

Worse than that was the feeling of having failed. Again. Why couldn't I make the right kind of life for my son? Why couldn't I make the right kind of love? I concluded there must be something terribly wrong with me. All the Mrs. Cravitzes of the world were right.

"The thing about a forest fire," says my hippie girlfriend, "is that the biggest trees need the heat in order for their seeds to germinate."

"Hmm?" I say so she'll think I'm listening.

"The forest has to get burned in order to grow."

That's a pretty good analogy for the postmarriage moment. You feel like you're the last stump standing—sawed-off, charred, and brittle. But in the aftermath there's a hidden gift of growing. It's imperceptible at first. You wouldn't know it was there if you tried to feel for it. But it is there. Just under the blackened surface of the earth. The seed of something new and the freedom to start working toward your own rebirth.

I have learned something from every man who broke my heart. The thing I learned from this man was the art of the sell. And I was determined to use it well.

EIGHT

CHAIN REACTION

"Lookin' good, Lance! Lookin' good!" I called.

As he came closer he slowed down enough for me to jog along beside him.

"You're doin' great, son! Thatta boy, Lance! Thatta boy!"

I handed off a water bottle. Lance chugged half and poured the rest over his head. I handed him the other one and he tucked it under his arm so he could grab a chunk of banana bread. We always carried plenty of banana bread, and I'm not talking about any old pale, store-bought, fluffed-up stuff. I'm talking about real southern grandma–caliber banana bread that weighs about eighteen pounds per slice and actually has some substantially gratifying impact. I don't mean to brag, but my banana bread is not just *good*. It's *way* good. It's *forget your middle name* good. It's—well, see for yourself. Here's what you need:

1 stick butter (softened, of course)
1½ cups sugar
2 eggs
1 cup buttermilk (and don't even think about substituting something gutless like 2%)
1½ teaspoons baking soda
2 cups flour
2 mashed bananas (try to catch them when they're just a little past their prime, looking for their last chance to contribute something meaningful to the world)
½ teaspoon salt
½ cup chopped nuts (walnuts or pecans)
1 teaspoon vanilla

Now, don't just plop everything into a bowl. You're doing this for someone you love, so you want to do it right. Heat up the oven to 350 degrees. Cream the butter, sugar, eggs, bananas, and vanilla into a lovely, ooey-gooey mess. Mix the buttermilk and soda together. Add that to the sweet, creamy banana mess. *Gradually* add the flour and salt so you don't have that clumpy lumpy flour thing going on, and when you've got all that thoroughly stirred up, add the chopped nuts. Pour your batter into a greased and floured loaf pan and bake for one hour or until the center is cooked. Use a toothpick to test if the center is done. You may want to have your loved one standing by with a serrated knife and a cup of coffee, because it's best to sit right down and have some together while it's still warm.

"Did you know that a bicycle wheel is a gyroscope?" says my hippie girlfriend.

"What's a gyroscope?" I ask without opening my eyes.

"It's something that stays upright when it's spinning because of this sort of invisible force. I mean, there's a totally scientific explanation for it, but I have no idea what it is, so to me it's like this supernatural defiance of the laws of gravity."

"Hmm. Interesting," I say, because sometimes there's not much point in trying to join in the conversation with her. You might as well try to play gin rummy with a hummingbird.

"And I was just thinking," she says, doing some kind of sweeping chigong movements in the water, "that you were Lance's gyroscope. You were the invisible force that allowed him to totally defy the laws of physics."

"No, he did that all on his own," I tell her, because I never want anyone to think I take credit for any of my son's accomplishments. I don't.

But inside, I'm thinking, *Ah-ha. So that's what it was. . . .*

~

A couple of Lance's friends were old enough to drive that winter, so when a particularly harsh ice storm hit the Dallas–Fort Worth area, it didn't take long for them to head out sliding. They probably started with the little culverts and modest hills that were available in our neighborhood, but when those failed to provide action on a par with this amazing meteorological occurrence, they decided to tie a rope to the back of Ian's car and take turns being towed in circles on a big cardboard flap off a Panasonic television box.

They didn't see me when I pulled over to the side of the road across from the parking lot where they were playing. Lance was good about calling to let me know where he was, so I knew right where to find them. I scrunched down in the seat, holding my hands close by the car heater vent.

Whooping and shouting, the boy on the ground picked himself up and brushed his gloves over the ice-encrusted seat of his pants. Lance piled out of the car and took the rope from him, saddling down on the cardboard flap and bracing himself for the ride. As soon as the other boy was back in the car, Ian gunned the motor. Frost sprayed back into Lance's face as the tires spun, then grabbed the glazed cement, jerking the rope and dragging him forward. He became a cowboy, a surfer, and the tip of a whip-crack all at once. Ian careened back and forth across the snowy asphalt with Lance skiing and hollering along behind.

"Doughnuuuuut!" someone bellowed, and the car spun out, slinging Lance full circle before he let go of the rope and slid, first on the cardboard and then just the seat of his jeans, rolling to a stop at the edge of the parking lot. He leaped up and ran toward the car, skidding and slipping, scooping up the cardboard and waving it over his head. His voice echoed off the hard night sky. The cold stars vibrated with his pure adrenaline energy.

It was like watching a circus act. Breathtaking, heart-stopping, death-defying stunts so beautiful you can't take your eyes away. Of course, it scared the fool out of me, but I didn't get out of the car. I didn't tell him, *No! Stop! It's too dangerous!* Because I didn't want him raised to be afraid. But I felt like I had to stay there watching him. Like if I kept my eyes on him, if I focused all my will and hope directly on him, he wouldn't get hurt.

It was like that at races too. I felt in my heart that if I was there, something about the very karma we shared would keep him upright and not let him fall. We'd witnessed some spectacular crashes over the years, and when Lance ended up in the middle of a pile, I could feel every bone-jarring moment of it. It knocked the wind out of me, even if I was seeing it on video for the eleventy-seventh time. This sport, I learned, is like the old nursery rhyme: when it's good, it's very very good, and when it's bad, it's horrid. On rainy days, on windy straightaways, on mind-bending curves—my whole being went out to him, surrounding him with a protective force, keeping him upright.

Watching him pour all of himself into everything he did—it always left me breathless with gratitude and love and inspired me in the most clichéd "when the going gets tough the tough get going" sort of way.

The going got tough, for sure, after the departure of my husband. A few days after he left, Lance and I drove to Louisiana for a junior cycling event. I have to say, my hands were shaking a little as I made out the check for the entry. As I filled in the amount I was removing items from my mental grocery cart. I had a fleeting thought that Sales might be right—that maybe God wanted me to need him so I would avoid the sin of divorce or that maybe depending on him was retribution for not saving myself for marriage. Maybe I really couldn't provide for my son without him.

Or *maybe,* I'd finally tell myself when the self-Osterizing started getting out of hand, *maybe* he was a big ol' horse's ass. And maybe he only said those things to throw me off the scent of his philandering. *Suck it up, buttercup,* I sternly told myself. This is one little ostrich who'd better take her head out of the sand and see that she's stronger and smarter than anyone ever gave her credit for.

As I signed my name, I made the conscious decision to write "Linda Armstrong." I'd attached that name to my son, and my son was attached to me. There was no going back. Signing this check that I was going to cover, thanks to nothing but my own elbow grease, I took ownership of that name. The Armstrong family tree starts here and now, I decided. Me and my son. Whatever Armstrong sons and daughters come after us, we are their root. Whatever history this family someday claims, the first chapter is the two of us.

On the way home from the event Lance and Ian sat in the backseat, timing themselves in a farting contest and laughing their heads off. There was no place available for them to shower or swim, so they smelled like a couple of llamas, and when they drifted off to sleep they stuck their feet up into the front seat. I had to drive with the window down all the way back to Dallas. My hair was a mess, but I couldn't stop smiling. The spring in my stomach slowly unwound, and I settled into the idea that we could be happy again, that we could do a lot better than just get by.

It's like that old story about frogs in a pot. One gets thrown into scalding hot water, which is noticeably uncomfortable, so of course he jumps right on out. But the second one gets put in a pot of cold water with the burner on just a little, and it's comfortable enough, so he sits there. And because one moment isn't so terribly much hotter than the moment before, he sits there until it boils. It wasn't until Sales walked out that door that I fully realized my life had become a steaming bucket of frog soup. As tough as it was to be a single mom, I was back in charge of my own lily pad and liking it fine.

When I watched Lance power through junior triathlon events, he was a dolphin in the water, then he jumped on his bike and became a machine, then he hopped off the bike and took off like a pony down the running path. The element in which he was competing seemed to recreate and feed him. He simply became whatever he needed to be. I could do that too. I knew I could. I could be a mother and a father and a pit crew and a taxi driver and a cheerleader and a friend and maybe some other things I hadn't even thought of yet.

No matter how I finessed the numbers, however, I couldn't see how I'd be able to afford the house on my own, so Lance and I went out and scouted around a few apartment complexes. It felt like such a huge step backward. The places we could afford were on a par with the places where I'd grown up, and having had something better for a while, I knew now how bad it really was. Like when you've been out in the sunshine and you walk into a closed-up room. It seems so much darker than it did before you went out. There was no way I was taking Lance back to the scuzzy housing project world we'd come from. I took a second job and spent my lunch hours searching and applying for something with benefits. Knowing we had no health insurance took some of the fun out of watching Lance rip around the racecourse. Every sharp corner made me hold my breath; I felt every near-miss in the back of my neck.

On a regular day, Lance would get home from school, go out for a bike ride, then come home and make spaghetti for himself. Not for dinner. This was just a snack. I was still doing my homework, just like when he was a baby, and the stats said carbo-load after training, so I'd make a huge pot of my "extremely terrific if I do say so myself" spaghetti sauce and leave it in the fridge for him. When I got home, I made dinner, always with a properly set table, including candles. We'd talk. His day, my day, upcoming swim meets, triathlons, bike-racing events. He worried when I seemed sad or tired, but despite the punishing schedule, I actually felt easier about my life than I had in years.

My son was pretty savvy about the realities of where we were at and did whatever he could to help me out. He stayed out of the kind of trouble that had always seemed to find him during middle school. With all his energy in demand at every event, he stopped channeling so much of it toward getting angry at people. Conscious of our tight finances, he worked his Rolodex to get sponsors for every event and was thrilled when he won any amount of money, large or small. With each cycling event, he improved his rank until he was the state champion, which meant—among other things—he no longer had to pay an entry fee for certain events. And he was adamant about not paying when we didn't have to.

"Check the regulations," he impatiently told a guy at the registration table in one small North Texas town. "I'm state champion, and that means I get to race without the fee. Look, here's my—"

"Yeah, I see that," said the guy, "but I don't know anything about waiving any entry fee. All I know is I'm supposed to collect twenty-five dollars before I can give you a number."

"Lance, why don't I write a check, and we can straighten it out later," I suggested gently. I usually tried to let him fight his own battles, but we were running late and I didn't want him to be distracted from the task at hand.

"No way!" he insisted. "It's waived. I'm the state champion."

He wasn't about to let anybody take that away from him. We'd driven all over kingdom come as he edged up the categories. A lot of blood, sweat, and banana bread had gone into getting where we were, and my son was genuinely appreciative of my support. After all that money and gas and time and heat, saving me the cost of this entry fee—it meant something to him. He set his jaw and stuck to his guns and eventually got registered without the fee.

That night we stayed in a particularly seedy motel. We could only afford a single, so I always slept on the floor. Lance needed the best rest possible to prepare for the next day's event. Walking to the course the next morning was like stepping back into the 1960s. Deputy types swaggered through the crowd with pistols on their hips, acting tough and giving rednecks a bad name. Beehive hairdos and bright red lipstick were everywhere. Between races, Lance and I strolled over to the town's single-screen movie theater and saw *Pretty Woman*. He was always a good sport about going to chick flicks, but back at the track that evening it was all testosterone again. He tore the place up, and I hollered myself hoarse on the sidelines.

"Go, Lance! You got it, son, you got it! *Go, Lance! Woohooooooooo!*"

What can I say? It's the drill team captain in me. I believe in the power of being *cheered on*. I've seen it work for a baby taking his first step, for a battered marathon runner on the track, for the little boys' football team on their last living legs, for a secretary struggling to pull together a proposal by five. Cheering someone on is a noble endeavor. It's such a purely giving thing, and giving feels *good*. I feel sorry for anyone who hasn't discovered that firsthand. There is a special bond between the cheering and the cheered. When you care enough about someone to show up for them, love them enough to get all emotionally involved and be a complete bellering fool, all in the cause of encouragement—you know, I think there must be some sort of love-induced chemical reaction. Somehow a little of your soul gets transferred into their system and gives them this little *snap-crackle-pop* of energy.

Maybe that's what made me such a good administrative assistant.

(I never liked being called a "secretary.") As an admin, I told every boss I ever worked for, "My job is to make you look like a million bucks." And I delivered.

"That's why I'm sending you to Ericsson," my boss at the temp agency told me back when I was still gathering my courage to throw Sales out.

"The thing is . . . I really need something full-time." I chose my words carefully. I didn't bring my personal life to work. Ever. Nobody at the agency needed to know that my marriage was about to crash and burn, but I was desperate for something full-time and rock-steady—with benefits. (Qualities every woman needs from her job, especially if she doesn't find them in her husband.)

"Linda, you're our top candidate. They don't want to take a lot of risks until they see what caliber of people we can supply. But this is a great little company. And pretty soon it's going to be a great big company. So I'm counting on you to open some doors for us. There's no one I'd rather have making our first impression there. If you knock their socks off, we'll be able to place a lot more people."

Oh, the power of being cheered on! He talked up what a great place it would be to work and how everybody was hoping to get in there.

"What will I be doing?" I asked.

"Well, just some filing, sorting, stapling, and that kind of thing to start with," he said. "It's entry-level in the human resources department, but the telecom industry is just beginning to take shape. You never know where it could lead."

The word *telecom* hadn't really entered the popular vocabulary yet, so I had no idea what that meant. Finding out was my first order of business.

"Mobile phones, computers—a whole lot of Star Trekky kind of technology" is how Jeanine, my new supervisor, explained it. "Basically, we supply the equipment that makes it possible for the phone company to connect people without phone lines."

There was a tremendous amount of activity in the office. We were sorting through hundreds of résumés every day, working through lunch and long into the evening. Since the telecom industry was so new, there weren't a whole lot of fantastically qualified people, and the few who were available had to be aggressively courted, so the company had brought in two consultants—professional headhunters—to guide the rapid expansion of its workforce. These guys were great at what they did, but they were pretty arrogant and didn't display a lot of respect for Jeanine, who was very young and brand-new to her position in HR.

"Did you get hold of this guy?" one of them asked her, holding up the résumé of a top candidate for an important position.

"Not yet," Jeanine said. "I haven't been able to get him on the phone."

"You haven't been able to get him on the phone?" The way the consultant pronounced each word made it sound like an unpardonable failure, and he did it loud enough for the whole office to hear. "This is our number-one candidate. We need this guy."

"I'll get him," Jeanine said. "I've left several messages at—"

"Messages!" The consultant made a disdainful sort of huffing sound. "Oh, right. 'Cause you *can't get him on the phone.*" He ceremoniously brandished a five-dollar bill, slapped it on the desk in front of her, and leaned down to get right in her face. "I'll bet you five dollars I can get this guy on the phone right now."

There was a *High Noon* hush over the entire room as he flipped open a manila folder, traced his finger down the page, and started punching a number into the phone.

"Actually, that's his work number," Jeanine started to say. "I don't think it's appropriate to call him at—"

"Hey, Dan!" the headhunter boomed. "Listen, sorry to bother you at the office, but I'm calling from the HR department over at Ericsson. One of our little gals has been trying to reach you about a position we have opening up. . . ." And he loudly blathered on from there.

Jeanine sat quietly until he wound up the conversation and clapped the phone triumphantly down in front of her. Then she stood up, her lower lip trembling. She picked up the five-dollar bill, ripped it in half, and stormed out of the room as the two pieces fluttered down to the desktop. A few minutes later I followed her to the ladies' room and tapped on the stall where I could hear her sobbing.

"Jeanine? Are you okay?"

"Yeah." She came out and ran some cold water over her wrists. "It's just been a very long week and . . . God, that guy is a jerk."

"Here." I handed her some tissues and my makeup kit.

"Thanks," she said. "I'm so glad you're here, Linda. I can't believe you're sticking with it. We went through three temps last week alone."

"What? You're kidding!" Funny how that little detail had gotten left out of the temp agency boss's whole setup speech.

"Yeah." Jeanine sniffed into the wadded tissues. "Nobody's willing to put in the crazy hours and put up with the crap, and if you leave I don't know what—"

"Well, I'm not leaving," I said, handing her some concealer and a compact. "Guys like that stopped scaring me a long time ago. And you shouldn't be intimidated either. You're sharp, Jeanine. You're well educated and professional. You're just as smart as they are! My job is to help you look like a million bucks, and I'm gonna do it. But you're the boss, girl! So get out there and *be* the boss."

"Okay." She took a deep, shaky breath. "You're right. I will."

"And Jeanine," I said seriously, "never *ever* let them see you cry."

Our eyes met in the mirror, and she nodded.

We were coming from two different worlds—the preceding fifteen years had made that much difference for working women. She was the one with the education and the position, but I was the one who'd been in the trenches for a while, and Jeanine respected that. She straightened her shoulders, and we went back to work. And somewhere between the overtime and the piles of files and the frustrations and the successes of the next several months, she and I became good friends. "Kindred spirits" my hippie girlfriend would call it. She would say that when you connect with someone the moment you meet them and you know you're going to be friends, that means you knew them in a past life. If I believed in that sort of thing, I would definitely apply it to Jeanine and me. She was definitely one of the best and completely unexpected benefits of the job.

She was from Minnesota, so she had that accent that made her words sound like they're bouncing on a trampoline. She was petite, very young, and incredibly bright—no matter how you define that word. Bright as in smart, bright as in sparkling, bright as in—well, *bright*. Sparking like a jumper cable all the time, Jeanine kept things interesting on a job that would have otherwise been sort of mind-numbing. We'd be laughing and talking about an entire world of topics while we worked without missing a beat. She cared about people and about her work, and she took an immediate liking to Lance. Sometimes he would stop by on his way home from school, and I guess it was natural for them to spar with each other like they did. She was such an easygoing person—and she was actually closer to his age than mine, now that I think of it.

One thing I loved about Ericsson was the lunchtime running group. The company had installed showers and lockers to accommodate people who wanted to get out and go jogging—a fashionable new trend at the time. My lunch hour gave me just enough time to change, run a three-mile circuit, shower, and put my hair and makeup back together for the afternoon. Sometimes I jogged along with the others. We chatted about weekend plans and workday hassles. I asked a million questions about the projects on their desks. There was always something new and fascinating going on in this new and fascinating industry. Other times I ran by myself, sorting through numbers and scenarios and the puzzle pieces of my life. I reconnected with that sweat-induced serenity I'd first discovered back on drill team. My mind became centered and focused as my breathing became deep and rhythmic.

"What do you think about?" I asked Lance one evening. "When you're running, I mean. Or when you're riding your bike or swimming. What's going through your head?"

"Music," he said between bites of fried chicken.

"Music?"

"Yeah. Like Metallica and stuff."

Lance was heavily into his obsession with Metallica. Seems like there was a heavy metal sound track to almost every road trip. Sometimes when Lance went on long training rides in the evening, he'd ask me to drive along beside him with that Metallica tape blasting. It wasn't my kind of music, but it seemed to help him focus his thoughts and frame his rhythm.

Focusing on school wasn't quite so easy.

"Lance is such a bright boy," his teachers told me year after year. "If only he'd learn to apply himself!"

They couldn't understand that he *did* apply himself—big time! Just not to schoolwork. He was smart, and he loved to learn. He had a dictionary on his desk and faithfully learned a word a day for years. But homework and lectures and standardized tests just weren't his thing. Academics made sort of a square peg out of him. When it all got too frustrating, there was only one piece of advice I could give him: "Run."

"People keep telling me they saw me out jogging on my lunch hour," Jeanine told me one day as we stood knee-deep in manila folders and hanging files. "I don't know if I should take it as a compliment that they think I'm in that good a shape or an insult 'cause they're confusing me with somebody who's ten years older than me!"

"Take it as a compliment," I laughed. "Or better yet, start running with me."

"Oh, Lord. No thanks. I couldn't run a mile if there was an ax murderer chasing after me."

"Well, you don't run away from something when you're running," I told her. "You run toward something."

"Maybe so. Still, I'm in no condition to be doing either one."

"But you could be! Jeanine," I said seriously, "today is the first day of the rest of your life. Now, do you want to spend the rest of your life sittin' on the couch eating potato chips or do you want to get out there and do something?"

"Oh, God, you really are a relentless motivator, aren't you?" Jeanine handed me a stack of folders and leaned back in her chair. "You oughta be in HR."

"Is there an opening?" I asked, not even half-joking.

"Well, not exactly," she said. "I do need a fourth person to interview for this admin position in engineering support. Sylvia pretty well has it. They like to promote from within, and she's been working hard for the last year or so. But you know the drill. I have to send four people. I hate to bring somebody in off the street, knowing they're not going to get the job. So you'd be helping me out and saving some poor schmo the disappointment if you could spare an hour on Thursday."

"Sure!" That was my standard response to everything too. "It'll be a good opportunity to practice my interview skills."

A few weeks later I was shelving office supplies when Jeanine tapped me on the shoulder.

"Hey, girl!" I said. "Did you decide to start running this week?"

"Well, apparently I'll have to if I want to keep up with you," said Jeanine. "You got the job."

"What job?"

"The admin position. Remember? You were supposed to be just a warm body for the interview, but it turns out—well, they loved you."

"Oh, Jeanine! That's fantastic! But . . . what about Sylvia?"

"She definitely doesn't love you."

"No, I suppose not," I sighed. "What happened?"

"Who knows?" Jeanine shrugged. "She was having a bad day, I guess. Hadn't gotten enough sleep or something. Anyway, you outshined her."

"Oh, great," I said, though I was really thinking, *Oh . . . shit!*

I hate those moments when the thing you want to have and the person you want to be come into conflict. The devil on one shoulder starts debating with the angel on the other, rationalizing how the not-so-nice thing you're about to do to somebody actually serves a higher purpose and may even be for that person's own good.

But the fact of the matter is, while the working world had become a little easier for women than it was in the early seventies, I hadn't forgotten what it felt like to be undercut and overwhelmed. I vividly remembered what it meant to have my expectations raised and dashed. And I believed then, as I do now, that women have to back each other up. We have to support each other and help each other up, because God knows the rest of the world loves to knock us down sometimes. Sylvia was a single mother of two—one still in diapers. She *had* worked a long hard time for this promotion, and over the months I'd been temping at Ericsson I'd grown to like and respect her.

Oh, Lord, help me know the right thing to do, I silently prayed, and when I felt the answer in my heart, I prayed even harder. *Actually, Lord, I think you must be mistaken about that, because I really really need this job!*

"I'm not going to take the job, Jeanine." She was almost as surprised as I was to hear the words coming out of my mouth. "It wouldn't be right. You should give it to Sylvia."

"Are you sure?"

"No, but that's my answer."

Jeanine squeezed my hand, and the look on her face—it meant something to me. It was like she thought I was . . . oh, I don't know, like I was a stand-up gal. And over the next several years, as Jeanine became my best friend and running partner and travel pal and confidante, I always kept that moment in my heart. It's a precious thing to have someone you love think you're a stand-up gal.

Sylvia still didn't love me. For some reason, she was madder than a cat and hardly ever spoke to me again. I guess this was her big moment, and I'd taken some of the joy out of it.

"So are you sorry you did it?" asked Lance.

"No, son, I'm not. You're never sorry when you do what you feel is right."

"I would've said screw her!" he said doubtfully.

"Gee, now why didn't I think of that?"

I handed him a box of matches, and he lit two tall candles on the dinner table. It doesn't matter if you're having macaroni and cheese with hot dogs, when you light a couple candles it's "dinner" instead of just supper. It's dinnertime with dinner conversation and dinner table manners. I always thought that was important.

"Anyway," I said, "it's all going to work out. Jeanine came back later and said she had another job for me in the accounting department."

I guess I didn't sound very enthusiastic about it, because Lance put his arm around my shoulder to console me. It's not that I thought I was too good for clerical work or anything like that, but it sank my heart a little when I realized I was living a life so similar to my mother's. It just wasn't what I had in mind for myself. And it made me uncomfortably aware of the fact that it wasn't quite so easy to pass judgment on her anymore.

"It's fine," I told him. "It's not as good as the other job, but I don't care if you're slinging burgers and fries or managing a Fortune 500 corporation, your work isn't just what you do, it's who you are. And why would you want to be someone who does less than their best? If you always do your best, well, then even when you have to do a job you don't especially like, you still have your self-respect."

"Maybe something better will come along," he said hopefully. "I mean, Jeanine said they promote from within, and now—look at you, Mom! You're *within*!"

"That's right! I am. And this is a good job. It doesn't pay that great, but it's full-time—*plus benefits!*" The thought of having insurance again was enough to bring tears to my eyes. "And if I come in on weekends and shred and bag paper, I'll be able to make a lot more than the temp agency is paying me. Enough to make the mortgage and bills and start putting away a little for your college."

"Congratulations, Mom," Lance said, clinking his glass against mine. "That's great."

And it was great, I decided. Things were getting easier. We relaxed into our standard suppertime banter. Lance updated me on who was going out with whom and what his old girlfriend said to his current girlfriend in the hall and which kids were the wimpiest about dissecting an earthworm in science and how somebody's locker got toilet-papered because it was her birthday. The phone rang, and Lance sat up on the counter talking while I cleared the table and started the dishes.

"You're joking. . . . No way. . . . Really? Since when?"

"What?" I nudged. I always had to get in there and know what was going on.

"Cherry Miles and Tom Delong broke up," he said. "No, man, I was talking to my mom. Hey, hang on a sec."

He put the phone down, went and got his little Instamatic camera from the kitchen drawer, and snapped a picture of the cat, who was draped over the back of the sofa.

"Yeah, I'm back," he said to whoever was on the other end of the phone. "Had to take a picture of my cat."

For some reason this struck me as absolutely hilarious. Or maybe I was just laughing out of relief and joy and the wonderfully easy feeling of a happy home.

~

The next morning I was in my new office fifteen minutes early, wearing a sharp red suit with a designer scarf from Dress for Less, looking like today was the first day of the rest of my life. My job was to make my boss look like a million bucks, and I was proud of that. I suppose someone who wants to *be* the boss or who has poor self-esteem about what they're doing in the world might have a hard time taking that attitude, but not me. I always felt like when you support someone, when you help them and make it possible for them to succeed, well, you share in the joy of that victory. The real things that are won and lost in the business world go far beyond dollars and cents. All those transactions eventually add up to your life. That makes every challenge worth meeting for its own sake, I think. Unlike the quick wheels and deals that pay off in ego.

I had plenty of time to contemplate this and many other more practical issues that were weighing on my mind during the Spenco 500, an event in Waco, Texas, sponsored by Spenco 2nd Skin—a clear, lightweight bandage known and loved by anyone who has had firsthand experience with the browned hamburger skin condition that is road rash. Lance was well acquainted with road rash. It was something he simply learned to live with. He was fairly stoic about the pain and shrugged off the ribbing from the girls on swim team, who teased him unmercifully as the summer wore on and the abrasions refused to heal because Lance was in the water so much. Bike racers are big customers for Spenco 2nd Skin. We should have bought stock in the company.

Anyway, the Spenco 500 must have been sometime in the mid-1980s, because I remember Jeanine and I were in our post-perm phase but well into the jewel-tone blazer period. Lance and his friends trained hard for the event. Relay teams of riders were challenged to get on their bikes and pedal five hundred miles through the heat by day and dark by night. Winning the race required speed, strength, and strategy coupled with the endurance of an armadillo, so my fifteen-year-old son was in his element.

His pit crew (me) wasn't quite as hardy, however, having started the previous day at 5:00 A.M. with morning chores and the necessary time investment required for putting myself together so I could get to the office early. I skipped lunch so I could put in the full day's work and leave a couple hours early. Lance and I packed the trunk and drove three hours to Waco, roasting like potatoes in our cramped car. Since the race would run all night, there was no need for a motel. When we hit town, I located a gas station with a relatively semi-undisgusting bathroom where I could put my limp hair and faded makeup back together again. Then we went to the track to set up our lawn chairs, pup tents, coolers, and all. I made the rounds, visiting the other pit crews, trying to learn what they were doing—gathering information and trying to sort out a method for the coming madness.

Between pit stops, Jeanine and I set up the grill and fed the boys burgers and salad for dinner. The night wore on, and Jeanine finally crashed, leaving me alone to face midnight. Struggling to stay propped up in my lawn chair, I waited with two bottles of water and a protein bar so that when Lance cruised by, he'd be able to reach out and grab it. I must admit, I was beginning to flag a bit. And I'm fairly certain I've looked better in my life. Finally, three shadowy riders took shape in the dry darkness, and I recognized one of them as Lance.

"How ya doin', Lance? Are you okay?"

"I'm all right," he nodded. "I'm good."

"You're great! You're the greatest!" I shouted after him as he picked up speed and pulled away from me into the night.

Along about three in the morning it all started to seem very symbolic. My role as his mother was to help him train for the laps of life, then stand back and watch him fly. I was ready to give him something warm to eat whenever he swooped in for a moment and shouted myself hoarse every time he came by.

The next time Lance came around the circuit, it was almost 4:00 A.M. He was pushing hard just to get the pedals to go around.

"Go, Lance! You got it, son! You're tearing it up!"

I jogged beside him with the open water bottle. He took a few slugs, struggling to find enough wind to talk to me.

"I'm about done," he panted. "I gotta stop."

"Okay, son. You're okay. Next time you come around, Ian'll be ready."

"No, get Adam."

"Okay, son. He'll be here. Keep going, Lance. You got it. You got it! You got it goin' on, kid!"

I put my hand out but didn't touch him. I didn't want to mess up his wobbly balance as he pulled away again.

~

I gave that job in the accounting department my best, but I missed the family-friendly atmosphere in the HR office, where Lance could swing by to say hello on his way home from school. I also missed working with Jeanine, but we had lunch, and she often joined me and Lance on our weekend expeditions. I'd gotten my GED when Lance was little, but I was lacking even the little bit of tech school training that would have put me on track to move up. Which was okay. I was able to leave every day at five and spend the evening with Lance.

But it doesn't take long for a workaholic to make herself indispensable. Over time my responsibilities in the accounting department grew. Not officially. There was no actual avenue to advance, but you know how it is when you let people know you're the Go-to Girl. I loved the challenges and responsibilities—the fact that people trusted and depended on me—even though it didn't come with any tangible bennies (silly little things like money or stock options) or even intangible ones (like respect or appreciation).

Younger women came in with their degrees in business or marketing or computer science. For them, the job was a stepping-stone, and they quickly moved onward and upward. Company policy dictated that without a college education, I wasn't going anywhere. But that's okay,

I decided. That's fine for now. I resolutely found satisfaction in knowing that in this tiny corner of the world I was the queen bee. I had all the answers, the solution for any problem that came up. I knew all the macros and shortcuts and formats, and when something huge had to get pulled together, I knew how to break it down and get it done. I was an important cog in the corporate wheel. I couldn't even think about leaving. The place would fall apart without me, everybody said.

This was all fine and dandy until the day I've come to think of as the "when worlds collide" episode.

Lance had called me as usual to let me know he got home from school okay and was going out for a long training ride.

"I'm going to be late," I told him. "We've got this huge thing we're putting together for the Securities and Exchange Commission, and everybody's going crazy over it. We just got the data this afternoon, and I'm trying to break it out into some usable format so we can type it up and assemble a couple dozen binders for a meeting tomorrow morning."

"You can do it, Mom. It'll come together."

"Thanks, Lance."

"I love you, Mom."

"I love you too, son. Have a good ride."

I wasn't expecting him to call me back two hours later, and I knew by the choked sound of his voice he was struggling not to cry.

"*Mom . . .*"

"Lance, are you okay?"

"*Huh-uh*" was all he could say.

"Son, what's wrong? Lance?" He just made a gulping sort of sound. I tried to make my voice as sure and steady and calm as I could. "Son, take a deep breath and tell me what's wrong."

"I dropped the—the glass pot and—and I cut my toe off."

"*Oh, my God!*"

"There's a lot of blood. And it hurts bad."

"Okay. Oh, God." My mind started racing, searching for some far corner of my brain where I might have tossed some first aid information. "Just stay calm. I'm on my way."

"No—Ian's gonna drive me to the emergency room. I don't think I can wait."

"Okay. Okay, good plan," I said steadily. "You guys go, and I'll meet you there."

"*Mom.*" He was struggling again. "It really hurts, Mom. There's a lot of blood."

"I know, son. Hang in there. I'll be right there."

I stood up and grabbed my purse from under the desk as I hung up the phone.

"Carole!" I called over my shoulder. "I have to go. Phyllis, I'm sorry, but my son's on his way to the hospital. I have to leave."

"*What?*" was the general response. The panic in the room was almost as palpable as the panic on the other end of the phone had been. My boss hurried over as I rifled my purse for car keys.

"Linda, you can't be serious!" she said. "You cannot leave us right in the middle of—of—you can't leave, Linda!"

"My son's on his way to the emergency room!"

"Well, he's in good hands then. He doesn't need you to sit there waiting around, does he? I mean—there's always *hours* of waiting."

I stared at her, completely without words. She was telling *me,* "You can't be serious," while expecting me to leave my kid alone and terrified in the emergency room?

"Phyllis, I have to be there for—well, for the insurance, if nothing else!" I said, trying to offer some concrete rationale even she could grasp. "There's going to be paperwork!"

"Okay, but what about his father or a neighbor or somebody? Isn't there somebody else who can—come on, Linda! It makes no sense for you to be sitting down there doing nothing, when you should be here, making sure the SEC doesn't nail our hide to the wall tomorrow morning!"

I was already on my way out the door. She followed me to the elevator.

"Linda, this thing has to be on that conference table tomorrow morning at eight. *This* is an emergency! It's going to take us all night to get it together without you—if we're able to sort through it at all!"

"I'll be back as soon as I can," I told her, punching the button and heading for the stairs when the doors didn't immediately open. "I'm sorry! That's the best I can do."

"Great." She glared after me. "That's just great!"

When I got to the ER, Lance was sitting in a wheelchair, ashen and nauseous, with a huge wad of bloody towels around his foot. He managed to tell me that the Pyrex pot he'd used to cook his spaghetti had broken in two when he set it on the cold countertop. A large, heavy section had fallen as he stood there in his bare feet.

A triage nurse had determined the deep gash across the top of his foot was going to require numerous stitches, but the toe wasn't actually completely severed, and this moved him down the waiting list. She wouldn't let him have anything to eat or drink until she was sure he wouldn't need anesthesia, and while I know this made good sense, it left Lance in a bad way. He'd just been on a long, hard training ride. He was dehydrated and starving hungry. I finally cajoled her into letting me scrounge up some saltine crackers and Sprite, which took the edge off enough for him to doze against my shoulder as another two hours ticked by.

There should be a rule: only one crisis at a time. But I guess that would come in conflict with the unwritten laws of the universe that decree there will never be a pen by the phone when you need one and your kid can only have an emergency when your office is in the middle of an all-out hurricane. I sat there stroking Lance's forehead, softly humming a little Motown tune to him, the way I did when he was a baby.

Nothing you could say could tear me away from my guy . . .

I couldn't help but worry about what was going on at the office. I wasn't one to take responsibility lightly. I felt torn and guilty about leaving. But whatever anyone else thought about it, I knew I was in the right place.

Another hour and many stitches later, I dropped Lance off at home and returned to a stony silence in the secretarial pool. It was late. No one was thrilled to be there, the project was miles from done, and somehow it was all my fault.

Not one person asked me if my son was okay.

We worked in silence until almost eleven. When everyone was gone, I went to the conference room and walked around the table, placing two binders—blue on the bottom, white on top—in front of each fancy leather chair. At the very last place I paused, looked over my shoulder, and sat down. Pretty comfy. Not as huge as it looked, really. My feet barely touched the floor, but I was wearing fairly low heels, I figured. Sitting there, it seemed to me that if you're going to catch hell for the bad things that go on, you ought to reap some of the benefits for the good. I was always telling Lance that privilege came with responsibility, but so far I was only in on the latter.

"There's only one thing you can do with a day that bad," I told Lance over dinner the next night. "Learn something from it. Use it as a catalyst for change."

"What do you mean?"

"I mean everybody's been telling me I don't have the college education required to get promoted. Company policy. But nobody recognizes I've got a whole different kind of education. And I say that counts for something. Do we always have to blindly march along according to policy? If they're so gung-ho on . . . *hey!* Lance, what are you doing there?"

He'd gone to the kitchen and come back with a pair of garden scissors in one hand and his shoe in the other. He'd already managed to jab one blade through the side of the sneaker.

"I'm cutting the top open."

"Lance! Those were expensive!"

"I know, but it hurts too much when I try to run or ride my bike. I can't stand it rubbing on the stitches."

"Son, the doctor told you to stay off it for a week or so."

"So?" Lance grinned. "Do we have to march along according to policy?"

There was a triathlon event in eight days, and he wasn't about to stop training for it. So he adjusted. He bent the rules a little and—spaghetti pots be damned, full speed ahead—he was there on race day. He didn't win, and his foot hurt like a son of a bean, especially on the bicycle course's steep hills. But he went home happy because he knew he'd tried.

And I went home inspired to begin my own steady climb upward.

NINE

UP THE LADDER TO THE ROOF

Raising children is like an armadillo race. You tend to this little life and feed him well and put something out in front of him and teach him to want to chase after it. But at the end of the day he's still a wild thing. All you can do is let him go and hope he stays on track. And maybe, just maybe, he'll be a little faster than the other armadillos that day.

My son was putting on some serious speed, and I wasn't the only one noticing.

On the downside was the local constable. Within about five seconds of getting his driver's license, Lance started racking up speeding tickets. I started recognizing the tone as soon as I picked up the phone.

"Um . . . Mom?" he'd say contritely, and I knew. I just knew there was going to be another two-hour wait in line to pay another big fat fine and another hike in our insurance rate—*if* I could successfully beg the insurance agent to give us another chance.

"Oh, *Lance!*"

"I'm sorry, Mom." He didn't bother promising he'd never ever do it again. We both knew he would.

On the more positive flip side to this were the people who'd taken an interest in Lance as an athlete. Jim Hoyt, the owner of Richardson Bike Mart, helped Lance get into better equipment than we could afford and encouraged him to come out riding every weekend with a bunch of locals—all grown men who didn't know quite what to make of this kid who wanted to know everything about the science of bicycling and was willing to spend every Saturday pedaling around the industrial park while his friends were hanging out at Burger King. They invited him to show up for the Tuesday Night Criterium, where you earned your category rank and maybe even took home a gift certificate from the hardware store or a Nike T-shirt or some other prize that was far more valuable than its price tag, because it meant you *won*. These guys taught Lance the dynamics and vocabulary of bike racing, words like *peleton* and *drafting* and *domestique*. They took him under their wings—or so they thought until he started beating them.

Another important mentor in Lance's life was Chris MacCurdy, the same swim coach who'd seen him lumber down the lane that very first day at the Plano Aquatics Center. He took me aside at practice one day and told me my son could be a serious contender.

"We're talking U.S. national team. He could be at the Olympics two years from now," Chris said. "We're talking about a career as a nationally recognized swimmer. If he's this good as a tenth-grader, by the time he graduates—well, he could get himself a full-ride scholarship to a good college."

"*Seriously?*" I actually felt my eyes get big. "That would be fantastic!"

"The thing is, Linda, he's going to have to get serious about training. He can't be missing practices like he has been the last couple weeks."

"Oh, that's just because he had this triathlon that—"

"I know, I know. There's always something going on. And you know whatever Lance does, Ian and Adam have to do it too, so then I end up missing all three of them. Look, the triathlons, the bike races—those are great activities, but they take time and energy away from swimming, and that's where his focus needs to be. If he doesn't want to focus his time and energy here, then—well, why am I spending all my time and energy on him, you know?"

"Yes. I do. Believe me, I know." I reached out and took Chris's hand. "But please, just be patient with him, okay? Please."

I stayed long enough to cheer for Lance in the 1,500, then went over to the office to put in five or six hours of overtime shredding and bagging paper. Feeding forms and printouts into the machine was always sort of therapeutic for me. The noise of the shredder provided a scoured blank backdrop for my thoughts.

A full-ride scholarship. That was the magic carrot. My dream was to continue to hammer away while Lance was in high school, and then we'd both go to college. He'd get a computer science degree just like the up-and-coming young people in the engineering department where I was now working as a project admin. I would study—well, anything I wanted! I've always loved the entirely positive act of *learning*. I'd always wanted to get my real estate license, so maybe that plus a degree in business.

Trouble was, I'd moved to a different department—which I loved—but I was still a non-exempt-level employee, earning pretty minimal money and making the mortgage payments on my own. After years of working overtime and temp jobs whatever evenings and weekends I could, I'd eked out only a small nest egg. The dream had remained distant. Until today.

When I showed up at the industrial park, the sun was almost touching the horizon. They were calling it a day, but Lance didn't want a ride home. He preferred to take his bike. I had dinner started when he walked in the door and on the table by the time he got out of the shower. As he lit the candles and laid napkins and silverware on the table, I asked him about his day, and he told me, and even though it was not a remarkable day, I relished listening to the buoyantly comic way he described it.

"I had an interesting conversation with Chris this morning," I mentioned in that absolutely nonconfrontational way mothers and other managers have of bringing up an issue that might turn into a bone of contention.

"Yeah?"

"He was talking about how, if a person was really dedicated, if he really narrowed his focus, he could be in the Olympics. Even get a college scholarship."

"Wow. He should do that then."

"Maybe you should think about it."

"Yeah, I know. He told me all that, but the thing is—Mom, I *like* doing triathlons. I *like* riding my bike. I don't want to give those things up, because I'm really good at it, and it's fun, and—I don't know about the whole college plan anymore."

"Lance," I said carefully, "not going to college has set me back. A lot. And you've always talked about how cool it would be to go to UT. How you could get a degree in computer science or engineering."

"But I don't want to *be* an engineer! Mom, those guys I'm up against—the professional triathletes—those guys are making huge money. Six figures, some of 'em. And I could do it too. I could turn pro and get good enough to beat those suckers. But if I go to college—I'm afraid I'd screw away my chance to do it, you know? Probably when you get old—like forty or something—you probably wouldn't be able to do it anymore," Lance said, leaning back in his chair. "So then I'll get millions of dollars of endorsement deals, and I'll buy us one of those huge houses over in West Plano."

Thank goodness our kids don't always do what we want them to do.

It occurs to me now that I could have made him do it. I could have said, "Son, I'm putting my foot down and da-da-da, and you'll be at swim practice every day, lapping that pool till you wrinkle up like a prune, and then you're going to get a degree and good job and have the same kind of life that I—well, that I *would have* had if only *my* mother had been as smart as yours!"

Let's see a show of hands: how many of you, in the same situation, would have made him do it? C'mon . . . be honest. I mean, isn't it your sacred duty as a parent to shove your opinion down your child's throat? *For his own good,* of course! Because you go to all this trouble, growing this kid like a prize pumpkin—it seems like you ought to be able to enter him in the county fair and take home a blue ribbon.

But this person was turning out so different from the child I'd imagined swimming around inside me when I was expecting.

Expecting. I love that word.

That about says it all, doesn't it? From that moment you know you're going to be a parent, you have it all mapped out. And you usually forget to put things like stubbornness and willfulness and an entirely unpredictable sense of style on the chart. It's easy to see anything that falls outside your expectations as faults, failings, or a thorn in your own side. Like a serious need for speed.

Looking across the candlelight at this young man, I was amazed. He was turning out so well. Despite my worst mistakes and best intentions, he was blossoming into an actual human being, right before my very eyes. He had this thing he was passionate about, this thing for which he was willing to work and sacrifice. How could I not respect that? Even if it wasn't the thing everybody else was doing?

"Son," I said, "how serious are you about all this?"

"I'm serious, Mom. Seriously."

"Okay." I took a deep breath and let go of a dream that had never really belonged to me anyway. "Then that's where your focus should be. From now on, all you have to do is train and race. Let me worry about the rest."

~

Three guesses as to why they call a bike race scheduled every August in Wichita Falls, Texas, "The Hotter 'N Hell Hundred." That's right. It's a hundred miles long, and if it's not hotter 'n hell, then hell needs a new marketing strategy.

The way Lance explained it to me, it did sound like a devil of a time compared to the merely grueling events he'd been involved in up till now. He didn't expect to win. His goal was to finish something better than dead last. Or just plain dead. True to its name, the event inflicts searing punishment on its participants and has claimed several lives over the years. Train and race, I told him. I'll take care of the rest.

Standing at the Tuesday night Crits, I brushed fire ants off my foot and thought about putting together the money we'd need for the trip—for the entry fee, for the new brake lines on his bike, and for everything from Gatorade to sunscreen. Motel, cases of water, gas, food. I figured I could entice Jeanine to come along and envisioned us catching the last of the late-afternoon sun, working on our tans and talking about life's greatest challenges: work, men, and the Foley's Red Apple Sale.

"So are you coming?" I asked Jeanine.

"Oh, Lord," she said. "I'm still trying to recover from that last thing."

"It'll be fun!" I nudged. "It'll be a blast!"

"Well, that's what I keep telling you about that club downtown, and we still haven't been there. C'mon. I hear it's very upscale. Not like a singles bar meat market thing at all."

"So if I go out dancing, you'll go to Wichita Falls?"

"Yeah, that sounds fair."

"We have to have an ironclad pact," I said seriously. "If we arrive together, we leave together."

"Agreed," Jeanine nodded. "Friday night then?"

What is it about getting out of a bad marriage that makes a woman feel like dancing? A friend of mine put it like this: "Somebody locked me in the trunk of his car, drove around for nine years, then dumped me on the side of a desert road. I had no idea what state I was in, but I couldn't wait to get that road under my feet and find out where it went to."

I put my arm around Jeanine's shoulder.

"You're a bad influence on me, girlfriend," I told her, and in my heart I was sincerely grateful for that.

The peleton approached, rounded the corner, and scrolled by like chaser lights on a movie marquee. Lance was positioned deep in the center, a look of ferocious concentration on his face. There were several laps to go before he'd break away. I focused on the familiar set of his shoulders among the flock of riders, willing him to stay upright, surrounding him with a protective shield, and feeling that the force of my love was almost enough to make him fly.

"I'll need to put in some overtime so we can afford a motel," I said.

"Why don't we camp out?" Jeanine suggested.

"*Camp out?*" I fanned myself with my hand. "Honey, not this Dallas dawg."

"Sorry," she laughed. "My Minnesota was showing."

"Did I mention we have to leave at four A.M. next Saturday?"

"Did I mention happy hour starts at four P.M. this Friday?"

It wasn't easy getting up the morning after my first real night out. The shredder roared like a freight train in my head, and I had to wear sneakers because of the blisters on my feet from a pair of stylish but user-unfriendly shoes. Still, a delicious sort of buzz carried me through the day. I'd never had the opportunity to sow any wild oats, so even though Jeanine was nine years younger than me—still in her early twenties—we were great party partners. We looked out for each other. If I was getting mashed on by some loser, Jeanine knew just when to pretend to have a splitting headache or an urgent need to get home and check on an aging aunt. If Jeanine met someone she wanted to talk to, I knew how to be the supporting actress and make her the star of the conversation.

Stretched out side by side under the broiling sun of a Wichita Falls afternoon, we must have looked like a couple of escapees from *Beach Blanket Bingo*. Between the boys' pit stops, we didn't have energy to do more than lie there and soak up the rays. Fortunately, we met somebody who actually could afford a motel with a pool, which—believe you me—had lots of visitors that week. Lance looked like a lobster shambling toward the water after riding the whole hundred miles. He stumbled to the side of the pool and collapsed into the water fully clothed. Floating on his back, he basked in the satisfaction.

He wasn't at all disappointed that he didn't win. Winning wasn't always the goal. Winning was awesome because—let's face it—nobody ever remembers second place.

"But losing is awesome too," I always told him. "That's when you really learn. That's when you grow."

I remember one time when another kid got frustrated and threw his bicycle across the track at the end of a race.

"You'd better never let me see you do anything like that," I said, and Lance replied, "Don't worry!" Even at that age, he had the right attitude about competition. He was an enthusiastic but gracious winner and a gracious but philosophical loser, because instead of ambition or greed, he was entirely taken up with the discovery of this uncharted territory inside himself.

He was always interested in advice from the older riders and was probably a lot more open-minded than I was. Once when his back was hurting him after a particularly tough week, he asked me to take him to an appointment he'd made with a "special doctor sort of guy" one morning before work.

The moment we opened the door, I was all but knocked out by the smell of sandalwood incense and patchouli oil and I don't know what all. The lights were dim and hazy, and some sort of spacey opium den music was playing.

"Lance," I hedged, "what sort of doctor did you say this was?"

"Don't worry about it," he said. "Jim was telling me about this guy."

"Oh . . . kay . . ."

A man emerged from behind a beaded curtain, and I eyed him suspiciously. He reminded me for all the world of that Punjab character in the old "Little Orphan Annie" cartoons. He led Lance to a back room, and I sat on a madras love seat, perusing the selection of magazines, which mostly had to do with things like being a vegetarian and solar heating and identifying who you might have been in a past life. This was well before the days of Andrew Weil and Deepak Chopra, remember, so I had no idea what to think. After what seemed like a very long time—in this world or any other—I started to get a little nervous. I tiptoed to the door where Lance had disappeared and listened. Nothing came to me from the other side but the same spacey music. I pushed the door open a crack and saw Lance stretched out on a gurney, long silver needles sprouting all over his body like quills on a porcupine.

"Is everything okay in here?" I asked, not wanting to startle Dr. Sort Of, who was poised to skewer my son with another long needle.

He looked up and smiled, nodded, and went back to—well, whatever that was he was doing. I stepped back from the door and sat very still on the madras sofa until Lance came out.

"That was an interesting experience," I said cautiously. "How do you feel?"

"Great! You gotta try this, Mom."

"Um . . . no thanks."

My hippie girlfriend doesn't understand why I can't bring myself to try this kind of thing. I know, I know, I tell her, the whole vital energy chi thing or whatever, but—no. Over the years Lance has encouraged me to take advantage of the soigneurs who are always on hand to give the riders a rubdown after a race, but there's just something about human-on-human touch that I find entirely too personal to share with a great big guy called "Bear," no matter how many people tell me his hands are pure magic. It's one of those things that reminds me that I am the product of a place and time very different from the place and time that produced my son. I'm proud of that, really. I was glad to make available to him experiences and opportunities that weren't available to me.

While I wrote out a check for Sort-of-Dr. Punjab, he wrote up a list of organic foods, vitamins, herbal supplements, and that sort of thing, which he was suggesting Lance eat exclusively from now on.

"Can we stop off at Whole Foods?" Lance asked. "I don't think they have most of this at the regular grocery store."

"I'm going to stop off at home long enough for you to get out of the car," I said, "and then I'm going to work. And when I get home tonight, I'm going to fix you a plate of chicken fried steak, mashed potatoes, and gravy." That was my idea of health food. And being a good southern mama, I served it to him already plated. My idea of portion control. Good, old-fashioned, "brown, hot, and a heck of a lot" home cooking made with plain old Kroger groceries had gotten him this far. I didn't see any reason to go out and pay twelve dollars a pound for some fancy-schmancy free-range chicken raised on caviar and Ritz crackers.

I have to say, though, I was impressed with Lance's open-mindedness. None of that new age complementary therapy stuff had really come into vogue yet, so this was pretty out there for a fourteen-year-old.

Early on, Lance became interested in the science of himself. The mechanics of the athletic body. He and his coaches devoted untold hours to calculating and tweaking and maximizing his potential. How much oxygen was in his blood. How many steps he could take per second. How much pressure in pounds per square centimeter it took to push a pedal all the way around.

It makes me laugh, because when he was just a little guy, he absolutely loved that show about the Bionic Man. I used to look out the kitchen window and watch him in the yard while I made dinner. He'd be out there leaping off the upturned wheelbarrow and brandishing a yardstick, kicking the tails of unseen bad guys, safeguarding the meek, fighting for justice.

"We can rebuild him! We have the technology! We have the capability! Steve Austin will be better! Faster! Stronger!"

And then every time he jumped off a tall building (stump) or crushed a nuclear warhead (pinecone) in his bare fist or crashed through a brick wall (azalea hedge), he'd make this sound like "*hunnn-nun-nun-nun-nun!*"

Sometimes, when he gets discouraged, I wish he could see it all the way I do. From the kitchen windows of his life. From my perspective, each race he runs begins with the Green Machine, dodging between the big kids on their skateboards and bikes in the apartment complex parking lot. Then I see my father pumping up the tires of that first little bicycle on Christmas morning. Then there's his BMX from Richardson Bike Mart, the girls on swim team teasing him about his road rash, all the older riders mentoring him at the Tuesday Night Crits.

And there's me.

Even when I couldn't be there, I was there, and I think Lance knew that. I never took vacation days for anything except races and triathlons, but when my vacation days ran out, Lance had to go alone. And I didn't worry. I knew he could handle himself. During all those years of swim meets, if another kid left his goggles at home, his mother would tongue-lash him, then go rushing off to buy another pair. If Lance left his goggles at home, I said, "Wow, too bad you didn't double-check your equipment." I didn't castigate or yell at him if he made a mistake. But I didn't facilitate him making it twice.

Still, the world was a pretty big place sometimes. His hotel reservation got messed up at an event in Chicago once.

"Mom," he said, when he called my office, "they're telling me they don't have a room for me."

"No, that's not possible," I said. "I made the reservation myself. I have a confirmation number."

"I know! I tried to give it to them, but they didn't care."

"Put the manager on the phone," I said, and Lance could tell from the tone of my voice that he might want to stand back a few feet. I spoke with the manager, and let's just say I was polite but extremely firm regarding arrangements for my son's lodging. Lance called me back a little while later to tell me he was in a great big room on the top floor. Turns out all they had left was one of their bridal suites, and of course, they hadn't wanted to put Lance and his buddy in there until I strongly encouraged them to do so.

"Mom, there's a phone in the bathroom!" Lance crowed. "I'm calling you from the bathroom!"

But here's the part that was classic Lance: all that luxury ended up distracting him from his goal. He was late getting up the next morning and even later arriving at the event.

"And then when I rode into the transition area, my stupid bag got hung up in the front wheel of my bike," he glumly reported the following evening. "And then when I came in from the swim, I went to get on and the handlebars were all buggered up."

"Oh, bummer!" I said. "And you practiced that a thousand times too."

We worked those transitions until they were as smooth as mercy in a milk shake, but this one was slow and clumsy and cost him the race. Being able to call me from the toilet and tell me he'd lost wasn't much consolation. He was philosophical about it, though.

"I guess I won't be late again," he said, and as far as I know, he wasn't.

~

Lance decided he was ready for the adult division of the President's Triathlon. He'd won the junior event a couple years running, so he figured it must be getting too easy. He didn't really expect to win against the seasoned adult triathletes, some of whom were professionals, but he decided that to stretch himself and lose was better than going the easy route and winning without a challenge.

We mapped a running course—10 miles instead of the 6.2 to which he was accustomed—and I drove along beside him, blasting Metallica as he loped along.

"Mom! Turn it up!"

"What?"

"Louder!"

"I can't hear you!"

"TURN UP THE MUSIC!"

"OH! OKAY!"

There wasn't any more conversation than that. I didn't want to break the wave of concentration that carried him forward. On Saturdays I took him to Lake Levon so he could practice the cold open-water swim. In the evening after work we tried to trace the bike route but ended up getting hopelessly lost.

After all this, when I went to register him for the event, some guy dressed as Superman started hassling me about Lance being old enough to enter. The triathlon audience spends a lot of time waiting around for the competitors to come by, and Superman was the event mascot or cheerleader or something, and while I have the utmost respect for cheer practitioners, I never really got what this guy was doing there. In tights. Though no one else had to supply proof of age, I was sent home for Lance's birth certificate.

On the way home to get it, I stopped off for Wite-Out and a black pen, so Lance would be fifteen by the time I got back. I admit, it stretched the limits of my conscience, but fudging the number to make it harder on yourself could hardly be considered cheating. Lance had worked for it. He had trained for it. And Mr. Super-tights notwithstanding, he was ready for it. To my way of thinking, it would have been far more unfair to pit Lance against a younger group of competitors who didn't stand a chance with him in the race.

When it came to the rules of engagement—in a triathlon, a bike race, a business deal—Lance and I lived by a strict code of conduct. Beginning with the thousand or so games of "Rescuers" we played, spreading the board open on the coffee table and setting up the pieces as soon as he was big enough to count the dots on the dice, I'd taught my son that cheating is self-defeating. What have you won if you win by becoming something you don't want to be? But those nebulous unwritten rules of life are a different matter. The freeing thing about being forced to forge a life outside the mainstream is this: those rules no longer apply to you. Gingerbread fortresses like "it's always been done that way" and "that's just the way it is" no longer hold you back. Old folkways and prejudices never come into play. The fussier elements of etiquette are a luxury you can't afford, because they haven't been afforded you. Act like a lady? Act your age? I'd rather be Rollerblading.

Lance didn't win the President's Triathlon that year. But he did well enough to get noticed. He was training harder and winning more. His name got to be familiar among people who follow those sports, so getting sponsors got easier. Meanwhile, I was accepting increasing responsibilities and reaping greater rewards at work, plus I was finally able to go to some night classes. For years I'd been wanting to take some business courses and get my real estate license, and with that in hand, I started making some money on the side selling houses. Most of the extra money went toward travel, gear, and whatever Lance needed to participate in all these events, but we also managed to take a few trips for fun. We went skiing in Colorado with Jeanine just before she moved away to take a job in Minnesota, and another time we went to the beach. At a time when a lot of people dream of taking vacations without their kids, my idea of luxury was taking a few days away from the blur of activity to remember how it was when we used to play.

Life became a spinning cycle of über-projects for me and high-speed victories for Lance, but we still made time to sit together most evenings, eating supper by candlelight. This was a good boy, I knew in my heart. But my son was starting to stretch definitions and limits. He no longer fit the rank and file. He had friends, and though I loved every last one of them, some were stretching their own limits, without the benefit of a healthy outlet like Lance had. Most of them were drinking, a few smoking pot. I knew—because Lance told me right up front—

that certain guys were spending a lot of time partying out in a field just beyond our neighborhood. It saddened me to see these wonderful boys making these catastrophically bad choices, and it scared me to see them doing it in such close proximity to my son.

Lance was a very sociable kid. I guess when you're an only child, you're more open to developing close friendships and lots of them. But because he got along with just about everyone, he had people pulling him in different directions. The athletes on one side, rowdy people on the other. He was in the process of figuring out which side of the tracks he wanted to be on.

When he started driving, all those clichés people bandy about started to come true—complaints about teenage mouthiness and lack of gratitude and how the adolescent brain scans the same way as a person with severe mental illness. At times he was truly on my last nerve. Thank God, I didn't know about the fireballs.

"Mom, I need the car tonight."

This was a common opening statement that year, but on one particularly trashy evening, I wasn't feeling quite as easygoing about it as I usually did.

"Lance, the weather is lousy," I told him. "Maybe you should stay in."

"Mom, c'mon. It's Clay's birthday."

"Well, then why don't I drive you? They're saying it could get really icy later on."

He went off on the various injustices of the world in general and me in particular, but you know, why do parents sit there and argue with kids when they do that? Rather than respond to any of that, I used to set my hand on his arm and say, "*Hey*. Look at the way you're talking to your mother." This almost always brought him down a notch so we could discuss the actual issue at hand.

"I told those guys I'd pick them up," he said. "I'll be careful. I promise."

"What about that English homework you were supposed to make up? Miss Angelo called me yesterday and—"

"Mom, she *hates* me. She's a *bitch*! She won't listen to anything I say!"

"Well, I'm listening, Lance. I'm standing right here, waiting to hear your side of it. Do you want to tell me what happened in class on Tuesday?"

"Oh, this is bullshit! She's a liar. And this doesn't have anything to do with me getting the car! You just never want me to do anything. You don't trust me!"

"I trust you fine," I said sharply. "I just don't think it's a good idea. But it doesn't really matter what I think, because I'm not the one who has to face the consequences of the decision. You are. So I guess what matters is whether or not *you've* thought about *that*."

He flipped me the old double-eye-roll-lock-jaw-shoulder-shrug combination, then sat there, sullen, with his arms crossed over his chest. There was a long, uncomfortable silence.

"So do I get the car or not?" he finally asked impatiently.

I stood there, looking at this almost man and thinking, *I carry it myself, Mama! I carry it myself!* I weighed the keys in my hand for a moment, then dropped them into his.

"Please be careful, son."

I tried to stay awake, but the long day caught up with me, and I was asleep when he came home. The next morning I got in my car to go to work and . . . *what the—oh, God*. It was blood. And not just a drop or two. The red stain seeped across the passenger seat and spattered across the floor. I bolted back into the house and threw open Lance's bedroom door.

"Lance! What happened? Are you all right? *Lance! Wake up!*"

I shook his shoulder, and he rolled over and sat up, blinking, bleary-eyed, and yawning. My heart started beating again when I saw that he was in fact here and still in one beautiful piece.

"Hi," he said. "What time is it?"

It was one of those parenting moments when you can't decide whether you want to hug your child or throttle the living daylights out of him.

"Where were you last night?" I asked in the calmest tone I could muster. "And why is there blood all over my car?"

"Oh . . . that. Clay was being an idiot and broke a beer bottle and gashed open his hand and I took him to the hospital to get stitches. Sorry about the car seat. I'll go get some stain stuff after school."

"Well, is he—is he okay?"

"Yeah, he's fine."

"And you just . . ."

"I took him to the emergency room, and then I took him home."

"Why didn't you call me?" I asked, and Lance just looked up at me and shrugged as if to say, *What for?* And I didn't have an answer to that. He'd done exactly what I would have done. And exactly what I told him to do. He took responsibility for the decision and its consequences. Just like . . . a grown-up.

"Have a nice day," he said, burrowing back under the covers.

~

One upside of Lance's ornery streak was that it showed he had a mind of his own. Peer pressure didn't seem to have a huge effect on him. He had his own style, and it didn't bother him a bit that it was unlike everyone else's. He genuinely didn't care what anyone else thought of him—at least not enough to let their disapproval get in the way of the things he did care about.

Once when we arrived at an early-morning race, it was a lot colder than we had anticipated, and Lance realized he'd forgotten his jacket. We ransacked our bags, but all we could come up with was a cute little pink windbreaker I'd brought for myself. He stayed in the car with the heater blasting until it was time to saddle up, then went out and sat there on his bike, wearing that girly little coat, his bare forearms sticking out several inches beyond the sleeves.

As he and I both began to realize that he had a future as a professional athlete, he seemed to turn away from those friends who had a tendency to lead him into temptation. Now my major worry was his driving. It was the Green Machine all over again, this discovery of untapped *go fast* potential. Only now, instead of navigating between kids on skates and dodging neighborhood dogs, he was weaving in and out of traffic and evading the local police. I was continually finagling with the insurance agent and throwing myself on the mercy of the traffic court in the wake of a steady parade of moving violations. He had an attitude that did less than endear him to authority figures. He could be mouthy, and that's just not appreciated in the southern culture. Children are to be seen and not heard. They are taught to address their elders with respect. *Yes, ma'am. No, sir.* That just wasn't Lance's style. And it wasn't my style to bully him into it.

Enabler, I scolded myself as I waited in line to bail him out of another jam. *Where's the tough love? Where's the strict code of conduct?*

My granny did day care when I was young, and I remember her raising one eyebrow and slowly drawing a ruler from behind her chair. Silence and order reigned the moment she started to reach for it. I don't think she ever actually did anything with it. The threat alone was enough. Lance never had any such fear of me. Remember that old song "You and Me Against the World"? Well, that's how it was with us. I ran interference and did damage control all the time. It's not that I thought my kid was perfect and never did anything wrong, but I simply could not take someone else's side against him. Whether this was good or bad, it just wasn't in my biology. There were a lot of raised eyebrows over the level of freedom Lance was allowed, but I never invested much mental real estate wondering what other people thought of us.

When Lance flipped off the wrong trucker, the guy trashed my son's brand-new bike. Lance took off running, but not without the trucker's license plate number. In court it was Peterbilt vs. the Wrath of Mama Barracuda (and guess who's gonna win *that* battle every time). When the local police or disgruntled teachers came around to complain about his various shenanigans, I turned on my sales charm and did my best to deflect their irritation.

"Mrs. Armstrong!" Even though we'd moved to a new subdivision, there was still some neighbor lady hot on my trail. "Your son was up on the roof hanging Christmas lights yesterday, and I personally witnessed him mooning at least three passing vehicles!"

"Oh, my," I said. "But didn't he do a beautiful job with the lights?"

I'm not saying all this was exactly swell with me, but I knew early on I wasn't going to have any more success controlling Lance than my mother had controlling me. I knew we'd both be better off if I devoted myself to searching out opportunities that interested him, teaching him to set goals, and helping him invest as much energy as possible in meeting those challenges.

Lance's saving grace during all this was that he literally didn't have time to get into too much trouble. As we sat going over his calendar, planning events, and working through his schedule, he could see that that kind of stuff simply didn't fit into his life. And more importantly, that kind of stuff didn't fit in with the goals he had set and the direction he'd chosen. Most nights he'd be crashed out in bed by nine. His friends would come over and try to coax him out, but he was too tired.

~

So many parents want to be the wind beneath their teenagers' wings. But they also want to keep those pinfeathers trimmed to keep them from flying the coop. Well, I'm here to tell you, you can't have it both ways. And that's okay. Too often I hear people complaining about this or that idiosyncrasy in their teenager. They perceive it as a flaw, but maybe it's the thing that sets that person apart. Maybe her stubbornness will keep her in med school. Maybe his obsession with video games will translate into a career in computer animation. And all those quirky childhood behavior "problems"—the unzipped decibels of energy and sound, the constant questions, the ditch-leaping daring that generates more gray hair than all the henna in Egypt could color—these are the very qualities that fortify a person as an adult. Maybe that thing about your kid that's driving you crazy isn't a fault at all. Maybe it's just a different aspect of his personality and he needs a little help finding the silver lining to it.

Not long ago, I stood on a mountainside in France and watched my son whip by on the razor-sharp blur of his bicycle, fully engaged with every ounce of that vast reservoir of *go fast* he's always had in him. That need for speed, that utter lack of fear—such a thorn in my side once upon a time—these are the very qualities that enable him to do what he does.

Quicker than the thought itself, he was down the hill and gone.

TEN

THE FIRST TO SAY GOOD-BYE

Thank heaven the gol-dang dog finally died.

I hate to be harsh, but this was not a dog I had ever loved or wanted. It was a ghost-white spitz that came home with Sales one day when Lance was about twelve and haunted us until he was a junior in high school.

"The spitz is the national dog of Finland," Lance read from the encyclopedia when we were first trying to figure out what to do with the thing, and that right there should have been an indication that this animal did not belong in Plano, Texas. He was forever panting and drooling and shedding a haze of dandelion feathers all over the house. When I went to change Lance's bedding every week, I'd shake out clouds of pale hair from the sheets. This dog chewed. He dug. He barked. He tossed his stomach on the hallway carpet, and toward the end he got so bad, he'd lose his bladder.

"Why on earth did you keep it?" asks my hippie girlfriend.

"Well . . . *because*." I'm not sure how to explain it to her. "I couldn't just get rid of him. He was a living thing. I didn't like him, but he had a heartbeat like you or me."

It was part loyalty, I guess, and part empathy. I understood the deep-down dog-pound yearning for a home and family of one's own. So the husband left and the dog remained—my last shred of hope for the nondisposable nature of love.

After two titanic bad choices, I had strong reservations about letting anyone into my life. My second marriage had left me feeling burned and jaded, and I wasn't looking for anyone to restore my shaken faith in the institution. Isn't that the surest way to stumble on something, though? To not be looking out for it? Why is it that love, so elusive when you want it, follows you home when you're finally happy to be alone? It mugs you on a street corner, pulls the cosmic rug out from under your feet.

Think Richard Kimble. You know—the David Janssen character in *The Fugitive.* An upright but terribly put-upon hero. Innocent pawn of blind injustice. Decent and kind, but shadowed by tragedy. An intelligent, gentle man, with a generous spirit, slightly sad eyes, and a vaguely unsettling history.

Only my Kimble was funny. He made me laugh. And every man who's ever considered investing in hair plugs should know that the ability to make a woman laugh is the most potent aphrodisiac there is. Jeanine and I met him while we were out one night, and the three of us talked for hours. No one but Lance had ever been able to make me laugh like that. He was book-smart and interested in life and ready to discuss anything and everything with this quiet, unassuming mindfulness. Once he'd gained the official Jeanine Stamp of Approval, he somehow sidestepped all my defense mechanisms.

It wasn't that he swept me off my feet. It was that he *fit.* He brought a different sort of balance at the dinner table. The conversation flowed better. We laughed more. There were no power plays; he was understanding about the fact that my seventeen-year-old son and I had had our way of doing things and weren't interested in changing. He and Lance quickly became fast friends. If they hadn't, Kimble wouldn't have made it past the door. The chemistry between the two of them made it easy for me to let him in. Perhaps a little too easy, I think in retrospect. With simple kindness—a commodity so rare in this world—he opened a hidden door in my heart. And once that door was opened, an astonishing store of passion rushed out.

We'd been seeing each other for a while when Kimble's house was robbed.

"They ransacked the place," he told me, his voice shaking with frustration. "It's completely trashed. The landlord says the insurance will cover repairs, but I guess I'm going to be living in a hotel for a while."

It was like I was standing on a high dive board. You've climbed all the way up. Do you jump? Do you cast yourself into the open air and free fall, with nothing but faith in the blue water below?

"Look," I said, "why don't you . . . I mean—if you want to . . . it would make better sense for you to move in here."

"Are you sure?" he asked.

No. Yes. I mean, no! Or maybe . . . kind of.

"Sure I'm sure," I said. *Yeah, right. And this is my real hair color.*

I held my breath and hit the deep water. And for a while, it felt fine to be a married woman again.

~

Lance was out there with a motor on his tail, "gut-checkin," as he used to say, and bringing home an impressive assortment of trophies and cash awards. The world he lived in was spinning faster by the day, so I wanted to make sure our home life was relaxed and loving. I tried to cover all the bases I could, making good on my promise: "All you have to do is train and race. I'll do the rest." But he was growing past the point where I could handle everything. He needed to make connections with people who could help him navigate the politics and business aspects of professional sports. As those people came into his life, his opportunities expanded. He traveled to places I hadn't dreamed of when I was that age—South America, New Mexico, Colorado, Russia. Getting passports and travel lined up for people was something I routinely did in my job, but placing that passport in Lance's hand was a different matter. It thrilled me right down to my shoes to see him open this door on the whole wide world.

Unfortunately, the wide world is a tough concept for people with narrow minds. Lance was getting the opposite of support from the faculty of Plano East High. As the school year rolled forward, I tried to juggle and negotiate as best I could to keep everyone happy, but Lance's teachers grew surlier, Lance grew more frustrated, and I had no idea how it was all going to work out.

Meanwhile, I had been promoted to project admin in the engineering department at Ericsson, and I loved it. I worked through a terrific project with a manager who'd come in from Canada. He was like my little puppy the last three months. Wouldn't even take a meeting without me there.

"What can I say, Linda? You know the project better than I do," he told me.

"Maybe," I said, "but my job is to make—"

"To make me look like a million bucks. I know," he smiled. "Keep it up."

I *did* know that project better than he did. I was glad to hear him say it, because of course I never would. I'd brief him or make suggestions or whatever, but not in front of other people. Just in private so he could come out looking like he really had a handle on things. The project was a spectacular success, and I couldn't have been happier. Just before he left, my manager came into my office, closed the door, and handed me a bottle of champagne.

"I just wanted to tell you, Linda—you're a gem."

"Well, thank you! Wow. You're so sweet."

"No, I really mean it," he said. "I'm leaving tomorrow, and I just wanted to tell you that there is a job waiting for you in Canada as soon as you're ready to move into project coordination. And you are ready, you know. You could do this job better than a lot of people I know. In fact, I keep wondering—why *aren't* you doing this job?"

"Well," I smiled, "it's a long story."

"Party time!" Lance crowed, when I set the magnum of expensive champagne on the table.

"Here, here!" Kimble agreed. "Let's pop that sucker!"

"No way!" I told them. "I'm saving it for a special occasion."

But I'll tell you what—that was a special occasion for me. It was an enormous confidence booster. It had been drilled into my head that I could never move from the non-exempt to the exempt level because I didn't have a college education. Every time a project coordinator position opened up, I'd march down to HR and beat that dead horse, and I never even got to apply for the job. Year after year I watched the fresh-faced college grads come in at the entry level and quickly move up, cruising past me without breaking a sweat.

"But you know what?" I said as I set dinner on the table. "I *do* know this stuff inside and out. Moving up to project coordinator—that would be a lot more money. And *fun*. And it's not just a job, it's a real career path."

"So when are we moving to Canada?" Kimble asked. "And can you demand hockey tickets in your relocation package?"

"Hockey tickets!" Lance called from the kitchen. "Cool!"

"Cool is right," I said. "This Dallas girl would be Fanny the Frozen Belle up there."

"Who cares if it's cold?" Lance said. "I just want to get the hell out of Plano."

"Son," I chided gently.

The sentiment bothered me more than the cuss word. I knew his days with me were numbered, but his leaving was something I couldn't even let myself think about. He'd been the core meaning of my entire adult existence. He was seventeen now—the same age I was when I had him. We'd been together for half of my life and all of his. How my daily life would go on without him—it was beyond my comprehension.

I tried hard to be excited about all that senior year stuff. Pictures, prom, graduation announcements, tassels, and plans. But the hassle over Lance's traveling quickly devolved from a three-way dialogue down to plain old BS. Here he was, gaining national attention at the top of his sport, but it wasn't the official sport of small-town Texas. It was some *weird* sport where guys wore Spandex shorts and shaved their legs. People couldn't wrap their head around the idea that he wasn't just out there playing hooky. What we saw as an amazing opportunity for world travel, they saw as an unexcused absence. We battled them till we were blue in the face, but ultimately it came down to a choice between his high school diploma and an opportunity to travel to Moscow for the Junior World Championships.

Lance was trembling with anger and frustration when we came out of the final meeting on the matter. One of the school administrators made the unfortunate suggestion that Lance was "a quitter," and that didn't exactly go down like a spoonful of sugar with my son.

"I can't wait to get out of this piece-of-crap town!" he raged, striding down the hall toward his locker.

"Hey, what do I always say? All you have to do is train and race," I told him. "I'll worry about the details."

"It's not a *detail,* Mom, it's my friggin' diploma!"

"Just calm down. Let me think," I said. "Go back to class. Stay here in school for the rest of today, and do what you can. By the time you get home, I'll have it worked out."

"How?" he asked miserably.

"*Somehow!* This is a problem. That's all. Every problem has a solution. We just have to get our heads around it."

I hugged my son right there in the hallway. He was never one of those guys who wouldn't be caught dead giving his mother a hug at school.

"In every obstacle . . ."

". . . there's an opportunity. I know," he said. "I just wish there weren't so many opportunities all the time, you know?"

Amen to that, I was thinking as I hugged him again.

Back at my office, I rifled the yellow pages and started turning the town upside down, searching for a private school that would let my son graduate with the credits he had plus what he could do during the next six weeks. And when I got them to agree to that, I had to mention the additional fact that I couldn't afford to pay tuition.

"But it would only be for the few remaining weeks of the school year," I pleaded. "And this is a remarkable young man. He is really going somewhere. Someday your school will be able to say, 'Mr. Lance Armstrong was a graduating member of the class of '89!' "

"Bending Oaks Academy," I told Lance that night, "would be thrilled to have Mr. Lance Armstrong as a graduating member of the class of '89."

I didn't bother mentioning the dozen or so schools that were less receptive. Bending Oaks didn't have a lot of swanky families and highbrow bragging rights like the others. It was a small, caring place where a lot of outside-the-mainstream kids found a place to fit in. They were used to dealing with far worse problems than someone being an Olympic prospect and welcomed Lance with open arms. I have to laugh when I look at the pictures of him there on graduation day. Since we'd already paid for the cap and gown at Plano East, he marched forward with a gold tassel on his cap, while the other kids wore maroon. He looked like the valedictorian or something.

We'd also paid for a Plano East prom ticket, so Lance rented a tux and made a date. That night he invited me to ride around in the limo for a little while before they went to the dance, and I have to say, that was a pretty sweet moment for me. Lance was devastatingly handsome in that tux, and his date looked like a princess. They wore the limo well.

~

Summer was hot, muggy, full of mosquitoes—and not nearly long enough. Lance and his friends cruised around every evening and slept in every morning. They worked summer jobs, he raced, and they all swam and played ball until late August, when things started winding down to a few "last hurrah" parties and picnics. The last Sunday morning after the final Saturday night, I was cooking Lance and Kimble breakfast, and when I went to toss some eggshells into the trash, I saw an empty bottle.

"Where did you boys get—*hey!* That was my champagne!"

"Oh, yeah," he said. "Me and Ian drank it. We didn't think you'd mind."

"*Lance!*" I started sputtering. "What were you—how could you think—"

"Ian's taking off today. He starts school this week. We were celebrating."

I stood there, my mouth opening and closing, but no words coming out.

"That wasn't very nice," I finally managed to mutter, and then turned back to the stove. On the one hand, I was a little stunned that he and a friend would so casually drink in our home—and more than a little pissed off that it was *my* celebratory confidence booster champagne they'd chosen for their aperitif. But on the other hand was the huge realization that Ian's mother was at this very moment saying goodbye to her baby, while my baby was still sitting here at the kitchen table. I set Lance's breakfast in front of him, but he didn't dive into it like he usually did.

"So," Kimble said, laying a hand on his shoulder. "Everyone's off to college now."

"Yeah," Lance sighed. He looked toward the window, watching his childhood disappear down the road. "Hey, Mom?"

"Yes, son?"

"I want you to get me up at six tomorrow so I can start some serious training."

~

If you want to conjure up a mental picture of J.T. Neal, all you have to do is think of Jiminy Cricket. Slight of build, dapper, and charming. The perfect sidekick for a young man who already had a conscience but maybe needed a little help listening to it. He was a lawyer who invested wisely and was successful enough to have a second career as a soigneur and guardian angel to up-and-coming athletes. He and his wife, Frances (who always wore enormous chunky jewelry that suggested a flare for the artistic and a taste for exotic travel), took Lance under their wing when he decided it was time to leave Plano.

"We've got a small carriage house out behind our home," J.T. told me the day we met at a race in Austin. "The rent is reasonable, and I'll keep an eye on him. And I'll make sure he calls you at least a couple times a week."

I forced a smile and nodded in agreement. I didn't trust myself to speak.

"Austin's a great town for him to have a home base too. It's a college town, you know? Younger, hipper, less conventional kind of people. It's virtually impossible to not fit in here. You've got a little of everything. And the training opportunities—well, I'm sure Lance has been saying."

I smiled and nodded again. The peleton approached, flocked past, and disappeared around the bend.

"*Whoo.*" J.T. gave a low whistle. "Look at that boy fly."

Back in Plano, helping Lance pack and sort his things and gather all the belongings a person needs to launch his very own life, I felt more indebted to J.T. than he would ever know. Letting Lance go was by far the toughest thing I'd ever had to do, and it greatly comforted me to know that he would be just a few yards from this unlikely but loving surrogate mom. J.T. didn't hold back if you asked for his opinion—and sometimes if you didn't. He'd tell you exactly what he thought. You always knew where you stood. He had a colorful background, an unconventional life. He was different, which is what Lance and I loved about him. And I knew he had Lance's best interest at heart. He genuinely cared. He was there for Lance long before a lot of other people came to hover and hang on, and he was there for me during all the peaks and valleys of the coming years.

Lance and I shopped for furniture and dishes, and he was seriously into it. He selected classic bachelor decor, including a very manly man's sofa and an enormous tooled-leather longhorn head to hang over his mantel. I rented a Ryder truck, and Kimble and I helped him load his things—his mattress (*Oh, please, not his bed*), his clothes on hangers (*But wait, I should iron those!*), his boxes and assorted gear. His bicycle. Every item that went into the truck put him that much closer to *away from me* and piled another jagged stone on my heart.

The day my son went away to be a man in the world, I tried—oh, I did try to keep my game face on, but it was no use. I was a mess. I wrapped my arms around him and held on tight until I felt him firmly tugging away.

"Call me if you need anything," I said, struggling to keep my voice unbroken.

"I will, Mom."

"Call me, and I'll be there. It doesn't matter where *there* is."

"Okay."

"I mean it!"

"I know, Mom."

"You take care, all right?" Kimble said, gripping Lance's hand. "Stay cool."

"Yeah, you too," said Lance.

"All right then. So . . ." Kimble clapped him on the shoulder and firmly took hold of my hand. This was it. But not one of us could actually say the word *good-bye*. Lance climbed into the driver's seat of the truck. Kimble checked the latch on the back of the moving van and gave him the thumbs-up.

"Good to go!"

Lance roared the motor, but before he put the truck in gear, he leaned out the open window.

"Hey, Mom," he called. "Thank you."

And he drove away, taking what felt like my whole world with him.

I let myself cry for a couple of days. I set aside the weekend to be inconsolable. Jeanine called me from Minnesota, but I couldn't even talk on the phone. Debbie called a little later, but I was still sobbing. Kimble tried to comfort me, but there was really nothing to say or do but let me grieve for a little while, and that seemed to be hard for him to handle. Late that evening he came and tried to rub my shoulders, but I was feeling so utterly shattered, it felt like he was kneading me like a loaf of bread.

"Just—*don't*." I brushed his hands away.

"Okay. Sorry. Umm, I'm gonna go get a beer."

"Whatever," I said bleakly.

"Do you want to come?"

"No thanks."

"Linda—"

"*I know!* Okay? I know how wonderful it is that he's earning his own living and doing so well. I know it's absolutely right that he should go off and make his own way in the world. I'm proud of him. I have total confidence in him. I want him to spread his wings."

"But I guess all that doesn't necessarily keep it from breaking your heart," Kimble said gently.

"He's my baby," was all I could say.

"It's the great paradox of parenthood," says my hippie girlfriend.

"You don't want your child to leave you, but you can't want him to stay. Your fondest hope and deepest dread are one and the same—his independence."

When our children leave home, they take us with them in a thousand small ways. The Rolodex I helped Lance organize back when sponsors had to be lobbied and begged. The way I stagger the glasses in a dishwasher and fold towels so they fit in the linen closet. The habit of reading the paper first thing in the morning or wiping the counter after making a sandwich. These are the things we unselfishly give our children: everything they need to make a life that doesn't include us. To dissuade them from taking risks, to relieve them of responsibility, to slay their dragons in the name of protecting them—those are things we selfishly do for ourselves, so we won't have to worry or wonder or wait. Or be left behind.

~

Monday morning, I was in my office, ready for something new and desperately needing it to be something good. I knew that what I needed right now was to run and work and stay focused on whatever task was at hand. I'd heard about an opening—a project coordinator position in the new Global Systems Mobility department. *I know this. I can do this,* I told myself. Now if only I could convince a few other people. I knew the HR recruiter. I'd been vigilant about networking over the last few years.

"This is a great group," he told me. "You'd like these people. Everyone's young and totally energized and full of ideas. It's a whole new technology we're dealing with, so really, the rule book is being written as we speak. This guy you'd be working for, Jack Farmer, he's sharp. He knows his stuff, but he really needs somebody to come in and orchestrate all the details so he can be the hero, you know?"

I interviewed with Jack Farmer, and he was favorably impressed.

"Linda, as far as I'm concerned, you're in," he told me. "I'd love to have you on my team. The only thing is—well, technically, you know—"

"I can't be an exempt-level employee without a college degree," I said. "So I've been told. But I'm just not willing to accept that anymore.

There must be some way to break through that. And if I can't break through it, I'll climb over it. One way or another, I'm getting this job."

"Well. All right then," he said. "Let's see what we can do." And he followed through. A few days later he called me in to tell me he'd gotten an interview set up with a VP who might be persuaded to authorize my promotion.

"Now when you go into this meeting," he coached, "be sharp, but very demure."

"Demure," I said. "Got it."

"This guy's going out into uncharted territory with all this new technology, so he needs to put the best people in there."

"Right," I nodded.

"Okay. Go get 'em," said Jack. "Tomorrow morning. Nine-fifteen."

"I'm there!"

"Look stunning."

"Not a problem."

I went back to my desk and rummaged for the old dictionary Lance used to use for learning his word of the day. *Demography . . . demolition . . . demonstration . . . demulcent . . .*

Demure!

demure *adj* **1:** Sober; modest **2:** affectedly modest, reserved, or serious

Okay . . . so in other words, act like a nice girl. I could do that.

~

Guy Jablonski sat back in his chair and smiled a well-groomed *I am the vice president of your destiny* smile.

"You've got quite a fan club around here," he said.

"Well, I'm so pleased to hear that," I answered, demure as a magnolia blossom.

We talked for a while about the new department and what they would be doing; about Ericsson and the upper management in Sweden; about company policy and the importance of structure, especially when one is venturing out into uncharted territory.

"You know we have certain standards for exempt-level employees," he said, finally coming to the point. "And one that's really cast in stone is the college degree."

"Yes," I said, and I made a conscious decision to step off the ledge. "Yes, I've been hearing that for six years now—longer than I would have spent in college getting the degree. Instead, I've been here, acquiring the expertise necessary to do this job. And I did go to night school to get my real estate license last year, so I do have some continuing education—and some sales experience as well. Mr. Jablonski, the fact that I haven't had the opportunity to go to college doesn't mean I'm not smart. I know a lot about what goes on around here, and what I don't know, I'll make the extra effort and learn. I'm willing to work as hard as I have to in order to make a real difference in this department. We both know I can do it. But somebody's got to be the first one to step out on the limb and give me a chance."

I'm not sure how demure all that sounded, but I got the job. I was so elated, I practically danced up the driveway. I couldn't wait to call Lance and tell him.

"That's fantastic, honey," Kimble said that night at dinner. "You're on the up escalator now."

He raised his glass and smiled, but there was a shadow of . . . something. I don't know what. I didn't want to know. This was my moment.

~

"*Three hundred million dollars,*" Jack Farmer enunciated. "That's what's at stake here. We're going to convince Pac Bell that they just can't live without this brand-new GSM technology. And that we are the only ones on God's green earth who can deliver it. Now, our claim to fame is wireless, right? We were the first provider of wireless equipment in this country and Europe. So a lot of people around here are thinking we ought to dance with the guy that brung us to the prom. They're in a nice comfy place—fat, dumb, and happy—and they like it. Now here we come with this GSM thing. It's going to take some finessing. That's where our project coordinator comes in."

Eyes around the conference table shifted toward me.

"Good morning, everyone. I'm Linda Armstrong. And I'm incredibly excited to be a part of this team. We're going to accomplish something really extraordinary here. We're going to take the technology one step further into the future. And we're going to do it together."

Enough with the drill team captain. I hefted two four-inch binders onto the table in front of me.

"Here's the contract."

Jack and I let them absorb that for a moment, then started laying out a plan to make it happen. Basically, we were going to go into every department in Ericsson and say, "This is what the customer needs. Can we deliver it? If not, why not? And if so, how?" It would be my responsibility to digest all this information and put it into some kind of user-friendly format that could be pitched to the client.

"The ability to ask questions—that's one of your strengths," Jack told me. "People like you."

"I think this is going to be a blast," I said. "Get me in front of them, and I know I can get the job done."

"I don't know," one of the team members said doubtfully. "It's a lot to wade through."

"Oh, we're not gonna wade through it," Jack grinned. "We're gonna climb over it."

~

We put in unbelievable hours over the next few months, which suited me fine, because I was learning something new every day. I traveled a lot and talked with so many new and fascinating people. My horizon was expanding daily—I could feel it. And I loved that feeling. A lot of the technical stuff really went in one ear and out the other, but I figured it would be like Lance learning French and Spanish and Italian as he competed around the world. Immersion. You don't sit there worrying about what you don't know, you just dive in and soak it up. I made these engineers explain things to me in simple terms. I needed to understand the mechanics just well enough to be able to communicate, and since I would ultimately be communicating it to someone who was no more mechanically inclined than I was, throwing around a lot of engineerese wouldn't help us get the contract signed.

A lot of people didn't believe we'd ever get that far, so getting them to even give me the time of day took all the blonde power and southern charm I could come up with. I spent a lot of evenings meeting with managers who weren't willing to make time for me before five. Jack would arm me with a list of questions to ask and send me into the lions' den. They would look at me like I was an idiot, but so what? I wonder how many people have been held back because they were too proud to put themselves out there and ask for the information they needed to move forward. That's a false, silly sort of pride that never had any practical value for me. I'd rather admit right up front that I don't know, gather the information, accomplish the goal, and have something to be genuinely proud of.

"Your son is trying to reach you," my admin said as I came into the office. "He says it's urgent."

The fact that the message was from him and not his coach comforted me a little. If he'd been hurt, someone from the team would have called. Still, my hands were trembling a little as I took the pink message slip from her. Shades of that old SEC-toe-amputation debacle flashed across my mind. He was racing abroad for the U.S. national team, planning to ride as an amateur until after the Olympics. In the United States he was riding for the Subaru-Montgomery team. It kept him incredibly busy, training hard and traveling a lot. I had a hard time keeping up with his schedule, but I knew he was in Italy at the moment. I called the number on the pink slip. He was out riding. I didn't want to move from my chair until he called back.

"Mom! I'm so glad I finally got through. These weird phones here are—"

"Son, what's going on?"

He was so upset and frustrated, he could hardly put the story together for me, but esentially, he'd found himself in a tug-of-war position where the two teams he raced for were competing. He was smack

Me, Alan, Daddy, and Debbie, 1968. He came to visit just before he left for Vietnam.

That Mooneyham girl in 1968, a few years before I discovered that I'm a natural blonde!

Me in all my Adamson Leopardette splendor, 1970. Don't even tell me I didn't have what it takes to be a real Rangerette!

Captain Linda, flanked by the high-kickin' Rusk Rams drill-team officers.

My mom and baby Lance, rocking in the American flag chair.

Daddy and Lance, out back barbecue wrangling in 1974. Daddy turned his life around after Lance was born. Don't know what I'd have done without him.

Lance on his first day of second grade, 1978. That smile still gets me!

What a trooper! Lance woke up with the flu on Christmas morning (1978) and still managed to smile for the camera.

Lance got his first really good bike for his birthday in 1979. Guess that explains the big grin.

Daddy went with us every year to this triathlon event in Waco. He used to wear a shirt that proudly proclaimed I'M LANCE'S PAPA!

Mom,

Congradulations on all your schooling. I really do admire you verymuch. Whenever I see a 17 or 18 year old girl having a baby, I sort of think It will have a bad life. If all those girls turned out to be great mothers like yourself. Their kids would be great. thanks

I love you!

(Above) A sweet note from my sweet boy.

(Left) Me and my boy, 1992.

During Lance's chemo: smiling from the eye of a hurricane.

Carpe diem! Celebrating Lance's first year of survivorship, October 1997.

A quick hug before the final time trial in Futuroscope, 1999. A few hours later, Lance won his first Tour de France.

Mom (with Lance's dog, Boone), Lance, Luke, and me. Four generations celebrating Christmas 2000.

Me and Ed Kelly, the love of my life, celebrating our wedding day in June 2002.

Honeymooners! Ed and I enjoyed a once-in-a-lifetime cruise. First stop on the love boat—Key West, Florida.

A devoted daddy having a swingin' time with the kids. Lance, Luke, Isabelle, and Grace, December 2003.

Four five-timers! Hinault, Merckx, Armstrong, and Indurain at the Centennial Tour de France in 2003.

Five-oh fabulous! Ed and the kids threw a spectacular bash for my fiftieth birthday in February 2004.

in the middle, caught between everything he'd learned about being a team player and everything he felt about winning.

"The Subaru director is telling me I have to help Nate win. And the U.S. director is telling me I should try to beat him. And these people here—the Italian fans—Mom, they *hate* me. They're yelling stuff and spitting on me and throwing broken glass in front of my bike tires and—and I just wanted to talk to you, Mom. I don't want to mess up my deal with Subaru, but . . . what do you think?"

"Lance, if you think you can win, you do it."

"I think I can."

"Then to hell with 'they think.' Don't let anybody intimidate you. You put your head down, and you *race*."

He was the first American to win the Settimana Bergamasca. And by the time he reached the finish line, the Italian fans were cheering him on. It made me look around at my own situation: I was trying to build my own career and still be a team player, trying to do something that hadn't been done before and change the hearts and minds of people who, on a fundamental level, didn't like change. What Lance was accomplishing on the other side of the globe inspired me to forge ahead in my own little corner of the world.

I started to have a reputation as someone who was interested in getting things done and knew how to have fun doing it. People started to be more receptive. Little by little, we were diverting them to a new way of thinking. I began meeting with the customer's people in California, helping them organize test equipment and offices, checking materials, learning more about what they were going to need from us. I'd never had such a rollicking good time in my life.

I remember the day we signed the contract. The second largest GSM contract in the United States at that time.

"Holy cow, Mom! That's huge!" Lance said when I called to tell him about it, and that was a wonderful moment for me. Like the huge grandstand full of applause that doesn't matter at all, until you see that one face in the crowd—that one person who loves you enough to show up and cheer you on.

I was already in the middle of a new project when he called me from Oslo a few weeks later. With just a few days left before the World Championships, he was feeling the pressure of all the expectations and the daunting competition—including a cyclist who'd just won a third Tour de France victory. I'd already burned most of my vacation days and all my frequent flyer miles, but he asked me to come, and I'd told him a thousand times, "If you call me, I'll be there—no matter where *there* is." It would take a lot more than walk-up ticket prices to keep me away. All the pit crew duties I'd performed for all those years as he worked his way toward this moment—all that was in the hands of professionals now. He didn't really need me to wash his laundry in the sink, or feed him the right food, or answer his phone—but I went and did all those things anyway. Because what he needed was *Mom*. He needed that one person who loves you enough to show up.

As the day of the race drew closer I felt him turn in toward the core of himself. He became very quiet, very focused. I bought a little reading lamp so I could catch up on some things while he lay on his bed, staring at the invisible gears spinning across the ceiling until he fell asleep.

Rain slashed across the track the morning of the event. I sat on the metal bleachers with Stephanie, a rep from Oakley, one of Lance's sponsors. We watched the huge projection screen in disbelief as riders slipped and fell, sliding into each other, bashing into side rails.

"Linda, I've got to go warm up for a while," Stephanie told me after a couple of hours. "C'mon, let's get some coffee."

"No thanks. I'll stay here."

"Are you sure? I'm buying."

"No thanks. Really. I'm fine. You go."

I couldn't move. I had to be there to hold him up, to keep him safe. He came around the bend, and before his wheels went out from under him, I felt him falling.

"*Lance!* Oh, God! You're okay! You're okay. Get up. *Son, get up!*"

He struggled back onto his bike, rode on, slid again, but managed to stay upright. Hours passed without a break in the relentless, stinging rain. Stephanie came back after a while, bringing a cup of coffee I could wrap my hands around to warm them. She stayed for a long while, then went for coffee again. When she came back, she took my arm and rubbed it between her hands.

"Linda, you've gotta get out of here for a while. It's been almost six hours."

"Has it really?"

"You must be frozen."

"No, I'm—*Oh, no!*"

Lance went down again, crashing hard against the pavement. Every bone in my body felt him hit the ground. He flailed his way back onto the bike, pushing hard to get the pedals around, wobbling to a start, taking off again. The race dragged on for another hour. Suddenly, I looked up and saw my son's face on the giant screen. And in his eyes I saw . . .

"Stephanie." I gripped her gloved hand. "Something's happening."

"What? Where is he?"

"He's doing it. *He's doing it!*"

Lance stood up and crushed down on the pedals. The rest of the peleton fell away behind him. There was a surge of surprise, a tidal rush of reaction from the crowd. Excitement vibrated through the metal bleachers. He soared over a hill, bringing us to our feet, and I would not have been the slightest bit surprised at that moment to see him take flight. As he hurtled down the impossibly steep and slippery descent, my heart clenched like a fist inside my chest. My whole soul went out to him, reaching for him, seeking to encircle him. I laced my fingers together, holding all my power to pray and every moment of his life between the palms of my hands—terrified, exhilarated, and overwhelmed with love for this precious and extraordinary being, my baby, my boy.

We are not big weepers, Lance and I. But we did weep. I fought my way toward him, through the crowd that always forms a whirlpool around the winner (the *winner!*—the one who *won!*). Lance held me in his arms, my feet barely skimming the ground, and we buried our faces in each other's shoulders and we cried.

"*We did it! We did it!*" he said over and over.

"Mr. Armstrong!" A gentleman in official costume wrestled through the crowd and tried to make himself heard while maintaining his courtly manner. "King Harold of Norway wishes to extend his congratulations, sir, and would very much like to greet you."

~

"You're kidding," says my hippie girlfriend. "Norway has a king?"

"Apparently," I nod, dropping a couple of extra ice cubes in my tea.

"So then what happened?"

"Well, Lance said, 'C'mon, Mom! Let's go meet the king!' and I said, 'Okay!' just like we were going off to get tacos or something, and there was all kinds of hoopla, of course, and they took us to the security checkpoint, where this guy stopped us and told Lance I couldn't go any further, because the king would be greeting just him alone. And Lance—I just have to laugh—he goes, 'I don't check my mother at the door!' And the guy was pretty surprised, but Lance was already headed out the door, so he gave in. He took us both in."

"To see the king. Of Norway."

"Uh-huh. He seemed like a nice guy."

It felt like a finish line of sorts, Lance said later, for the race we two had run together. Everything we had at that moment, we'd given to each other. It was the sum total of all those years of hardship and happiness and struggle and love. But there was no time to say all that at the time. King Harold was waiting. And my son was showing no signs of slowing down.

ELEVEN

MERCY MERCY ME

Lance was walking through the door of his very own house for the very first time. I wanted him to have that threshold moment all to himself, so I purposely lingered in the garage for a few extra minutes, pretending to fuss with luggage and things, listening for Lance's reaction. I'd taken great pains to make sure everything was ready. All he had to do was set his bags down and start living there.

Lance had put me in charge of finding a designer, overseeing the construction, and hiring the movers. I was indescribably proud of him, and I loved getting my hands around the particulars of building, furnishing, and decorating the place. I'd been selling real estate for years and worked through the building process a few times. This wasn't my first rodeo, and I let everyone from the contractor to the carpenters know they weren't dealing with some ivory tower socialite. I'm what you might call an aggressive consumer (though I'm sure there are a few people who might call me something else). I'm not shy about asking for what I want and insisting on what I need. But I'm also quick to express appreciation for a job well done—and this truly was.

The first time I spread the blueprints out in front of Lance, I said, "Study this. It's the book that will build your *home*." And he did. Even though his schedule kept him training and racing in Europe most of the year, he carved out a plan for this place and made it happen. He carefully selected all the furniture and art. As project manager, I made sure that everything from the ultramodern kitchen to the beautifully appointed master bath—the silverware and saucers, the andirons by the fireplace—every detail was seriously considered and gently tweaked to make the place completely, uniquely Lance's house. His haven, his Alamo. And he loved it. *Loved* it.

We walked through the house, looking over every last square inch of the place, laughing and talking as I pointed out this feature and that.

"Mom," he told me when we finally stood out on the sun-warmed porch, looking over Lake Austin, "this is better than I ever imagined. This is awesome."

"I'm really glad for you, son."

"I know what I'm going to call it," he said. "Casa Linda."

I turned out toward the water, so he wouldn't see the tears in my eyes.

Lance squeezed my hand, and then we stood there quietly for a while, taking in the satisfying climate of absolute peace. I wondered if I would ever find that sort of sanctuary for myself.

I was hardly ever home anymore. Traveling and working late was easier than being home with Kimble. In the few years since Lance had left, Kimble's drinking seemed to be cementing the same stone wall that had separated me from my father the first seventeen years of my life. It cost him his job—and then another job—leaving me to support the household, while managing Lance's finances and overseeing the design and construction of the house. I was beginning to feel the weight of it all in the back of my neck. Sometimes late at night it made my stomach feel shallow and tight. I could see the shadow of it when I smoothed moisturizer around my eyes in the morning.

It didn't help matters that the honeymoon with Pac Bell ended almost as soon as it began. After the contract was signed, I was responsible for doing a contract summary. I was assigned to go through it line by line, comparing the contract with every last little thing we were doing and verifying—well, every last little thing. Yes, we can do this. No, we really can't do that. I put together a matrix of deliverables—what we could and couldn't do—and it got pretty interesting. There's a lot of territory between power lunch promises and the actual shipping of product out the door, and my job was to cover every inch of the course, rounding up stray cats and putting out brushfires along the way.

"Just give me the facts." I started to sound like Captain Joe Friday. It was hard, because there were some things that were promised that we simply could not do.

"Okay . . ." Jack rubbed the heel of his hand against his temple, trying to prepare himself for the dust storm that was headed our way. "This is solvable. It's not a new problem. It has a solution."

He set me to work organizing all the stuff Ericsson was not responsible for—all the third-party stuff. We knew how to make the widgets, and we knew we were going to deliver them, but third-party stuff like repair and return is a little tricky. That group had never been part of our project. And it turns out, that was kinda like having a bachelor party and forgetting to invite the stripper. You wheel in this giant cake, and nobody jumps out.

There was a certain piece of equipment that was failing out in the field, and I mean it was failing bad. The customer was sending it back to our repair and return department, and I discovered (not nearly as soon as I wish I had) that our repair and return department could neither repair nor return it. They had to send it to Sweden. To Gävle—which is actually pronounced "Yav-lah" I discovered during the first of many lengthy phone calls.

"Ah, yah, the transceiver unit," my Swedish counterpart nodded—or at least he always sounded like he was nodding. "Yah, that's important. You could say that's the heartbeat. That's the thing you need to make the signal."

"The transceiver unit," I echoed, furiously taking down every word he said, trying to decipher it all through the heavy accent and technospeak.

"Yah," he said noddingly, "the *very very expensive* transceiver unit."

"Oh. Great."

I loved those new GSM cell phones. These were the next generation—the very first really cool little phones. A giant step forward from those old things that made you look like you were hitting yourself in the head with a brick. Unfortunately, the repair center in Plano did not love them. They weren't set up to love them and wouldn't have known how to fix a transceiver unit had I dropped one on their head. Somehow, in the middle of all the research and the sales pitches and the math and physics and geography of this whole project, we'd missed that vital link. These guys were only interested in repairing the equipment for the old technology. That was our bread and butter, they kept reminding me, because—let's face it—people don't like change. Change takes effort. It introduces unknowns, and for a lot of people the unfamiliar thing is scarier than the bad thing they're already familiar with. They didn't want to get involved in the new stuff, because they didn't think it involved them. These guys wouldn't even make time during the day to meet with me. I had to stay after six, track them down like a bounty hunter, and practically tie them to a chair just to get them to explain to me why we were now in this pickle of a situation.

Once I got involved in the Plano operations and test station and got my head around the clockwork there, I realized they didn't have the components to repair the new equipment if they'd wanted to. They didn't even have the documentation.

"Everything goes to that *Gavel* over there," I was told by the beefy plant manager.

"Actually, it's pronounced 'Yav-lah,' " I smiled.

"It figures," he said grimly.

I made a trip to Sweden and learned that we couldn't even draw the dotted line from Plano to Gävle. There was no traceability at all. No communication, no cooperation, and, consequently, no results. So—first things first. Any major conquest begins inside people's heads, so I organized a monthly meeting with the Plano people, the Gävle people, and the executive committee and devoted my inner Rangerette to convincing them all this could be sorted out. Meanwhile, I devoted every ounce of southern belle I could muster to sweet-talking the customers, who'd been complaining for months and were, understandably, not talking very sweet at me.

The next phase was to get repair stations set up in Plano, have the barge-load of documentation (which was all Swedish as a lingonberry pancake) translated and organized, and instigate all the training and tooling and tap dancing that was going to have to happen in order to fulfill the commitments we'd made to our customer. It was a huge co-ordinating effort, a logistical nightmare. Good people—management people—were going to lose their jobs over it. I could have lost my own job over it. Nerves were unraveling like cheap cashmere. Tempers were flaring like Black Cat firecrackers. All of us in the department were flying by the seat of our pants, reinventing the wheel as we went along.

God help me, I loved it!

This is the kind of hair-straightening, blood-pumping business that makes you feel like you're rising right up the wrong side of the ski lift. Overseeing this tar pit was a chore nobody else wanted to touch with a vaccinated cattle prod, but that's exactly what made it so much *fun*. Pulling all the puzzle pieces together, we built the repair stations, located competent people to run them, and sent them to Sweden, where they could learn which widgets were needed to repair the whatchamacallits and which whatchamacallits were essential components for the thingamajigs. It was awesome. Every day was a new challenge, and I came home late every evening, entirely spent. Ready for bed.

I usually worked most of the weekend, but I managed to get away just long enough to make a brief appearance at Lance's twenty-fifth birthday party. It was a glorious September evening. He and his friends were going to a Jimmy Buffett concert later that evening, so of course, preshow margaritas were mandatory. Lance had rented a machine and was playing bartender. He placed a tall, icy glass in my hand and put his arm around my shoulder.

"Mom," he said, as full of life and love and joy as I'd ever seen him, "I'm the happiest man in the world."

I held that moment close to the front of my heart for a long time.

About a week later I was out on the patio, my feet propped up at the end of a long day, reading a recent issue of *Velo*, a magazine that helped me stay current with the people and events of bike racing. When the phone rang, I couldn't help but sigh a deeply weary sigh. I almost didn't answer. But then I thought it might be Lance, so I picked up.

"Mom, where's my flashlight?" he asked.

"Bathroom, second shelf, right-hand side, back corner." (Yes, I know, but that's just the way I am.) "Got it?"

"Yeah. Okay. Thanks, Mom."

"What's going on?"

"Oh, nothing," he said.

He said "nothing." That's what he said. He didn't say he'd been sick and coughing up blood. He didn't say he needed the flashlight so the doctor who lived down the street could look up his nostrils. I never harbored the illusion that my son told me everything, but just a few days earlier he'd talked to me about having sinus trouble. A bad headache. Allergies, he thought, because he'd been at that outside concert. Or maybe too many birthday margaritas.

"And now I've gotta go to Beaverton, Oregon, this weekend," he said wearily, "and I really don't feel like going. I think I'm gonna cancel."

"Son, they're counting on you," I said. "You really should go."

I said that because that's the kind of thing I always say. The encouraging thing. The cheering-on, "you go, kid" thing. I never pressured Lance to win, but I always pushed him to finish. There were times as a kid when he'd bonk in the middle of a race and end up walking his bike across the finish line with me urging him on. *Don't give up, son! Son, you never quit!* These guys from Nike were designing shoes for him and wanted to ride with him for the weekend. He'd made a commitment, taken on a responsibility. So I told him that.

And a few days later he told me "nothing."

For a long time I couldn't replay this moment in my mind without a thousand unasked questions haunting me. Why didn't he tell me "Something's very wrong and I'm scared?" Why didn't he say, "Mom, I need you," so I could have rushed right over there and made it all right? But it occurred to me after a while—maybe that's why. Maybe he didn't want me to rush in and make it all right. He wanted to handle it on his own.

It also occurred to me that he could have easily found his own flashlight. The logic with which I put away everything in his house was the same organizational logic he'd grown up with. And this makes me think that maybe—even though he was all grown-up, on his own, didn't want to worry me, whatever—maybe in that moment he just needed to hear my voice.

~

There's an old joke about a freighter captain who sees a light in the distance and flashes the message: "Change course to avoid collision."

A message flashes back: "No, you change course to avoid collision."

Incensed, the captain flashes: "I will not change course! I am the captain of a very large ship!"

"Suit yourself," the distant light replies. "I am the keeper of a lighthouse."

This is what is known as a shift in paradigm. And I was about to learn exactly what that means. Moments before I left the office on October 2, 1996, I was discussing some aspect of the gargantuan repair center project with my boss.

"I'm on it," I assured him with full confidence. "It's my top priority."

I didn't know that it would be three weeks and two days before I would walk through my office door again. I didn't know—couldn't have imagined—that in just a few hours the phone would ring and my life would be utterly unrecognizable.

"Linda?"

"Yes?"

"It's Rick Parker. Linda, Lance asked me to call you."

Rick was Lance's neighbor. A plastic surgeon with a warm smile and quick sense of humor.

"Nice to meet you," Lance had said when I introduced them. "I think I've been seeing a lot of your work out there on the lake!"

We got to know each other while the house was under construction, and I was glad to know my son had good people surrounding him. I knew Rick. Rick was a friend. The fact that Rick was calling me didn't raise any alarms. But then he started saying words that couldn't possibly be . . . right. Words that didn't fit together in a sentence about my son. My son was young and invincible. My son was the number-one cyclist in the world. Everything he touched turned to gold. He was healthy and strong and safe in his beautiful house.

"Linda, there's no easy way to tell you," Rick said. "Lance has been diagnosed with cancer."

Something at the foundation of me crumbled away.

And I said—well, actually, I don't know what I said. I guess I said something. And I think I remember feeling the phone in my hand, and Rick talking in a doctor way instead of neighborly, and he kept talking about my son and this *thing* and *surgery*, and he said *tomorrow*—as if there could possibly be a tomorrow after you hear those words about your only child.

"I'll be right down," I told him. Yes. That was the right thing to say. So I said that. I said, "I'll be on the next flight."

I thanked him. I hung up. I walked down the hall, but it felt foggy and tilted, as if the entire house had been picked up and shaken like a snow globe. I dragged a small bag from the closet and started throwing things into it.

Blouse, makeup, one extra—no, two pairs of—and these shoes or—it doesn't matter! Just go go go. I can't still be here. Don't cry. Don't cry. Stop crying! Call Kimble. His favorite bar. Please be there, Kimble. Please don't be drunk yet. Come home, goddamn you, and be sober enough to drive me to the airport. I have to find my son. I have to hold him as hard as I can.

My hands trembled in my lap for the entire flight. Lance's lawyer and longtime friend, Bill Stapleton, came with his wife, Laura, to pick me up at the airport, and I was a mess as soon as I saw them on the concourse. Seems like I couldn't take a real breath until I had my arms around my child.

"Don't even try this with me," I told him, choking back my tears. "This thing is not going to get us. Not after everything else we've done and dealt with."

We cried a little, holding on to each other for dear life. And then I held him at arm's length and looked him in the face.

"Okay," I said. "What's next?" And we went forward.

~

I've gotta tell you—I knew nothing about cancer. Never knew anybody who'd had cancer. Not up close and personal. You hear about it, but mostly as a cause of death, an afterthought in an obituary. Not as something that happens to living, live people. I had never for a moment thought about cancer as something that had anything to do with my life—and I certainly never imagined it would have anything to do with my son's life.

The next morning we took Lance in for the surgery to remove the cancerous testicle. It was early, and none of us had actually slept.

"Have a seat," the admissions nurse said. "We just need you to fill out a few forms. Let's start by getting a copy of your driver's license and insurance card."

Lance seemed a little stunned. His face was gray as the dawn outside.

"Oh . . ." he said, "I guess I left my wallet back at the house."

He looked over at me, and I thought of all the trips he'd taken from the time he was a kid. Always organized. Always in charge of everything he needed. He'd stand there, intently looking down at his bags just before departure, scanning a mental checklist of everything he was going to do over the course of the trip and what he would need to do it. But neither of us had an inkling of where this journey would take him or what provisions would be called for.

"Why don't I take care of the paperwork?" I said before the nurse could comment or complain, and Lance nodded gratefully, pushing the pile of forms toward me across the desk.

I spent the dragging hours reading, rereading, and re-rereading an assortment of pamphlets about testicular cancer, forcing my eyes back and forth across pages and pages of terrifying statistics and incomprehensible spelling-bee words. The pamphlets were filled with numbers and diagrams and pie charts where entire pie slices represented dead men. "Testicular cancer affects about 6,000 men each year." That struck me as a low, low number. *So okay,* I thought, *how does this translate into quality and availability of care? Think like a project manager. This is not a new or unique problem, therefore it has a known solution. The first step is getting the information.* "Cancer is classified by the degree to which it has metastasized. This is called 'staging.' " *But which is the good stage? Do you want to be a one or a four? Okay.* I read on and discovered that stage one is—well, it's not good, but it's less horrible. *We want one. He's a one. I feel it. It's gonna be one, baby. Come on* one. *Oh, God—Lord, I'm begging you. Make him be a one.*

He wasn't a one. The doctor who diagnosed him had asked for a chest X-ray, which revealed mets to his lungs. And he wasn't a two. According to the tests he'd had so far, Lance was stage three. *Okay,* I sternly told myself. *At least it's not four. We can deal with three.*

"He's asking for you," the nurse said, startling me. I realized I'd been concentrating so hard on what I was reading, my forehead felt stiff and achy. I followed her into the recovery room, and though I'd just seen my son on his way into surgery three hours earlier, I felt as if he was coming back to me after a long voyage. I found my firmest voice again, speaking to him about how strong and full of life he was and would always be.

There was a small sofa in the room, so I stayed there through the night, fighting sleep. I needed to be awake in case he opened his eyes. I thought about that long night at the Spenco 500. If he came by, I had to be waiting with whatever he needed. A sip of water, a steady hand to help him drag his IV pole into the tiny bathroom, a dry towel to rub against his back when he woke up in a cold sweat.

There are moments of mothering—unique but universal moments—when the awesome responsibility and overwhelming love merge to form the instinct that guides our nurturing. When my son had chicken pox—I guess he was two or three—I rocked him for hours on end, singing softly. *No wind . . . no rain . . . no winter storm can stop me, babe . . . oh, baby. . . .* His mottled skin stung like scorpion bites and itched like an ant farm, and I was afraid he'd scratch and give himself a bunch of those little circular scars. So I held him. I took a little stuffed bunny and stroked his tummy and arms and legs. It soothed him enough that he could sleep. Sometimes I dozed off for a minute or two, but as soon as I felt him whimper or stir, I'd start stroking again, moving the soft fur over his forehead and face. *Shhh, baby . . . Mama's here.* I was in that same place now, and the blessing of it, the gift—the privilege of sharing a life with this amazing baby being—it was more than enough to make me cry.

The next morning Lance was weak and hungry. He squeezed my hand, and I leaned in close to hear what he was saying.

"We can rebuild him," he whispered. "We have the technology. . . . Steve Austin will be better . . . faster . . . stronger. . . ."

~

The next day Lance kept his brave face on as friends came and went and nurses moved through the background in that quiet, efficient nursing way. People made hospital-type conversation—a rallying, cheering-on sort of small talk that purposefully avoided the tubes and monitors and the cath port that had been installed in Lance's chest.

"What's with the neon pink?" Lance's friend Bart teased, peering at the dressing. While Lance was sleeping, I'd gone down to the gift shop and got these brightly colored Band-Aids. I don't know why. I guess they just seemed less painful than the wilting flesh-colored ones. Less bleak and *cancer*-like.

"There's no harm in making it look pretty," I said irritably. "It doesn't have to look like shit."

"Oh," he said, slightly taken aback. "Right."

"It glows in the dark," Lance grinned. "Seriously, Mom, I looked down in the middle of the night, and I could see that damn Band-Aid glowing at me."

It was anything but pretty the following day. When Lance woke up at home, he found a large unspeakable something oozing out of the port. Understandably alarmed, he called me into the bathroom. I calmly examined it, wiped away the dried blood and *stuff* as best and as gently as

I could, then went to the other room and picked up the phone with trembling hands.

"There's something—I don't know what—it's coming out of the cath port," I told the doctor. *"I think it's cancer!"*

"No, no, no—it's just a blood clot, Linda. It's perfectly normal."

"Normal?" I almost laughed. "Nothing about any of this is *normal."*

"Linda, trust me. It's fine. But I'm glad you called, because we've decided to move his first treatment up to Monday."

"No—you . . . he can't! He's going to San Antonio for—for the—you know . . . to bank sperm. They said he had to come every day. Just one day—that's not enough."

"I know, but the numbers are higher than we'd like to see. He needs to get started right away, okay, Linda?"

"Yes. Okay, but. . . ." *No, no, no. Not okay. This is not okay.* He would be a wonderful daddy. He loves babies. Always has. He was never afraid or uncomfortable around them. Not even a little bit. This was so vastly and horribly not okay.

"Linda?"

"Yes. I'll have him there."

We set out immediately for the clinic in San Antonio. God knows what they do there. Don't ask. That's what I told two friends who rode along for moral support.

"Not a word when he comes out of there," I hissed. *"Not one word."*

Athletes are generally pretty casual about their bodily functions, and Lance had always operated and maintained his physical self like a sports car. He was uninhibited. Comfortable in his skin. He and his friends could joke about road rash, saddle sores, "T. rex" flatulence, and the unseemly circumstances in which a triathlete is required to relieve his bladder. But this . . . I had no idea how he was going to feel about it, and I did not find it the least bit laughable.

After we got home, I went over to the chemo clinic to pick up Lance's prescriptions and supplies. What I saw there—I guess I wasn't prepared for it. Recliners. Like La-Z-Boy chairs, you know? They were everywhere. And people were sitting in them with these poles leashed to their bodies. Tubes snaked from a pole to a man's arm as he sat reading a newspaper. From a pole to a woman's chest as she sat and stared at the wall, dazed. From a pole to the shell of a person—I couldn't tell if some of them were men or women, because they were bald and sunken and shattered-looking.

"May I help you?"

I was standing at the nurses' station, I realized. They were busy. I was businesslike. Scrambling to absorb the information they fired at me, I scribbled in my spiral notebook and collected more pamphlets. Then I drove home and tried to prepare my son for what he was about to see. Without going into a lot of detail, I gave him a general idea of what it was like and reminded him that everyone there was on the same mission he was. They were there to get well. If they didn't have hope, they wouldn't show up.

Lance and I spent the weekend in "calm before the storm" mode. He slept on the couch and watched football, while I cooked and cleaned. We devoured piles of information on cancer and chemo.

"How are we going to get rid of this stuff?" he asked me wearily.

"We're going to leave no stone unturned," I said. "We're going to gather all the information and examine the options."

In preparation for the first treatment, I picked up Lance's prescriptions, organized a file for his medical records, and bought him a journal in which he could keep track of his appointments, medications, and visitors. I tried to set up a staggered schedule for friends stopping by, trying to strike a balance between keeping his spirits lifted up while not letting his energy get run down. But on the day of his first treatment, I wanted everyone to rally around.

"Look, let's call everybody to come," I said. "We'll just make it a party. That place needs a breath of fresh air."

Maybe it's that thing about being an only child. Lance has always had a lot of friends. He's quick to laugh and eager to encourage. He's *likable.* He was at the clinic for four or five hours, and during that time the place seemed to have more oxygen than it had the first time I was there. All day long his friends came and went. While they sat with him, I went and hired a nutritionist, and then I went to the Whole Foods

Market, looking for tofu, organic vegetables, and free-range chicken. That's right! Fancy-schmancy, ridiculously expensive free-range chickens, raised on caviar and Ritz crackers and retired to their luxury air-conditioned chicken coops only when it was time for high tea. Call it another shift in paradigm.

That first treatment was deceptively uneventful. Lance didn't get sick. In fact, he was out riding his bike the next day when two oncologists we'd contacted for a second opinion called from Houston. They discussed Lance's test results, asked me questions about the treatment he'd received, how he'd reacted to it. Then they asked me if he'd had an MRI of his brain.

"Well, no," I said. "Why would we need that?"

The doctor didn't hedge or try to couch his words in the phone-call equivalent of bedside manner.

"We believe the cancer has spread to his brain," he told me with blunt force.

"*Wh—what?* What do you mean?"

He said something about the numbers. That they were very high. And he said more about—I don't know—*words*. Words I couldn't even think about. Horrifying, hard-shelled nightmare words that scattered like roaches into the darkest corners in my mind.

"*What do you mean about that?*" I kept saying, my voice choked and small, sounding more childlike than it ever had when I was a child.

Numbers. Explanations. Jargon. Instructions. I tried to write it down, but my hands were shaking.

"You need to get him here as quickly as possible for an MRI," the doctor concluded. "How soon can we schedule it?"

"I—I'll have to call you back," I said.

"Look," said one of the doctors, "your son should be receiving a more aggressive treatment. He's not going to make it at this rate."

"No . . ." I tried to coordinate my thoughts and words, tried to speak them without oxygen. "Don't do this. Okay? *Don't do this!* I have fought for this child my whole life!"

"We feel he should come down and start treatment with us right away."

"I . . . will . . . call . . . you . . . back," I said, willing myself to stay calm, stand firm. "Lance will be home in a little while, and I'll talk to him, and we'll call you back."

Waiting for Lance to return from his ride, I understood why he'd sent Rick to call me and Bill and Laura to collect me from the airport. It was just too unbearably burdening. Loving someone so much and having to tell them something that will rip their world apart. Something more than enough to make a grown man cry.

He sat and listened intently, looking out at me from that concentrated quiet I'd seen him wrap around himself right before the most grueling races. He called the doctors back, and they repeated everything they'd said to me. Lance called his Austin oncologist, who told him he'd already planned an MRI based on the same suspicions. Leaving no stone unturned, Lance worked his way through a list of friends and advisers he'd been assembling.

From the start of this thing, we'd been reading everything we could get our hands on, including rafts of letters and e-mails from people all over the world who wanted to encourage Lance and share their cancer experiences. It's the first inkling I had of what people mean when they say "cancer community." These letters came from grandmothers, guys in prison, business executives, housewives. In addition to the hope and encouragement, there was valuable information, including a letter from a doctor who directed Lance to the specialist in Indianapolis, where he ultimately went for his brain surgery and continuing chemo.

Lance was shaken to his foundation, so I wasn't about to buckle in front of him. I was in project management mode—collecting data, coordinating options, orchestrating action items, and asking every question I could think of except the one I was really struggling to understand: *why?*

"It's bad," I told my boss, leaning against a white clinic wall beside the hallway pay phone. "It's in his lungs. It's in his brain. He's a stage four, they're saying now. Stage four is—it's as bad as it gets. And I don't . . . I just don't know. I can't leave him, Jack. I know this is incredible timing—"

"No," he cut in. "Family is the most important thing. Do what you need to do, and we'll figure it out when you get back."

"I'm sorry. I'm sorry."

"It's all going to work out, Linda. You'll see," he said, adding, "Is there anything I can do?"

"No, but thank you so much for asking," I said, because that's how I always answer when people say that. It's my biology.

"Is there anything we can do?" one of the admins called to ask.

"No. But thank you so much for—"

"Linda—look, we can help. Let us help."

"Well, I can't really think of anything . . ."

"I can," she said firmly. "I'm going to check your e-mail every day and sort it into files. That way you won't have to deal with any spam or low-priority stuff, and you can deal with the well-wishers when you have time. Pam's going to grab your voice and snail mail and sort them the same way."

"Thank you," I said, and I can't think of an occasion when I meant it more sincerely. "That would be incredibly helpful."

Being on the receiving end of a support network was a novel experience for me. I'd always been the helper, the facilitator, the spark plug. And I liked it that way. There's a lot of power and control—or at least the illusion of control—in being one of those people who lives by the credo "If you want something done right, do it yourself." A credo that (you eventually come to realize) makes the arrogantly flawed assumption that your way is invariably and uniquely right.

We went to Houston for the second opinion. The oncologist was arrogant and dramatic, telling Lance, "I'll cure you, but you're going to crawl out of here." Seems like I didn't take a breath the whole time he was talking. I looked over at Lance, and there were beads of sweat on his temples and upper lip.

"Look," the doctor told him, "your chances aren't great, but they're a lot better here than they are anywhere else."

We went to Indianapolis for a third opinion. Lance, me, Bart, and Lisa, Lance's girlfriend. Hotels, hospitals, waiting rooms, doctors, diagnostics, more waiting rooms, more doctors, another level of gripping sadness, fear, and directionless rage. Every time another radiologist shucked another picture of my son's interior onto the lighted viewscreen, the sterile room seemed to get a little colder. I hadn't packed anything warm to wear, so I swiped a blanket off one of the airplanes and clutched it around my shoulders as we hurried through the frozen morning air to Lance's next appointment.

I liked the doctors in Indianapolis. They were grave and serious but they had an attitude of hope. Instead of melodrama, they were all about the science. Instead of emphasizing the disastrous effects of chemo (which struck me as a disclaimer anyway—just a doctor's way of covering his you-know-what if things didn't go well), these guys started talking about protecting the quality of Lance's life and how they might preserve his career. They discussed treating the brain lesions with surgery instead of radiation in order to preserve Lance's coordination and balance. They suggested eliminating bleomycin from his chemo, because it wreaks havoc on the patient's lungs and heart. Basically, instead of explaining accepted protocol and laying out "doctor's orders," they took the time to understand Lance as an individual and built a protocol around him. We left and went to lunch, feeling more optimistic than we had in days, and I was relieved to hear Lance say he'd decided to pursue treatment with the Indianapolis team.

It's hard for me to sort out the events of that month. A thick fog rolls across my memory, beginning with that evening when I walked out of my office with one set of priorities and stepped off a cliff into a whole other life. There's a certain photograph of me, standing beside Lance's bed right after the brain surgery—and you know, I can't remember who took it. My face in this picture—it's two-dimensional. There's no soul behind my eyes. I'm just standing there with the other jigsaw-cutout spectators, smiling this impenetrable, aluminum smile.

After his brain surgery, Lance asked for me, and for a long time I just stood in the recovery room and held his hand without speaking. I know now that in the days following his diagnosis Lance was thinking some deep thoughts, but we've never been big on deep conversations. We lived in the moment, and in this moment all I could do was be there with him, holding his hand.

"Mom," he whispered without opening his eyes.

"I'm here, son."

"I love you, Mom. I love my life . . . and you gave it to me . . . and I owe you so much for that."

I gripped my son's hand. I laced my fingers through his and swallowed hard, holding him in my heart. I imagined us dancing to a soft slow tune, my baby's feet on top of mine, my boy's blue eyes filled with life and love and joy. It was the only way I could reach past the confusion of wires and tubes and monitors in an effort to find my child and cling to him.

~

Lance began his chemotherapy the next day. Everything we'd been reading indicated that the initial response to chemo was critical. A poor response was strongly associated with a poor survival rate. I compulsively studied those statistics and monitored those numbers, wanting to understand every test result and blood cell count.

There were moments of profound quiet inside the hurricane of necessary activity. The adrenaline-charged days were separated by long, silent nights. When Lance was in the hospital, I paced and prayed—conscious of the tick of the clock, the drip of the IV, the periodic sigh of the blood pressure cuff—until the morning shift started rustling around the nurses' station. While Lance slept, I sat beside his bed, making lists in a spiral notebook. I used a straightedge to draw a three-month calendar and mapped out the days in neat squares. The straight black lines that separated the days—those were the nights, I suppose. They defied time and intention. There was a little sofa in Lance's room, and I lay there, perfectly still, listening with my whole body, as if I had a newborn baby down the hall. I waited to hear him cry, and when I knew for certain he was asleep, I cried. I was just so very sad. I locked the bathroom door and covered my mouth with my hand, rocking back and forth with my arms tight across my heart. My ribs felt bony and frail. Seemed like I was losing weight by the day. Every time I tried to eat something, my stomach tightened to a constricted knot of panic right at the center of me. But I did not cry in front of my son. He didn't need that right now. He needed me strong, and that's exactly what I intended to be.

There were a few precious moments of good news. (Funny, isn't it, how our definition of "good" tends to operate on a sliding scale.) The doctor who did Lance's brain surgery told us that, astonishingly, one of the tumors had been fried by the single chemo treatment. Most of Lance's sponsors were sticking by him, which took a lot of financial worries off his back. I cherished even the smallest signs of hope. Every time his blood counts rose or his tumor markers fell, it was like coming up from black water for a precious gulp of air.

On the way back to Austin from Indianapolis, there were three first-class bump-ups available. I handed the coach ticket to Bart, and said, "Have fun." I collapsed into my seat up front and huddled there for the next few hours, grateful for the amenities I'd come to take for granted. The warm towel to press against my face. A glass of wine. A little white pillow and clean blanket. Kindness—even canned flight attendant kindness—was a priceless gift to me right then. To have someone nurture me, even for a moment.

Kindness was the thing I loved about Kimble, and my heart ached for him. He came to Indianapolis for Lance's brain surgery, but he didn't offer to come to Austin, and I didn't ask him. As much as he loved both me and Lance, he just didn't have it in him to be there. I closed my eyes and thought about how it would feel to have his arms around me.

"When are you coming home?" he asked me every time I called.

"I don't know," I kept telling him. "I can't leave."

"Well, do you think—"

"I can't think about anything but Lance," I said sharply.

He was quiet for a moment, then told me, "I love you."

Walking in the front door at Casa Linda with Lance, I hardly felt like we'd been gone. More like we'd all had the same bad dream and awakened disoriented, headachey, and sad. And I had to work the next day. I didn't want to leave, but I'd burned all my vacation time, plus a few days.

"You could take an unpaid leave," Bill Stapleton suggested.

"There's the Family Leave Act. They have to let you take time off for a family emergency."

"It's not an option," I told him, and left it at that. I didn't feel like explaining that The Fugitive was between jobs. He'd been in and out of work for the last couple years, and for the last couple months he'd been solidly out. It was nobody's business.

"Are you sure you're ready to go back?" Kimble asked.

"What choice do I have?" I answered bitterly. "One of us has to be working."

He looked at the floor and didn't say anything. Employment was a touchy topic. Even when I thought I was genuinely trying to encourage him, anything I said sounded like an indictment. And right now, I wasn't trying. I didn't care if I hurt him. I wanted to blame someone, hit someone, make someone on this earth feel as sad and gut-shot and wasted as I did. Like ballroom dancers, Kimble and I had established our pattern: accusations, arguments, silence, sex. Kimble sensed that right now I needed to cut straight to the silence and stay there.

Going back to work was actually a relief. There are moments in life when the healthiest thing you can do is go about your business as if your whole life isn't engulfed in flames. Embrace the denial. Go willingly with the distractions. And that's all they were now. Numbers with lots of zeros and a dollar sign. Not nearly as jolting as the numbers I'd been recently faced with. White counts and PSA factors and survival statistics. The melodrama of the office was comfortingly pale after the genuine drama of the preceding month.

Oh, God, I thought on my way up in the elevator, *I suppose people are going to want to hug me.* That's not a problem for me usually. I'm a warm, southern *hey, darlin'!* kind of gal most of the time. Only just now—I felt so fragile. Like I was made of spun-sugar skin and blown-glass bones. Every time I inhaled, I felt hollowed out and brittle. My wrists were pale and thin as a paper doll's. *If someone hugs me right now,* I thought, *I will turn to salt.* I've never been good at being comforted. My coworkers were wonderful, and I loved them, but I'd always kept my home life at home. Very few of them even knew who my son was. These were such good people. It was agony facing them, because they felt so bad for me. I couldn't bear that. It made me want to comfort them, and that required more energy than I had at the moment. Plus there was a little part of me that kept remembering that day Lance almost cut his toe off. Were people going to be annoyed that I'd been gone almost a month during the critical stage of a particularly explosive project?

This is probably where I learned the difference between a job and a career. I'm not sure when I crossed over from one to the other, but there's a definite difference between the two. Job is what you do, career is what you are. When you work a job, you know you're just passing through. When you build a career, you build a community, fraught with all the conflicts and caring of a family.

My coworkers met me with an outpouring of love and support. There were cards and gifts and hugs that made me feel stronger instead of breakable. True to their word, the secretaries had sorted a gigantic amount of mail into neat folders. Jack came in, closed my office door, and said, "You don't have to be here if you don't want to be."

"No," I said, "I do. I mean—I want to. There's the meeting with all the—the—it's all got to be prepared and all those contacts made. I need to be up to speed on everything and—and I need sticky notes. And . . . I have to—to just be here, Jack. It's just my way of coping. I take my sticky notes and my e-mail and I throw myself into my work."

He nodded and went to the door.

"Let me know . . . if there's anything I can do."

"I will," I said for once. "Thank you so much. I'm going to take you up on that."

~

I'm not going to grind through all the details of the whole chemo thing. Oh, my God. I cry when I even think about it, and if you have the luxury of going your entire life without ever having to think about it, I'm glad for you. Besides, it's my son's story, not mine. That's what makes it so hard. More than anything, I just wanted to breathe the same air. I wanted to put my hands on his head and take the cancer away from him. I wanted to be the one who had to have it. Not him.

Every week I worked frantically to accomplish what I needed to so I could spend weekends with Lance. I'd drive to Austin Friday afternoon and spend the evening cooking Lance's favorite white chicken chili, expanding the recipe to feed the steady parade of friends and well-wishers with plenty left over for the freezer. Saturday morning I'd wait for Lance to come back from his bike ride or his walk when he was too weak to get on the bike. Then I'd go out shopping for his groceries: tofu cheese, vegetables and fruit for juicing, organic everything.

Saturday and Sunday, friends came and went all day, and in the evening Lance and I sat together reading the continuing flood of mail and writing piles of thank-you notes. I was still in project manager mode, bird-dogging the appointment schedule and making sure Lance had everything he needed. If the nutritionist said he needed X number of milligrams of vitamin C, that's exactly what he got. The nurses had explained to me the importance of keeping him hydrated, so I bought tall bottles of purified water and numbered them so he'd know when he'd reached sixty-four ounces each day.

As he drove off to go somewhere with his girlfriend one afternoon, I discovered he'd left his water bottles, so I jumped in my car and took off after them, calling his cell phone to give him a heads-up.

"I'll get it when I get home," he said.

"No. You have to space it out properly," I insisted.

"Okay, fine," he sighed. "Just pull up alongside us and hand it off."

I suppose any normal mother would have said, "What, are you nuts? Pull over!" But you know, I kinda liked the idea. It was a brave and crazy and fun thing to do. In the middle of this all-out storm of sadness and fear and hard facts to live with, it felt like defying gravity for just that moment. I stepped on the gas and roared down the road until I caught up with Lance's car, then skimmed up next to the passenger side, and laughing and shouting, I passed the tall water bottles across the fast and furious divide.

I spent the weekends doing whatever I could to help, then drove home Sunday evening, feeling torn and exhausted, grateful for the friends who would see Lance through the week but wishing with all my heart I didn't have to leave. The long drives made for many hours of deep reflection. I prayed. And I mean really prayed. I talked to God about Lance's white count and his cath port not getting infected; about the future, the banked sperm, and how I could possibly help my son seek out some sort of blessing in this astonishing setback. To this day Lance thinks that prayer didn't help him, because he didn't pray. But I prayed for him, and I know in my heart of hearts I wasn't just talking to the windshield.

So much has been unspoken between us over the years, I wonder sometimes what I might have done differently to share with him my faith in God. Trouble is, actions speak so much louder than words. In my life I learned about God from my granny, who lived her faith every day, and from my father, who was transformed by faith and became an instrument of grace for me and my son. Lance learned about God from the Salesman and his preacher daddy and the preacher's compassionless wife, who practiced a harsh religion made up of strict creeds and antique rituals instead of encouraging words and genuine acts of loving kindness.

Ultimately, I came to respect the belief system Lance carved out for himself. As difficult as it may be for parents to accept it when children choose a different spiritual path, we have to recognize that it is their choice, and the fact that they find their own way in no way invalidates the choices we've made for ourselves.

Lance spent every third week in Indianapolis receiving chemo. That was the worst time, because I couldn't go with him, and sometimes he was too sick to talk to me on the phone. But the tide was turning. While the chemo drove him into the ground, it was driving the cancer out of his body.

"Nichols says I'm a responder," he told me proudly. "In just three weeks my HCG markers fell from 92,000 to about 9,000."

"Oh, Lance, that's fantastic!" I said. "How's your white count?"

This was the odd language we spoke now. As if we'd moved to a different country, and I suppose in a way we had. Lance endured his last chemo treatment just before Christmas 1996. Afterward, his HCG count was normal. Technically, he no longer had cancer. But that's not the way it felt. There was something that had stayed with me—haunted me—since the day I went to pick up Lance's chemo supplies before his very first treatment: a lot of those people were there for the second or third or even fourth time. This was our first rodeo. But would it be our last? Even if the cancer was gone for good, we had no idea what the long-term and late effects of the chemo would be.

I brought Lance home to spend Christmas with Kimble and me, and it was not the happiest holiday we've ever spent. Lance always put a lot of energy into stringing lights and setting out decorations when he was a kid, but after he left home, I never felt like going to all that trouble. This year, though, I dragged out the strings of icicle lights and hung them along the eaves. I even dragged out these goofy plastic reindeer we'd been lugging from place to place over the years. I cooked all his favorite foods and tried hard to keep the mood light and cheerful, but I could tell Lance was struggling with a lot of conflicting emotions. Anger, sorrow, uncertainty.

Where is the big moment? I kept wondering. Because isn't there supposed to be a heartstring-twanging, tear-milking moment where everything turns out fine? A happy ending? There's talk from time to time from people wanting to make a movie about Lance's life, and if they ever get it off the ground—well, what do you want to bet they'll manufacture that moment? Some scene where Alec Baldwin or whoever is playing the doctor says, "Congratulations, Lance, you've beaten the cancer! Now get out there and win one for the Gipper!" And Brad Pitt or whoever is playing Lance will grin and stride right out the door and hop on his bike and win the Tour de France like thirty seconds later. And Susan Sarandon or whoever is playing me will brush a tear from her eye and say, "That's my boy!"

But life isn't a movie. And cancer doesn't have a tidy happy-ending moment. It has remission. You know, I looked that word up, and it means "to release or lay aside partly or wholly." There's a tentative feeling to that word. A sense that the thing you fear most isn't really gone; it's just set aside. Partly or wholly. Maybe forever. Maybe not.

The end of chemo was a welcome release, but there would be years of follow-up. Fearful moments. Overcompensation. A grieving process.

Because even though Lance lived (oh boy, did he ever live!), there was a loss. Something vague and indefinable. Innocence maybe.

Lance took a spectacular fall in the 2003 Tour. Support people hand riders food and water in these yellow bags called musettes, and spectators collect or buy them as souvenirs. A kid by the side of the road was swinging a musette by its long strap, the strap caught Lance's handlebars as he whipped by, and down he went. Hard. He hit the cement like a ton of bricks, and some incredibly lucky cameraman was right there to capture the incident close-up in all its bone-jarring glory. It's a great shot. I understood why Outdoor Life Network used it in a montage advertising their 2004 Tour coverage. But every time I see him go down, it hurts me—deep inside, deeper than my spine, somewhere beyond the reach of my reasonable self. Obviously, when I see that footage, I know he's going to be okay. I know he got up—injured and enraged, but burning with purpose—and went on to blow the stage away, even though the other riders practically tore their legs off trying to catch him. I know all this. But somehow it still hurts when I see him fall. It still scares me. I can't help but cry out, "*Lance! Oh, no! Oh, son!*"

The cancer thing is like that. He didn't just live—he lived large! And I think he's got a healthy attitude about what happened. So do I, for the most part. It's just every once in a while. Something will cause a particular moment to replay in my head, and it is still bone-jarring. Emotional and physical recovery take time. There are no shortcuts. You can't get around it. You have to get over it.

When the active phase of his cancer treatment ended, Lance still had an immense task ahead of him—a great mountain to climb. Proud and terrified, I stepped back to watch him rebuild his life, not sure where we would go from here, but knowing neither one of us would ever be the same.

~

The repair center project was successfully completed not long after Lance's last blast of chemo. We had a final videoconference with the executive committee, management personnel from every department, and everyone else who'd been battling for sixteen months to slay this dragon of a situation. Reports came in from Plano and Gävle. Smooth transactions and efficient transitions were happening on both continents.

"And I'd like to reiterate the rave reviews several other people have given our project coordinator, Linda Armstrong," said one of the department heads. "Spectacular job, Linda. A year ago, just looking at the scope of this problem—the magnitude, really—we frankly didn't think it could be done."

The big guy in Sweden always had the last word at these things. He praised everyone, thanking me individually, and then he rose to his feet and asked everyone to join him in a standing ovation for my excellent performance.

My applause. Here it was. I was being cheered on, and I wanted to enjoy it. I wanted it to be my day. My best moment. Instead, the bittersweet quality of life overwhelmed me. I felt a stiffness set in from my hard-set jaw, down the sides of my neck.

Never ever let them see you cry, I'd told Jeanine that day in what seemed like another lifetime. And I wasn't about to do it now.

~

" 'If you can meet with triumph and disaster,' " says my hippie girlfriend, quoting that Rudyard Kipling poem you always see on graduation cards, " 'and treat those two imposters just the same . . .' "

"Imposters." I smile without opening my eyes. "No kidding."

" '. . . Yours is the world,' " she says, " 'and everything in it.' "

TWELVE

SMILING FACES SOMETIMES

When Sammy came into my life, I was in desperate need of something fluffy. Being a sensitive man, Kimble sensed that and mentioned that someone at his office was trying to find a home for a little shih tzu she couldn't keep in her new apartment. I'd always been a cat person, and we had a cat at the time.

"Why don't you bring him for a visit?" I said. "We'll see if he gets along with Misty."

Well, if you've ever cuddled a Sammy dog in your lap, you know that saying he's there for a visit is like saying you're going to eat just one jelly bean. From the moment I set eyes on him, he was mine. And he loved that cat. Seems like he was enthusiastically demonstrating his love every time I came into the room, in fact. I'd have to chase him off her. He made me laugh, and *oh, boy*—did that feel good. To laugh again. That was the sweetest thing I'd felt in a long time.

I had grown to love the group I was working with at Ericsson. A lot of us started together on the Pac Bell project. We were all new, because we were doing things that hadn't really been done before. That made for strong camaraderie, but also for some pretty tough times. There were several instances where people left over bitter moments. Some people wore their hearts on their sleeves and just couldn't handle the crossfire that was going on all the time. I was fortunate to be working directly for Guy Jablonski now. He would always give me the hard jobs, because he knew there was nothing I loved more than that challenge. He would just sit back and watch me take it on and turn it around.

My son and I are alike that way.

Lance received a clean bill of health in January 1997 and began rebuilding himself, physically and mentally. I've seen him ride so hard the whites of his eyes turned bloodred, but I don't think I've ever seen him work harder than he did in the year following his chemotherapy. He struggled with his new role as cancer survivor, grappling with decisions about the direction his life would take, but finding his way at his own pace. He made me more proud than I've ever been in my life when he started the Lance Armstrong Foundation. Intensely caring and compelled to act, he created a way to turn the tables on this dark force. He no longer had that typical twentysomething ability to walk through the world and not see the suffering of others. His eyes were opened, and wherever he saw sickness and sadness, he felt driven to help. The foundation has since raised millions of dollars for cancer research and given Lance an avenue through which he personally reaches out to other survivors. I can't begin to tally the hours he's spent calling and e-mailing people in treatment, visiting children in cancer wards, and doing whatever he can to increase awareness. I personally think it empowered him, because after he started giving back some of the love and support that had come to him during his chemo, he discovered a whole different sort of power inside himself. After a period of uncertainty, he started riding again.

Best of all, he was happy. I could hear it in his voice on the telephone. There was an embracing of life and an appreciation of beauty and a readiness to move forward. *Of course,* I realized after a little while. *He's in love.* He'd been talking a lot lately about a certain young woman who was doing PR for the Lance Armstrong Foundation's "Ride for the Roses," an event that would raise a tremendous amount of money for cancer research. I didn't know a whole lot about her. Her name was Kristin, but everyone called her Kik. She was blond and beautiful and full of energy. And she made him happy, which was all I really needed to know.

We were sitting at my kitchen table one Saturday morning, drinking coffee and reading the paper, feeling like that was the only thing for which Saturday mornings had been invented.

"So what are you up to today?" he asked.

"Nothing much," I said, though he knew me better than that.

"Wanna go shopping with me?"

"What for?"

"Diamonds."

You know how sometimes when a person is smiling a certain way—with his whole spirit and the entire contents of his heart shining from his face—and we say he's *beaming*? Well, Lance was beaming. And I'm pretty sure I was too. Neither one of us knew what he would end up doing with the rest of his life at that point, but knowing he'd found a soul mate made the rest seem so much more doable, and it made the "carpe diem" celebration of his first year past his diagnosis all the sweeter.

Meanwhile, Kimble had gotten hired as a sales manager at a car dealership, and even though I suspected he might be sneaking away from work to go to the movies some afternoons, it seemed to be going all right. He seemed to be drinking less—or hiding it better. Either way, it worked for me. We were talking to each other, feeling like lovers, friends, and equals again.

Kimble wasn't totally on board with the idea of building a new house, but I still had my thumb on the real estate pulse in the area and decided the time was right. Our neighborhood was in decline, and the house was so heavy with the sadness and anger of the last two years, the very plumbing and foundation seemed to be giving way beneath the weight of the unpleasant memories. I was ready to move on and eager to work with the builder to make our new home exactly what I wanted it to be.

There was a glorious moment of feeling on track.

~

I was building a reputation within my company. I was the person who was willing to take the hard job and get it done—make it fun even—because I never looked at a difficult task as a Gordian knot or a royal pain in the backside. I saw it as another mountain to climb, and I started feeling like nothing could stop me. After years of banging my head against the low ceiling set by my lack of formal education, I had convinced people that I was a whole different kind of smart and what I lacked in academic qualifications I more than made up for in bulldozer determination.

I wanted to move into sales, to work directly with customers. I loved the game of give-and-take, not to mention the financial rewards. I could earn bonuses, while working with account managers from whom I could learn a lot. During all those years as an administrative assistant, I'd been observing how they interacted with customers. I went to the all-employee meetings and soaked up the strategies, the motivation. Everything I could learn about my company and what we did, I learned. Everything I could do to move the company forward, I did.

When Lance was a kid, I never wanted to move into a position of responsibility, because I wanted to be as flexible and as available as he needed me to be. Now I was ready to move up, and a terrific opportunity in the microelectronics division—which was kind of an unknown division at Ericsson—finally came my way. It was an account coordinator position—a promotion from the position of project coordinator.

The day of the interview, I got up early and dressed for success. Colorful, without being garish. Professional, but not too stodgy. Comfortable, yet crisply tailored.

"Good morning, I'm Linda Armstrong," I practiced in the mirror.

Dan Clancy was dynamic and knowledgeable (and would it be terrible if I add *gorgeous*?), very intelligent, with a great sense of humor. I left the interview impressed with him and hopeful about the job. He hired me. I knew nothing about the whole power angle of the work we were doing—you had to understand math, which is something I don't understand. I was fortunate to land in this small group of people who were willing to mentor me.

Another account coordinator had come in before me and was trying to show me the ropes, but sadly, her husband died shortly after we started working together. I tried hard to take up the slack and forge ahead without anyone to really train me, which was hard, but there was so much to learn and I enjoyed the job so thoroughly, I basically ended up working all the time.

"So since Dan was brought in as manager of the sales group," I told Kimble over a late dinner, "he's really turned it around. Him and Mitch . . . the sales guy . . ."

I stopped when I noticed the way Kimble was staring toward the window. After a little while he reached over and poured some scotch into a glass.

"Why are you telling me all this?" he asked.

"Well, I'm just sharing what . . . I don't know," I shrugged. "I'm sorry. I was just telling you about my day."

That was one of the things I missed most after Lance moved away from home. Sitting down to that candlelit dinner and telling each other about the day. I found it all so interesting! How could you not talk about it? And if it wasn't interesting enough to talk about, well, what the heck kind of day was that? And why would you trade a day of your life for it?

"When I get home," I said carefully, "I always ask you, 'How was your day?' And it would just be nice if someone ever cared enough to ask me that, as if they were actually interested in hearing the answer."

"Yes, you ask me how was my day, when what you really mean is, 'Why didn't you make any sales today?' You know, it's not all rosy opportunities and open doors out there, Linda."

"I know! I wasn't saying—"

"You set these punishingly high standards for yourself—you set the bar way up here—and then you think you have the right to expect everybody else to measure up to it."

I got up and started clearing the table, and Kimble got up to help me.

"I'm sorry," he said. "I just had a rotten afternoon, that's all."

"Do you want to tell me about it?"

"No."

As he rinsed his plate in the sink, I stood behind him, my arms around his waist. Resting my cheek against his back, I could feel the tension in his shoulders. He was struggling. Struggling to get up and go out every day, looking for work, and when he found it, struggling to hang on to the job, even when the weight of it started suffocating him. And the continuing expansion of my career seemed to magnify those struggles.

"Can you believe this crap?" he'd rage every morning, and then go off on whatever the morning news was grinding on. By the time I was ready to leave for work, I was exhausted.

"Kimble, you can't do this to me anymore," I finally had to tell him. "If the morning news bothers you so much, why do you insist on watching it? Could we please start the day with some quiet music or something instead of all this—this . . ." Chaos? Rage? Flailing? I didn't even know what to call it. But as the days wore on, I understood that it wasn't the news that bothered him—it was the morning. It was the facing of another day. He simply couldn't bear waking up and looking into the future or lying down and contemplating the past. He was just stuck in the tar pit of the moment.

After we'd been together for a while, I realized why Kimble was so easy to get along with. He never disagreed with me on anything. He always let me choose the restaurant, the drapery fabric, the tax accountant, the day trip destination. But that same undertow of laissez-faire that made him so unflappably agreeable left me making all the decisions and taking on all the responsibilities. I was beginning to feel very lonely, even those evenings when he wasn't out drinking. And those evenings were getting precious and few. Most nights I sat on the couch, waiting to see his lights in the driveway so I'd know he made it home in one piece.

~

Lance and Kristin were living in Europe, so I didn't have a whole lot of information about the wedding, and I couldn't help feeling a little left out. I secretly wanted them to have the Port Charles showcase wedding I never had, but after all he'd been through and all that lay ahead of them, more than anything, I just wanted them to find a quiet space where they could figure out how to be together. I was certainly in no position to be giving advice on how to forge a great marriage, but I knew a lot about how to have a lousy one, and I wondered if my son and prospective daughter-in-law were aware of how easy it is to fall into those quicksand pits that suck couples down. There was so much I wanted to say to Lance and Kristin before the big event, but at the end of the day I knew my duty as a good mother-of-the-groom was to simply show up, look smashing (in a nonthreatening, matronly sort of way), and love them.

Things were stressful, at best, when I loaded up the dysfunctional rodeo that is my family and set out for the wedding in Santa Barbara. Along with Kimble, who hardly came up for air between Bloody Marys on the airplane, there was my mother, my father, and (*thank God!*) Debbie and her two daughters. We all flew to L.A. together, where I'd made arrangements for a rental van so I could drive us all down to Santa Barbara.

"I have no idea what my role is here," I told my sister during the flight. "Nobody's said *boo* to me about the arrangements, except when Kristin asked if I was going to pay for the rehearsal dinner, and—well, is that the tradition? Is that the way it's done?"

"Don't ask me," Debbie shrugged. "Last wedding I went to was in somebody's backyard, and if they rehearsed it, it sure didn't show."

"It's a lot of money, and Kimble's between jobs again. And there's all this elaborate stuff planned out to the last detail and these wee little gifts for the bridesmaids—I mean, what's *that* about?"

"Linda," said Debbie, "you're fretting."

"I know. I'm trying to stop. I just feel very out of my element. And I want everything to be wonderful for them."

"It will be." She squeezed my hand. "Don't worry."

I pressed my fingertips to my temple. It took me a moment to identify the tight-stretched feeling just under my skin. I'd almost forgotten that old radar.

The night before the ceremony was the rehearsal dinner, which was also sort of an engagement party, at which the families and friends of the bride and groom gathered to celebrate their new life together and life in general. Everything was beautiful, from the elegantly appointed restaurant to the exquisite night sky above the moonlit beach. Lance introduced me to his in-laws-to-be, his new sponsors, his longtime friends.

There's something about my son that you don't always see with grown children—my son always made me feel *honored*. He's always been genuinely respectful toward me, and I've tried to live up to that. I've tried to make him as proud of me as I am of him. For better or worse, he was living the life of a public figure, and never once had I been an embarrassment to him. Until now.

By the time dinner was served, Kimble was utterly hammered.

He was never a loud or abusive drunk. He was the kind who would start out in an animated conversation about some social issue, then graduate, as the evening wore on, to pontificating about Shakespeare or something, and eventually isolate himself in a corner, where he could prop himself against a wall and allow the whole blurry world to spin around him like a carousel.

He was well into the Shakespearean stage when I nudged him over to our table to sit down, hoping it might help if he ate some dinner.

"It's a beautiful, beautiful evening, isn't it, honey? You're looking particularly gorgeous," he said warmly, and leaned in to plant a sloppy kiss on my neck. "And nothing is too good for our boy. I ordered a bottle of Dom Perignon for his table and another one for the parents of the bride!"

"What?"

"Dom Perignon," he enunciated with exaggerated patience. "It's a kind of—"

"I know what it is!" I whispered harshly. "And it's a pretty brassy order for someone who doesn't have a job."

I watched the words slowly sink into his head and tried hard not to care how deeply they hurt him. He drew back and fumbled with his bow tie.

"Excuse me," he said. "I think I need another scotch."

Lance had always liked Kimble. He'd brought a welcome feeling of generosity, love, and humor to our home just before Lance moved away. And Lance would be the last one to judge someone for getting a little too much party on, but—oh. Oh, God. *Kimble.* I didn't know whether to drag him outside and kick him in the ass or pull him into my arms and rock him like a baby. He did this whenever he was in an uncomfortable situation—which was pretty much anytime other people were around. (It's classic humanity, isn't it? How often do we slavishly work to fulfill our worst idea of ourselves?) Over dinner, he grew more rumpled and uncoordinated, dropping his silverware, mopping his glowing face with someone else's napkin. As we made awkward small talk around the table, he got quieter and quieter, his chin sinking down to his chest, his forehead drooping closer and closer to his plate. After dessert, I was asked to propose a toast, and I tried to step away from Kimble as I raised my glass.

"I just want to say how very glad I am that Lance has found his soul mate . . ."

Out of the corner of my eye, I saw Kimble's head bob sharply, like a person does when he's falling asleep at the wheel.

"And what a wonderful occasion this is . . ."

He looked up at me, nodding and smiling blearily.

"And . . . and we're all so very glad to be here."

There was a spatter of embarrassed but polite applause.

"Here, here!" Kimble stumbled to his feet and plopped his hands together.

The music started up again, and people began mingling. Kimble made his way over to the bar and sort of wedged himself in the corner. I started to go after him, but someone caught my arm.

"Linda! How wonderful to see you!"

"Oh, Stephanie. It's wonderful to see you too. How are you?"

I glanced over my shoulder toward the bar. Stephanie wanted to introduce me to some people, and then someone else wanted to take a picture with me. From across the room, I heard the sound of breaking glass, followed by Kimble's profuse apologies. I glanced over at the mother of the bride. Our eyes connected, and she was plainly not amused. She gripped her husband's arm, smiled icily at me, then quickly looked away.

"Mom?"

I felt Lance's hand on my elbow, and before I could say anything, he nodded awkwardly toward Kimble. For the first time in my life, I didn't know what to say to my son.

"Mom," he said as gently as he could, "you gotta take him home."

Debbie drove us back to the hotel. When we got there, he wouldn't get out of the car. Couldn't get out. Couldn't stand up. He was so drunk, my elderly father had to hold him up. Debbie and her daughters stood there, mute, mortified for me and painfully self-conscious about standing there on the street, unwilling participants in the whole scene. I couldn't even speculate on what my mother was thinking.

Daddy rescued me. Again. Without judgment or shame or the need to carp on the obvious, my dad—who'd been sober now for over twenty-five years—dragged my husband to the elevator and up to our room. While Daddy dumped Kimble on the bed and wrestled his top coat and tie off him, I stood in the hallway outside the door, shaking with grief and humiliation. It was one of the lowest moments of my life.

"I can't believe this," I told Debbie over and over. "I can't believe it."

"It's okay," she said weakly. "Really, Linda, I don't think anybody . . . I mean—lots of people were . . . you know . . . having a good time."

I, on the other hand, was not having a good time. After all the hills and valleys we'd traveled together, here was my son at the happiest, most momentous moment of his life, wanting to share it with me, and he had to come over and ask me to leave. And my family—*my nieces*—had to stand in the street and witness this drunken slob.

God, I hate irony. And it was so thick here, you couldn't cut a porthole in it. My reformed alcoholic father dragging my descending alcoholic husband up the stairs. My mother, whom I'd always judged harshly for staying married to a drunk, standing there watching. My baby sister, who I always liked to imagine was just a little bit jealous of me, standing there filled with pity. My marriage ending, just as my son's began.

All through the night Kimble stumbled and ranged around the room, knocking things over, falling down, hitting his head. He was like a bear in a cage. I huddled in a chair by the bathroom door, fearful that if I fell asleep, I'd wake up and he'd be dead. The next morning he was oblivious. No recollection. No worries. Just a dull headache he was so used to he didn't even wonder where it came from anymore.

"What's the matter, hon?" he asked with genuine concern. "Didn't you sleep well?"

I looked at him incredulously.

"Don't be nervous about today," he said kindly.

Oh, the kindness that was in him. Even now. It like to killed me.

"Lance is happier than I've ever seen him," Kimble went on. "And you, lovely lady—I really love that dress on you. You're going to be the most beautiful woman at the wedding. Tough luck for the bride."

"You know . . ." I said quietly, "you have ruined this moment for me."

"What?" He was genuinely taken aback. "What do you mean?"

"This moment. The most important moment of my son's life. You have ruined it. My son's getting married today, and instead of celebrating, I feel like I'm stuck taking care of another child."

"Linda . . . honey . . ." He tried to take hold of my hands, but I couldn't stand to have him touch me. "Look, everybody's nervous and tense and . . . *damn*. Where are my damn cuff links?"

He started rifling through his things. Somehow he'd lost his tuxedo buttons and cuff links. His bow tie was wilted and stained. Debbie had to take him out and buy new ones. When they came back, I grasped my sister's hand.

"Debbie, you've got to help me," I begged. "Please, promise me that you and Daddy will help me keep him away from the bar at the reception. *Please!* Maybe if we all three keep an eye on him . . . I just want to try to salvage some fragment of dignity and joy out of this occasion."

Debbie nodded, and Daddy promised too. But it was like trying to keep a boulder from rolling down a hill. During the intimately lovely wedding ceremony, I listened to the words about loving and cherishing in sickness and in health, for better or worse, about a wife joining unto her husband, and a husband being a tower of strength for her. I tried to focus on Lance and Kristin, my beautiful son and his radiant bride, so I could hear those words without every syllable breaking my heart.

Even as the operative problem-solving section of my brain clicked through action items—*counseling, rehab, AA, Al-Anon*—there was a growing certainty at the core of my being: *I've got to get out of this.*

Kristin's family was Catholic, so God knows what they must have thought of me already. But more painful than the lingering humiliation was knowing I had failed once again at the one thing I had always thought was most important. The binding of a good marriage. The making of a family. Kimble and I really did love each other. This would have been so much easier if we didn't! Unlike the clear choices I'd faced before—exits that were clearly marked for reasons I could easily put into words—this was like sailing into a dense fog.

"I feel like the ship is going down and taking me with it," I tried to tell Kimble once we were home again. "The idea of another failed marriage—I have to tell you, it makes me sick. It's unbearable. I don't know how I'm going to go through this again and not have it kill me. But this . . . this is like dying every day."

"Linda, I'm sorry. I know I've screwed up—"

"No, you don't know! You *don't know,* Kimble. You can't even remember!"

"I know that I am not some kind of monster! I know that I am a good and decent human being, whether you can see that or not. And I know that I love you. *I love you.* I do know that."

"But not as much as you love this," I said, taking the bottle of scotch from his hands. "It's like you're climbing a ladder, and every time you take a step the one below you falls off. And pretty soon . . ." I took his face between my hands. "Kimble, I'm telling you—you need to go to a hospital."

"Hospital?" he said, pulling away. "You mean rehab."

"Yes."

"Oh, that's great. It always comes back to that, doesn't it?"

"*Yes!*"

"Well, forget it, Linda!"

"Why?"

"Because we can't afford it, for one thing!"

"I set it up with my insurance," I told him. "Here. Here's the paperwork."

"Oh, well then! It's all settled! You've got it all figured out, don't you? Only one little monkey wrench in your plan—*I am not a goddamn alcoholic!*"

We sat there for a moment, not even able to look each other in the eye.

"Okay," I finally said. "Go or don't go. It's up to you. But I'm not going to enable—"

"Enable?" he scoffed. "Where did you pick that word up?"

"Al-Anon," I said without flinching. "And I am not going to *enable* you to destroy yourself and ruin my life. Get help, Kimble. Or don't get help. It's up to you. But if you don't go into a recovery program, then . . ."

"Then what?"

"Then . . . leave."

He left.

Sammy and I stood by the window and watched him go.

God, I really do hate irony.

THIRTEEN

WHAT BECOMES OF THE BROKENHEARTED

This one hurt me more than the other two combined. This breakup. Instead of an escape, it felt like a profound loss—more like a death than a divorce.

Maybe those other times were easier because I had Lance to take care of and that kept me from sinking into the mire. Or maybe because with Eddie Haskell and the Salesman I thought I needed them when in reality I didn't, and when I discovered that—well, I'd be lying if I said it wasn't a little exhilarating on some level. But with Kimble—the Fugitive I thought I could shelter—I held on as long as I did not because I needed him but because I loved him. I believed in him. And when I discovered that wasn't enough, the sadness felt like water filling up my lungs. Depression closed over my head like a muddy river.

Lance and his wife were living in Europe, adjusting to being a couple and already thinking about starting a family. I hadn't gotten off on the greatest footing with my new daughter-in-law, and Lance was training intensely for the Tour de France, so I didn't expect to hear much from them, and I didn't. That was okay in that I didn't really want Lance to see me like this, and I wanted to give them the space they needed to face the challenges of their life together. But feeling so separated from my son cut deeper than anything else.

You'd think someone who prides herself on her ability to gather information, organize resources, and solve problems would have been a little more open to the idea that she needed some help getting through this. But that same silly, false pride I'd always steered clear of kept me from reaching out until the darkness became unbearable.

Heartbreak sucks. It's so counterproductive. And for me, recovery mode is by definition productive. *When the going gets tough* and all that crap. I've always been strangely charged by hardship. Energized in a way. Galvanized by pure ornery purpose. *Find the opportunity in that obstacle! If life gives you lemons, then* . . . da-da-da. That was my nature. But I have to say, the old school spirit was wearing pretty thin. I finally came to that harsh realization and said to myself, *Get real, sister. This calls for pharmaceuticals.*

It took a little Zoloft, a lot of time alone, and some straight talk from an extremely insightful therapist for me to finally face the fact that—*Hello! Memo to Linda!*—I made bad choices when it came to men. (Why is that never a news flash to anyone except the person in charge of the choices?) It didn't make sense. I was intelligent and intuitive in my professional life. I made bold gestures, educated guesses, smart moves. Yet when it came to men, I consistently made stupid, self-undermining, counterintuitive, utterly *stinko* bad choices.

My mother made one mistake, then crawled into her shell, never to venture out again. But I believed in marriage. Believed it was God's plan for us. But there has to be give-and-take, and I was sick of being the person giving 150 percent. I didn't have it in me to give anymore. The sheer *inequity* of it just twisted a dead bolt inside me. It wasn't fair, and I was finished with it. My life was closed. It was locked, with only me and Sammy and my son's growing family inside. No man was ever going to put me through the ringer again. I didn't want to feel again. I didn't want to fail again. And honestly, I was sick of high-kicking myself silly, supporting other people, and living off the leftovers.

At the end of the day, Kimble did me a backhanded favor, really. I started to get my head around that after a year or so, when the pain was a little less blinding. He taught me a lesson about what you can and cannot do for people. A lesson about the limitations of love that extends only outward and not inward to yourself; love that makes excuses for someone instead of respecting him enough to hold him accountable; love that sets high standards and is self-respecting enough to declare,

"I will not accept less than the most excellent person you have it in you to be." He starkly highlighted for me the previously fine line between nurturing and enabling. It was a line I would never cross again, even if that meant spending the rest of my life alone.

Just me.

Myself.

This concept, which had always seemed scary and unnatural to me, was actually sort of appealing.

~

"Heard from Lance lately?" asked J.T.

"No, not for a while."

"I'm sorry," he said. "You doin' all right?"

"I'm doing great, J.T. I'm fine. And Lance is fine too. He's just busy. They've got a lot to handle," I told him. "How about you, J.T.? How are you doing these days?"

"Oh, I'm good. Going shopping later. Frances needs to get a birthday present for somebody. Buy her a purse! That's what I said. Get her a nice purse."

"Are you still on the same chemo, or did they end up changing it?" I asked him.

J.T. had been diagnosed with cancer, and it was always a challenge getting a straight answer about what was going on. He wasn't one to complain.

"Oh, you know. That whole thing. Now you tell your son I said hello."

"I will, J.T. Take care of yourself."

"Ah, don't you worry about me," he said. "Everything works out okay in the end. Am I right?"

"You're right, J.T."

I appreciated his concern, but he didn't understand—I needed this time alone. I didn't choose it, but I could feel it blessing me all the same. Just like Lance didn't choose chemo, but in a hideous way it gave a texture to his life that had not been there before. As much as any mother would love to have her son living right next door for the rest of his life, she knows in her heart this isn't right for him—or herself. I *wanted* Lance to go and do his own thing. "A son is a son till he takes him a wife," the old saying says. Lance had a life of his own now, and suddenly I realized . . .

So did I!

I could turn up the Motown as loud as I liked, eat dinner or not eat dinner as I pleased. I was living like the Mamas and Papas song—*Go where you wanna go, do what you wanna do*—without considering someone else's emotional or logistical issues. I got interested in a Bible study class. I planted flowers and read the newspaper. I took up golf, a game that combines the delicate arts of networking and recreation.

But most of all, I worked.

When I was selling houses, I used to tell prospective buyers, "The three most important things you'll grow to love about your house are location, location, and location." My house was located about eight minutes from my office. Draw your own conclusions. I came in early and stayed late after everyone left. There was no place else I wanted to go. Once my divorce became final, the papers signed, cried over, and filed, I felt the fog lifting. My mind opened up to a whole new breed of possibility, and I threw myself into my job.

Turns out there was a lot to learn about, and I was happy devoting every square inch of my mental real estate to learning it. I made it my mission to understand Ericsson equipment—how to power it up, what it took to maintain it, where and when and which competitors it could outperform, and why—so that I would be able to explain it clearly to prospective customers and implement it effectively for existing ones.

Our group required a lot of input from the switch engineering group, and it started to dawn on me—if we need this from them, there's probably something they need from us. Eventually we became part of their meetings and they became part of our meetings, and instead of holding on to the old attitude of *this is your stuff and this is my stuff*, we went out and met each other halfway, which had never been part of the old protocol. I immersed myself in phone conferences and message groups with different managers and just took in all the information I could. Eventually the technology began to look less and less like something off the space shuttle and the jargon started sounding less like pig Latin. The more and more familiar I became with the equipment—how to quote it, pricing, the computer system, components—the more I loved getting involved. I started seeing solutions instead of problems, and sometimes this amazed the product managers as much as it amazed me.

It consistently surprised people that I didn't have some private agenda. I loved the company, and I wanted it to do well. I was making a generous salary—more than I had ever imagined I would have an opportunity to earn—so I was grateful. And you're guaranteed joy when you adopt that old "attitude of gratitude," because the first step is to recognize the good things you have. The next step is recognizing that you don't have to have everything go your way. When it goes the other way, you regroup, glad for the opportunity to approach from a new direction.

My administrative style was (and is) centered on asking questions. Face to face, whenever possible. Communication is everything. But that doesn't leave any room for BS. I worked hard at being assertive without being overbearing, because I'd had to work hard when I was younger to get past a natural tendency to be easily intimidated.

I was put on a task team to explore a new technology that was being introduced, and a couple of major phone company pharaohs were giving the various equipment companies the opportunity to come before them with burnt offerings and plead their case. This was a great assignment. I was invited into the holy of holies to support sales heavyweights.

Back then, I worked in the GSM group—GSM being the European technology that gives you the ability to take your cell phone from Paris, Texas, to Paris, France, and still have the same phone number. But in the United States cell phones had to stay on the continent, because we used something called TDMA, and Ericsson had decided to stick with that technology instead of backing the new CDMA technology, which was being backed by Qualcom (which we later swallowed whole—*ha!*). Their claim to fame was a streamlined cellular ARP engineering that required less infrastructure and da-da-da.

It finally came down to us against them. We had some brilliant people on our team, and we spent an intense few weeks preparing to make our assault like a pinstriped battle brigade. The fortress to fall was a boardroom at the Sprint corporate headquarters in Kansas City.

When we arrived at the airport and the team (twenty men and me) marched down the concourse, following Dag Lundquist, our fearless leader, everybody except me was dragging a little rolling suitcase, grimly heading for a sign that said GROUND TRANSPORTATION.

"Whoa," I said, "I've got to stop at baggage claim and get my bags."

Our boss exploded. He let loose a torrent of displeasure that included every swear word you could come up with in two different languages, and everyone just stood there, cringing.

"Look," I said when he paused to inhale, "I'm the one who's responsible for getting all the documentation here, and it was *damn heavy*. I didn't want to lift it, so I checked my bag. My bag is checked. That dog's been walked. Now, we can either stand here cussing about it, or we can go to baggage claim."

To say we were all a little tense would be like calling Bull Run a difference of opinion. The day of the mega-meeting, we marched into the lobby and joined a gaggle of competitors who all wore the exact same chiseled collars and freshly starched faces we did. In the boardroom Sprint's purchasing person barely skimmed my outstretched hand.

"Do you know all these people?" she asked brusquely.

"Oh, yes," I said, even though I wasn't entirely sure.

"Here." She thrust a stack of business cards at me. "Line these up in the order in which they're sitting so I know who's who."

"No problem," I smiled.

I managed to do that, and we all sat down at a 747-sized conference table across from her and two other people. I listened to the dialogue back and forth, jotting down action items and questions she was going to need answered the following day. We went back to the hotel and debriefed. Our boss left us with instructions to work through the list I'd compiled, but the day was wearing long. People were hungry and tired, and after a while I started feeling like the drill team captain when half the girls have their period.

"Come on, guys. We need to do this. We've got to be able to explain these issues in a nontechnical way, because I'm getting a distinct feeling from this woman that she doesn't want to hear it. It's not the language she speaks. Now, we can pull this off if we just buckle down for a couple hours."

Half the guys were on the bus, but the other half—I could just as well have been shouting down a gopher hole. The next morning we were all meeting, and Dag asked me for this and that, and for the most part I was able to appease him.

"What about the figures on these other components?" he asked.

I didn't have them, and I didn't want to point any fingers, but all eyes at the table instinctively drifted to the individual responsible. And the boss proceeded to tear that guy up. I mean, he *ripped* that guy up one side and down the other.

There was a time I would have stepped up and taken the blame for something like that, just to make the conflict stop. But you know, I wasn't afraid of conflict anymore. I wasn't there to be the shock absorber. I was there to help all of us, not deflect the blame for someone who could have done the job had he wanted to. I used to get really frustrated when somebody didn't do something or something I thought should happen didn't happen. Maybe Kimble was right about that: I did set the bar high. But I did learn (maybe from him) that you can't control anyone but yourself. If another person doesn't share my commitment to making a difference, it's best to just back away from the situation and focus on another avenue through which I *will* make a difference.

This would have been the biggest contract ever written by Ericsson. Dag was in a barking bad mood heading into the meeting. He and the head sales guy managed to razzle-dazzle-dance their way around the missing info enough to get invited back the following week, but we headed for the airport frantically trying to tie up loose ends. In the terminal we were afraid to use our cell phones because all our competitors were in the same terminal, and considering how cell phone technology was their area of expertise, we thought it would be better to use a landline.

When Dag came over to ask me if a certain bunch of pages had been faxed, I was still standing in line for a phone booth.

"They've been sent," I said, "but I can't confirm that they were received."

"*What do you mean you can't confirm . . .*" and he was off on another barking rampage.

"That fax was not even my responsibility!" I barked back. "Now you lower your voice."

Back in Dallas the big joke on the jetway was, "Oh, Linda's such a princess. Linda checked her bag."

"That's right," I said, striding toward the carousel. "And you'd better not give me any shit about it."

When my bag came down, the boss's limo driver took it from my hand.

"Mr. Lundquist would like you to share his car," he said. "Mr. Lundquist is *waiting* for you." Which was not customary, I guess, but I didn't have the energy to be impressed.

"Damn right he is," I said.

"Damn right," the boss's voice came from behind us. "And you better not give her any shit about it."

Heads rolled after the deal went down the drain. Several people quit, saying, "I don't have to put up with that," or whatever the case may be, but I kept trying to tell people that Mr. Lundquist was actually a very good boss. You just had to get your head around his style. Answer his question, then shut up. He was very smart and very driven, and he had little patience for people who weren't as smart and as driven as he was. Problems came up when the people around him let him get away with his natural tendency to spontaneously combust. I respected him. And I insisted that he respect me. When he went off on a rampage, I just tried to see the humor in it.

One morning he charged into the office, barking out a list of files and items he wanted rounded up and delivered to his desk immediately. I waited until he ran out of steam, then looked up and smiled sweetly.

"Good morning, Dag," I said.

"Oh . . . uh, good morning, Linda," he said, entirely defused and even blushing a little.

By the time his limo dropped me off at my front door, I'd been promoted to a management position in the group that dealt with batteries and other power sources. I seized the opportunity and ran with it. I just loved going into a meeting and saying, "Good morning, everyone. I'm Linda Armstrong, the lady with all the power."

~

Dag ended up putting me in charge of one project after another, including a quality audit that we were nowhere near passing, because we just didn't have our handoffs down. There were too many disconnects.

"Think about a bike race," I told them. "The rider comes by and you run alongside with the water bottle or whatever, and if you don't have a smooth handoff, you lose time. He doesn't get what he needs, and the other team wins."

That was a great project. Before you knew it, we had binders at every desk, requirements were clarified, brown bag lunches were scheduled. I loved it. I don't know if this is necessarily good, but I was picking up the same tornado energy I'd been seeing Lance display again. Everything he loved about the sport, I loved about my job. Teamwork, strategy, getting into the other guy's head. I loved the competition, the speed, the head-spinning victories—even the spectacular crashes.

"But what about *life*?" Jeanine asked me during one of our not-nearly-often-enough phone conversations. "Is your whole life about this job?"

"Well, yeah, right now. Because—oh! I've been wanting to tell you about this. So I'm working late and a guy comes in from the RF engineering department and asks me if I'm interested in a promotion over there, but of course he hasn't said anything to Jack about this at all, so I tell him, 'Well, I really have to talk to my boss about that,' and when I did, he was just like, 'Oh, Linda! Don't go over there. You'd hate that department,' and da-da-da, and I said, 'Well, yeah, but this would be a pretty significant promotion for me,' and he says, 'Actually, we've been talking about offering you a promotion over here, and would you be interested in managing the Lynchburg account,' which is actually a much better opportunity to—"

"Linda, are you hearing yourself?" Jeanine cut in. "Everything is about work. You don't have any fun anymore."

"I have fun," I protested.

"Doing what?"

"Doing the Lynchburg account!"

"Okay," she laughed, "and what else? Do you ever go out anymore?"

"Of course! I play golf every Tuesday."

"That doesn't count, because if I know you, you're networking all over the course. What else?"

"Well, lots of things. I water the plants . . . and I throw the ball for Sammy." (There's something about a shih tzu with a raggedy tennis ball that keeps you from getting too serious about yourself.) "Anyway—you should talk, girlfriend! What do you do for fun?"

"Well," Jeanine said, "I'm going to have a baby."

And of course, that changed the whole conversation.

~

Putting in twelve- and fourteen-hour days, hardly looking up, I never noticed until one of the admins pointed out how thin I'd become. No one had ever questioned me about "work–life balance" before. *Work–life balance.* It sounded like something out of a Volvo commercial. In my mind, work and life had become the same thing.

But you've got to understand—this really was a *great* account! The biggest microelectronics account we had. The guy who'd tried to poach me from my department got his hand slapped and didn't much like me after that, but Jack had taught me a lot. I wasn't about to go behind his back. Loyalty and being up front—those are important qualities to me. *Honesty is the best policy* is what I always tried to teach my son as he was growing up, and I had to practice what I preached, knowing he was watching me.

Managing inventory for Lynchburg was a whole new rodeo. The

account was exhibiting a lot of potential—which is a nice way to say "mushrooming out of control." The client was about to take a hike, because they kept getting wrong information from the department and not getting the equipment they needed. My job was to pull people together, get the communication happening, find out what the customers needed, keep the great fountain of commerce flowing, and lasso any stray armadillos that threatened to clog up the drainpipes.

One of the first items on my agenda was the little matter of two million dollars in obsolete inventory we were sitting on. We had a weekly conference call with this client, but for months the subject never came up. With the account hanging by a thread, no one had been willing to light the fuse on this issue for fear it might turn out to be a real stink bomb.

"This is crazy," I said. "Nothing ever gets done. The chessboard's not moving. If we let this go on much longer, factory workers are going to lose their jobs."

"Well, I'm open to suggestions," said my sales manager. "What do you plan to do on it?"

Good question. But that only means that somewhere there's got to be a good answer. Once I'd had a chance to gently put my hands around the situation, finesse some of the problems on both sides, and develop a relationship with the client, I decided it was time to strike a match and see what happened.

"I'm going to ask them to pay for twenty thousand pieces," I told my SM before the meeting. "And if he takes ten off our hands, I'll be happy."

We did the call and were just about to wind it up.

"You know, Darrel," I said, "something that's been a real pickle of a situation for me is this obsolete inventory we've got down here. It's hanging up that other project, and we'd really like to do that one for you. I really do need some relief on that."

"Oh," he said. "Well, how about if we pay for ten thousand pieces. And you can just keep the inventory. Resell or recycle it or whatever."

There was stunned silence from my SM's leg of the phone line. All this time, no one had ever just laid the card on the table. And it turns out that's all that was standing between us and our two million dollars.

This moment ranks high on my top-ten list of learning experiences. From then on, I operated on what should be the most obvious strategy in business: ask and you shall receive!

The thrill of the game, whether it was golf or sales, entirely took me over. I found immense satisfaction in the alchemy, the daily juggling act, and the tangible rewards that came with success. And eventually I did make an effort to do some downtime. I took day trips with my girlfriends, and I even enjoyed an occasional dinner with some nice-looking man. I expected nothing but pleasant small talk, and I made it clear that they could expect nothing more than that from me.

Another lesson I learned from Lance was what it does for your life when you make time to do the soul-feeding work of a volunteer. I lobbied for cancer research and pitched in however I could with the foundation. I sat quietly with my paper and coffee each morning. I was in bed by ten every night. I was always a nurturer by nature, and now—for the first time in forty-three years—I was learning to nurture myself.

"Same time next week?" Darrel asked as we wrapped up our weekly conference call late one evening.

"Oh, actually I'm out of town," I said.

"Linda's off to Paris," my SM said, and I tried to head him off at the pass.

"Right, so maybe we could schedule—"

"What are you doing in Paris?" asked Darrel. "Don't tell me you're actually taking a vacation."

"Well, you know how it is. I don't get out much, but when I do, I like to do it up right. So shall we shoot for the first week of—"

"Actually," said the SM, "she's heading over for the Tour de France. You'll never believe this." I felt my forehead tighten. "Linda is Lance Armstrong's mom!"

"No kidding!" cried Darrel. Turns out he was a huge cycling enthusiast.

Now, I think it's pretty clear that I am incredibly proud of my son. If you ask me any given day on any given street corner, I'll proudly tell you all about my son the rock star, the superhero, the amazingly wonderful Lance Armstrong. I know people mean well when they share that information, and I think it's cool that they're so proud of this great Texan, this great American. But in addition to a long-standing tradition of keeping my personal and professional lives separate, I was always sensitive about any appearance of trading on Lance's celebrity in the business arena. I went golfing every Tuesday with a group of Ericsson managers, and none of them ever knew Lance was my son until he won his first Tour and there was a lot of publicity.

Frankly, it didn't come up a whole lot, because during all the years my life revolved around the sport of bicycle racing, I never saw a whole lot of other people in Texas give a flip about it. That changed in July 1999, when a certain young man from Austin powered down a mountainside in France and took the lead in this prestigious event. Suddenly, everyone was captivated—not by the race, but by this extraordinary young man who'd defeated cancer and was now taking on the rest of the world.

Because of the time difference, I hadn't been able to find out what happened until I saw the tape-delayed television coverage of the stage through the Alps to Sestriere.

"Look out! Look out! There he goes! *He's got it!*"

I danced Sammy around the room, hooting and hollering.

That last week or so before I left for Paris was torturous. I stayed up late, clicking between CNN and ESPN, trying to take in every possible glimpse of my son. Every time he came on the screen, I rocketed off the sofa, in full-on Kilgore Rangerette mode.

"*Go, Lance! Go, son, go!*" I knew the picture was several hours old and thousands of miles beyond the sound of my voice, but who cares? The Power of Cheer transcends time and space. "You got it, son! You got it! *Go, Lance, go!*"

The first day he showed up wearing the yellow jersey, I could have flown to Paris without even using the airplane. I couldn't sit in my office any longer. No matter what I tried to fix my mind on, my whole body and soul were taken up with wave on wave of giddy, gleeful realization: *Lance is winning the Tour de France!* He was speeding toward the dream he'd given everything to achieve. I had to be there.

I flew in for the second-to-last stage of the Tour. A time trial at

Futuroscope. Time trials scared me more than mountains, because this was where the gut-wrenching, metal-and-bone-twisting crashes happened. This was the stage that would determine the winner of the 1999 Tour, so I knew the competitors would be taking no prisoners. Lance arranged for me to ride in one of the follow cars, and I focused a lifetime of sheltering energy on him, asking God—no, *telling* God in no uncertain terms—to hold my child in the palm of His hand.

As Lance took the podium, I waved a flag and screamed myself hoarse, along with half of France and a surprising number of old friends who'd flown in from Texas. Amid the chaos of the crowd and the feeding frenzy of the paparazzi, he graciously credited his teammates and found a moment to say hello to a little girl in Fort Worth who was fighting cancer. That's my boy.

The next day, he rode into Paris, triumphant in more ways than anyone could know. Crying and laughing and crying some more, I fought my way through the thronging well-wishers to hug him and his wife, whose belly was round and warm and bountifully, beautifully big with my first grandchild.

"Madame Armstrong!" a French reporter called out from the crowd. "Do you say your son's victory is against the odds?"

"Are you kidding?" I cried. "His whole life has been against the odds!"

~

I'm not nervous. It's all good. I can do this.

I always loved the all-employee meetings at Ericsson. It was a great opportunity to see old friends, network with new ones, and hear some dynamic speaker. Only this year the speaker was me, and the butterflies in my stomach seemed to be multiplying every moment.

"And now it's my pleasure to introduce Ericsson's Mother of the Year—global account manager Linda Armstrong."

Swept along on the wave of applause, I made my way to the podium with the script I'd carefully prepared.

"I began my career with Ericsson in July of 1987 as a temporary employee," I said, adjusting the microphone a little lower. "My son,

Lance, was entering the challenging teenage years. He was driven by tremendous confidence along with an insatiable desire to win. Traits we both share. I always assured him he could be the very best at what he did as long as he gave 100 percent. We started setting goals and working toward the achievement of those goals. Each weekend we were on the go with 10Ks, cross-country meets, competitive swimming, triathlons, and cycling. My work colleagues looked forward to hearing about our weekend adventures. You see, Ericsson provided me with the opportunity to balance my life and my work."

I told them how Lance wore my pink windbreaker when he broke the record at the Junior American 20K time trial in New Mexico. How we worked as a team and accomplished what we set out to do.

"It took tremendous support, structure, and commitment to help Lance fulfill his dreams," I said. And it took the same for me to fulfill mine. "In 1996 I was working on a very critical project. Tage and Roland will remember this." I smiled when I saw several heads nodding. "I was managing this project with good results. My deadline was November of '96. On October 2, I was told that my son had been diagnosed with testicular cancer. My heart hit rock bottom." There wasn't a sound in the room as I described the frantic phone calls to my boss, the frenetic travel plans thrown together, the dark days of chemo, my homecoming—those neatly organized message folders that made such a difference to me that day—and finally, the standing ovation at the videoconference.

"Speaking from my heart, Ericsson—what a gift you've given me! You cared enough to help mentor me, provided me with excellent training, challenged me, helped me set goals, honored me as Ericsson's Mother of the Year, and encouraged me to pursue my dreams. I love my job! Eleanor Roosevelt once said, 'The future belongs to those who believe in their dreams.' Thank you, Ericsson, for your support along the way and providing me with the opportunities to pursue my career dreams while giving me the ability to put my family first. For this I am grateful."

~

There's a lot of crossover between the qualities of a good manager and the qualities of a good mother. Everything I learned in one role helped me to succeed in the other. Motherhood taught me about the necessity of relationship-building and the dangers of micromanagement. You don't just show up one day and say, "This is how it is." You cultivate respect and nurture communication first. As a manager and as a mother, you have to acknowledge and learn from your mistakes, set a powerful example, and know when to let go. Good managers and good moms know that respect is a two-way street. They know how to roll with the changes. A good mother is willing to give her life for her child—and a good manager *does* give her life, day by day, to her job (so she'd better be doing something she cares about!). As those two roles come together for more and more women, I hope companies will click to the fact that they get more out of people who are happy and whole, who maintain a healthy work–life balance.

I had recently discovered the only thing that even comes close to the joy of being a mother—being a grandmother. The night Luke was born, Lance and I went for a long walk through the same hospital corridors I'd paced while he was in surgery. Suddenly, in this place I'd tried so hard to forget, I wanted to remember. Everything. We passed by the room where he'd made a post-op joke about the Bionic Man. He'd made it come true. He'd shouldered the weight of the world and leaped over tall mountains. But at the end of the day he was something far greater than a superhero.

He was a daddy.

FOURTEEN

YOU CAN'T HURRY LOVE

My grandson started life as a locksmith. Without even trying, he slid aside the dead bolt with which I'd secured my heart. The first time I held him in my arms, the joy that flowed through me was so potent, I couldn't imagine being genuinely sad ever again. He was the living proof of the power of hope, the embodiment of the simple idea that *life goes on*. I was caught up in the same baby love that swept me forward when I was seventeen years old, and I ached for him during the long stretches Lance and his family spent overseas. Even when they were in Austin, they had a nonstop schedule that didn't intersect with mine very often.

"It's just time and miles working against us," I tried to tell J.T., but it bothered him to see how much I missed them.

J.T. took the European view of motherhood; your mother is some sort of queen bee dragon goddess in your life who should be revered, consulted, and included at every turn from your first diaper change to her last day in the old folks' home.

I remember sitting with Stephanie at a race in Norway, early on in Lance's career. As this young American upstart began tearing up the tracks, rumbling and booing erupted in the stands every time he rode by and could be seen up on the giant screen, mugging in a cocky American way.

"*Armstrong?*" an Italian gentleman below us on the bleachers grumbled loudly. "Who is this *Lance Armstrong*?"

"I don't know," Stephanie called down to him. "Maybe you should ask his *mother*!"

The gentleman turned, startled and absolutely abashed, apologizing profusely and doffing his hat in a respectful gesture. The next time my son came around, the man got to his feet, glancing over his shoulder at me and Stephanie. Cuffing the spectators to his right and left, he berated them in Italian and gestured toward the track until they reluctantly rose and joined him in a healthy round of applause.

"*Allez, Lance!*" he cheered enthusiastically. "*Allez! Allez!*"

But Lance learned about motherhood from me, and while I felt good about the example I'd set for him as a parent, I'd also set the example of an adult who lived completely separate—almost unknown, in fact—from her mother. What goes around comes around, I guess. Anyway, he had plenty of fish to fry without adding me to the long list of people trying to get a slice of his time. I missed him, but I tried to put the most positive spin possible on it.

"It's probably for the best, J.T. Given the chance, I would probably be one of those nosy grandmas, hovering and driving them crazy."

I remembered what it was like to have a new baby, so I respected my daughter-in-law's need for elbow room. We all have reasons for needing open spaces in our relationships. But still . . . I dearly longed for the opportunity to be the powerful undercurrent in Luke's life that my grandmother was in mine.

I didn't say that to J.T., however. He had enough on his plate. He was facing another round of chemo. Knowing what that meant, I could hardly stand there complaining about my life. My son was healthy and happy and had a beautiful family. I was healthy and happy and had a productive life full of good friends and great opportunities to grow. I loved my dog. I loved my work. I had a beautiful house, filled with beautiful things. I thought about the last time I saw my granny, rocking my baby boy on her lap.

"What a blessing!" she sighed. Sitting in her shabby old chair, she felt rich. And I felt the same way now.

Only when it was just me and Sammy out on the evening patio, and the late-autumn wind started getting a tiny bit too cool to be comfortable—that's when I'd feel the occasional twinges of loneliness. There's only just so many times you can throw a ball, just so many plants you can repot. Filling up the hours is easy. Filling up your life is more of a challenge.

I'm not proud of the fact I've been married more than once, but I can say this: I learned something new about myself from each of those men. And it was always something pretty darn amazing. Every time I got married, it was under the misconception that love and I could conquer all. And every time I got divorced, it was under the misconception that love and I had failed. But living alone, I finally learned what it really takes to be married: *two people*.

Not a princess and her frog.

Not an actress and her director.

Not a taskmaster and her task.

It takes two completely self-contained, happy, healed, individual people. I finally was one of those. I finally had a whole and balanced self to offer—something I'd never brought to a relationship.

After Kimble left, I had decided to start applying my business smarts to my personal life. They teach you in those morning seminars on career tracking and contact managing that a list is a commitment. A goal merely thought of or even spoken is still just an idea. Written down, it becomes something tangible. You're tethered to it, so to change your mind you have to consider it enough to physically remove or add an item on the list. My head is organized in a more three-dimensional way. I've never been a list-maker. But I was sitting at my desk one night, doodling on a notecard after paying some bills, when a list began to make itself.

Sophisticated, mature, stable
Shared values, ambitious
Commitment to a lifetime relationship
Spiritual, intellectual, emotional
Fun to be with—both friend and lover
Good communicator
Works out/takes care of himself

Respects and supports my work
Affectionate
Loves my family as I do

The list was a prayer, I realized. Below it, I added: *Father, I put my trust in your hands. May this prayer be your will, not my will. As I grow spiritually, let me walk with you daily in love and happiness. Amen.*

More importantly, it was a commitment to myself that I would happily make my life alone rather than accept less than what I needed. There was a time when I was willing to make any compromise asked of me, but that time had passed. All that remained of my Cleaver dream was a desire to share my life with an equal partner.

I gave the list to God, tucking it in my Bible before I went to bed, knowing I could be happy no matter what God decided to do with it. God took His time, but with His trademark grace and typical sense of humor, He eventually decided to send it back to me.

~

Ed Kelly was supposed to be lunch. That was it.

"Just a casual thing," insisted my friend Krissie. Her husband Chris was Lance's swim coach when he was a kid, and apparently Ed's son was on the team at roughly the same time. "I don't know if you remember, but he's a super-nice guy. His wife died about a year ago, and I just thought the three of us could get together for lunch."

"Sure," I shrugged. "Sounds like fun."

I don't know if it was strategy or circumstances, but at the last minute Krissie couldn't make it, and—well, I couldn't very well leave him sitting there, could I?

"I'm so sorry," she fretted. "It won't be awkward for you, will it?"

"Oh, heck no. You know me," I said. "I'm not shy. I'm always up for meeting people."

As I pulled into the parking lot at Café Max, which is this chic little place that's only open for lunch and invariably crowded with Richardson's fabulous telecom crowd, I spotted the red shirt I was supposed to be looking for. I waved as I cruised into a parking spot, just

La-la-la! How ya doin'? It was just lunch, for Pete's sake. But Mr. Kelly seemed nervous. It was sort of sweet.

"Butterflies in the tummy?" I asked.

"I'm still a little new to the whole dating thing," he said uncomfortably.

"Oh, don't worry about it," I reassured him. "This is just lunch with a friend. No sweat."

We had a great conversation about golf and work and all the ups and downs of the businesses we had our hands full of. I didn't usually settle in with someone enough to talk about my family, but Ed was more than eager to talk about his. There's something endearing about a guy who goes around with a wallet full of family photos. I've always found it charming when daddies brag.

"Here's my son Mike with his fiancée, Jenny. And this is Megan with her husband, Jeff. And Maureen—we call her Mo—she's a student at SMU."

"What a lovely family," I said.

"Oh, they're really terrific, terrific kids. All of them." He flipped to the last photograph. "And this is my late wife. This is Peggy."

"She's beautiful," I smiled.

"Yeah, she was," he said. "She was a beautiful person."

It wasn't misty-eyed or sloppy the way he said it. Not maudlin or sentimental. Just *sincere,* I guess. Full of gladness and appreciation. I found that very touching.

"And of course, I know all about your son," Ed moved on. "He's married now, isn't he?"

I decided to bend my rules and bring out my own brag book.

"Here he is with his beautiful wife. And here's my little Gogie. Luke is two already. Can't believe it. How precious is he? I can't wait to get my arms around him."

"Looks like quite an armful!"

"Oh, you're not kidding. He's rambunctious. I don't know how his mom does it. She's expecting again. *Twins!* And this is Lance last year in the Tour. *Love* that kid!" I tend to get pretty wrapped up in looking at my pictures, so I appreciated Ed Kelly's ample oohs and ahs. "So . . .

that's my family. I guess I sound like a regular old granny, making a big fuss over my grandbabies."

"Yeah," he said. "Only you don't look like any granny I ever met."

"Hey! Good answer!" I cheered. "All right. Score one for Mr. Kelly!"

Score two, actually. He also made me laugh.

As lunchtime stretched to early afternoon, I could tell he was sort of captivated. And looking back, I guess maybe it wasn't my riveting description of the project I was working on.

"I'd like to see you again," he said as we left the café. "Are you free for dinner tomorrow night?"

"Nope. Tuesday is golf night, remember? That's sacred."

"Oh. Right. How about Thursday?"

"I think I have a thing with somebody."

"Friday then? Or Saturday?"

"Actually, me and a couple girlfriends are going to this B&B up in the hill country for the whole weekend."

"Next week?"

"Well, I'm working on that Cisco thing, so I'll be back and forth to California a lot this month."

He looked crestfallen.

"But, hey," I said, "give me a call. We'll see if we can work something out."

Over the next two weeks, every time my admin handed me my messages, there was at least one from Ed Kelly.

"Whoever this guy is," she said, "he's certainly tenacious."

"You're a very busy person," Ed groused, when he finally got me on the phone.

We finally got a fix on a date for dinner and met at one of my favorite restaurants.

"How was your day?" he asked, holding my chair for me.

"My day?" I echoed.

"Yeah, did you have a good day? Tell me about it."

Such a small question. He couldn't possibly have had any idea what it meant to me to be asked. We spent a long pleasant evening together.

Lunch talk never takes you to the conversational places you go over a long pleasant evening with a leisurely meal and a glass of wine—and when things are really good, lingering over coffee and dessert.

"I have a confession to make," he said. "Before we had lunch, I checked you out on the Internet. And I read your son's book."

"You have me at a disadvantage then," I said. "You already know all about me."

I was incredibly proud of the success Lance had had with his book. I thought it was wonderfully well crafted by Sally Jenkins, and I was so honored when I read what my son had said about me. But it always made me feel a little odd that so many people knew so much about our life, so I was pretty cautious about sharing any personal details beyond that.

"Tell me about you," I said.

He cracked me up with stories about his childhood—very much the Cleaverworld upbringing I'd always longed for—and told me about his lake house and his career with IBM. We talked about golf and grandparenting and traveling the world for business and pleasure. Over another glass of wine, the conversation wandered on to things we had in common, things we loved about our lives. Ed was a true blue *Father Knows Best* throwback. He never got tired of talking about his family, and I found that so sweet. He spoke lovingly of his late wife and what he'd gone through when she died. He didn't go into a lot of detail about it, but he didn't have to. Loving someone with cancer was another thing we had in common.

You know, there are two kinds of cancer survivors. Lance Armstrong is one. Ed Kelly is the other. After thirty years of marriage, he saw his wife through the ravages of chemo and held her hand as she lay dying. Through my work as a volunteer in the cancer arena, I've tried to speak out about the need to care for the caregiver. The fact is, a family has cancer—it doesn't happen to just one person—and our compassion has to extend to the ones who are left to cope long after the person with cancer has found peace.

"I had a really nice time," I told Ed as he walked me to my car.

"Me too."

He opened the door for me, and I reached out to take his hand.

"Look . . . Ed . . . you are a very nice guy . . ."

"Uh-oh," he said. "I don't like the sound of this."

"An *extremely* nice guy . . ."

"Aw, hell."

"And I just wanted to tell you—be careful, okay?"

"Careful of what?"

"This town is full of women who are looking for a wealthy, attractive, eligible man, and you are just so sweet and kind and caring. And you're coming from kind of a vulnerable place right now. I would hate to see someone take unfair advantage of that."

"Wait a minute. Are you—am I getting the brush-off here?"

"It's not that," I said. "It's just—I don't have a lot of time in my schedule for socializing right now."

"I understand," he said. "I can work my schedule around yours."

"And I'm sort of dating someone else."

"Oh. So am I."

"Someone who understands that, at least for right now, I'm really not looking to get involved in any kind of . . . involvement."

"No involvement," he said. "So—no problem! I'll give you a call."

Before I could protest, he firmly helped me into my car and clapped the door shut. As I pulled away I saw him getting into a Mercedes convertible.

Dang, that's a nice car, I observed before I could help myself.

~

Ed Kelly wasn't kidding when he said he'd work around my schedule, despite an incredibly demanding schedule of his own. If he called my office and I said I had five minutes to talk, he would wind it down and hang up after four minutes and fifty-eight seconds. If I told him I was going out with my girlfriends Saturday night, he'd invite me to Sunday brunch. If I told him I could cook dinner, but not until after my seven o'clock spin class, he was in my driveway with the groceries when I got home at eight-fifteen. And you know somebody's got it bad when he sees you getting out of your car after spin class—road-hard and put-up wet, bedraggled, limp, and without lipstick—and the first words out of his mouth are "Wow! You look fantastic!"

And he did all this without coming off as needy or cloying. He had a high-powered job with lots of challenges and triumphs, and we loved trading daily war stories from the corporate trenches. The dynamics and deals, the office politics, the Trumpish work ethic we shared—that was the first level on which we really connected. I respected him as a peer, and he showed that same respect for me, which was a rare treat, frankly. No one in my personal life had ever fully understood this important aspect of who I am.

We went on like this for a while—casual, friendly, and comfortable. Neither of us mentioned that the people we'd been halfheartedly dating had drifted into the background, then disappeared completely. Ed invited me to his daughter Mo's twenty-first birthday bash, and I showed up in party mode. I mean, it's a party! Pass me a margarita, Chiquita! Apparently, some of his more straitlaced friends were a little scandalized, but Mr. Kelly didn't seem too put out. Late that afternoon he walked me to my car and surprised the heck out of me by sweeping me into his arms *Gone with the Wind* style, and I'm here to tell ya—he laid one on me like Atlanta was burning in the background. I couldn't remember the last time I felt a kiss clear down to my kneecaps—the kind of kiss that lasts all the way home and leaves you thinking all sorts of things.

"I approve," said J.T. "You look happy."

~

Ed wanted us to share Thanksgiving together with his family, but I ended up cooking a turkey and all the fixings and carting it to the hospital in Austin, where my twin granddaughters, Grace and Isabelle, were making their grand entrance.

"They are so so precious!" I told Ed on the phone. "You can't imagine how beautiful they are."

"Oh, I can imagine," he said, truly and warmly happy for me. "Must run in the family."

The baby girls brought a delicious glow to the whole holiday season for me. I don't think I've ever had so much fun shopping for presents. I'd never been able to linger in the frilliest section of the department stores. Now I reveled in all that pink and lace and angels.

It's possible that the opportunity to run around on the roof meant more to my adolescent son than Yuletide spirit, but whatever motivated him, he was up there every December, stringing lights from one end of the rooftop to the other. He was the best at that. He always made sure that entire roof was framed in multicolored lights and those goofy reindeer we trucked from place to place were posted out in the front yard.

"The only problem with that," I told Ed, "is that while he was up there stringing the lights, he'd sometimes moon passing vehicles."

Ed got a big hoot out of that. Ever the master handyman, he was replacing some solar screens at my house. He felt those regular old screens weren't good enough for me, and doesn't that simple thing say a thousand times more than the treacliest love poem? I'm not really a word person; I'm an action person. And this seemingly mundane action spoke eloquently about what a pragmatically gallant hero Ed Kelly is. He's the Home Depot equivalent of a swashbuckler.

"So how come you don't have a tree up yet?" he asked.

"Oh, I don't think I'll bother with it this year," I said. "The kids won't be coming up for Christmas, so it's just me."

Truth be told, I hadn't had a tree in years. I'd had that tree in '96—the Christmas right after Lance finished chemo. He was feeling so low. I just wanted him to have a nice Christmas. Since then, all the lights and decorations had been in the garage gathering dust, until I moved to this new house, where they were now gathering dust in my new garage.

"There's always a huge tree at the office," I told Ed. "I just enjoy that one."

A few days later I was coming home from a late-evening meeting, smiling at the soft glow of all the merrily lit houses in my neighborhood. One house up ahead caught my eye. The entire hedge was decked out in multicolored lights. As I came closer, I was astonished to realize it was *my* house. The whole place was fairly dancing with twinkle lights and Christmas spirit, and there in the middle of it all was Ed Kelly, posting my goofy reindeer out in the front yard.

"I saw that stuff in the garage, and I didn't think you'd mind," he said.

"Oh . . . oh my gosh . . ."

"I didn't want to rummage through your attic or anything, so I just brought this other stuff from home."

He opened the front door to unveil a beautifully decorated Christmas tree. The fresh festive scent of it, the aliveness of it, the joyful innocence of holly and ivy and bells seemed to fill up my whole house and heart. I walked into this Nutcracker scene that just a few hours earlier had been my orderly living room, and I couldn't help it—I started crying. It was *Christmas*! Joy to the world! Love was real, and someone had come to reveal it to me, opening my eyes to a multitude of blessing gifts and saving graces.

"I hope you don't mind," Ed said uncertainly.

I didn't know what to say, so I just kissed him.

~

We went to Cabo San Lucas to play golf after the holidays. We discussed the possibility of spending the rest of our lives together, but out of respect for his wife's memory and consideration for his children, who were having a difficult time facing the two-year anniversary of their mother's death, we waited a few months to make any big decisions. As Ed gradually opened up to me about what the experience of losing Peggy had been, I loved this man even more for the deep, deep passion and devotion he'd shared with her all those years.

Unbeknownst to me, he started plotting some kind of dramatic way to officially pop the question, including the brave idea of dropping a diamond ring in the eighteenth hole and letting me discover it after a perfect putt. Ultimately, he decided on the traditional route, and later that spring he caught me off guard with a romantic but straightforward proposal. Roses, champagne, down on one knee. The whole nine yards. I cherished every moment of the entire experience. Later that evening I called each one of his children and told them how much I loved their father, how much I admired their mother, and how glad I was to have them all in my life. I e-mailed Lance and Kik, because it was the middle of the night at their home in Spain, and they called the next day, thrilled for us.

I'd never actually had a real wedding with all the princess trimmings. It was something I'd always dreamed of when I was young, but when we started to make the arrangements, the thing I wanted most was for my son to be there.

"I know it complicates things," I told Ed, "but he's my family."

After a flurry of e-mails and phone calls, we set a date Lance had available the following summer. It might seem backward, but we just had a small window of time with him. Once we had a commitment for a day in June, I went forward with the whirlwind of arrangements in between critical projects I was working on at the office. But a month or so before the wedding, Lance sent word that the date wasn't going to work out for him after all. We pushed the date back, but that one didn't pan out either. We discussed pushing it back even further, but you know, at this stage in our lives, we figured, why should we wait? We wanted to start living our life together.

"Besides," Ed pointed out, "how do we know that date won't change too?"

This was a valid point. Through no fault of his own, Lance's fame sometimes overwhelmed occasions and distanced him from those he loved most. He couldn't help it that he drew a lot of attention wherever he went these days, but it did get a little exhausting. There was a time when I used to tell him, "All you have to do is train and race." But that was no longer true. Beyond the Herculean task of being the world's greatest cyclist, he had his family to think about now—a wife, three children, homes on two continents. Then there was the foundation, and all that he felt compelled to do personally and financially for the many, many people who contacted him for help and hope. And piled on top of that were business issues, endorsement deals, press junkets—the money-fueled machinery of success and all the plastic distractions that are supposed to make your life easier but somehow only add to the clutter. It was hard on him. He didn't ask for that. But he was gracious about it. He knew it came with the territory, and this particular territory was a damn lucky place to be.

"If you want to postpone, we'll postpone," Ed told me.

"I'm not sure it'll help," I sighed. "His schedule is a moving target. So . . . I don't know. What am I supposed to do?"

"You," said my soul mate, "are supposed to be the star of your own wedding day." He pulled me into his arms and waltzed me around my kitchen. "Let's get married. Soon. In June. And we'll croon and spoon on our honeymoon."

I'd already canceled Perkins Chapel at SMU, and because it was such a perfect fairy-tale place to have a wedding, there was no getting back on the dance card. We went ahead with plans at another location, which was going to be gorgeous, but it was hard for me to be excited about it, knowing Lance wouldn't be there. I wanted to share my joy with the most important people in my life. And though it might sound a little silly, I wanted him to see me doing this right. Being married was something at which I'd tried so hard and failed so miserably. Someone even made the unkind remark that Lance had been at my first three weddings, so what was the big deal. I indulged in a moment of self-pity, which brought to mind an unflattering image of me, waving my arms and trying to catch my son's attention.

Look at me, son! Look at me! See? I really mean it this time!

Not exactly what I wanted my wedding day to be all about.

Suck it up, buttercup, I sternly told myself.

"You gotta make hay while the sun shines," I told Lance. "That's just the way it is."

That same principle applies to a lot of things, I think. Love. Motherhood. Work. Life in general, really. It's like the old song says: "To everything there is a season."

~

When someone comes into your office and shuts the door, it's either bad news or juicy gossip. And everyone knew I wasn't much for gossip, so it always made me a little nervous.

"I've got to tell you something," a good friend from HR said, slumping into a chair across from my desk. "This is confidential. It isn't for general knowledge yet, but . . . your department is being sold."

"*What?*" I was absolutely stunned. "Why would they do that?"

"It's just the way the economy is right now," she said.

She didn't have to tell me. I lived it every day. The whole telecom industry was crossing some kind of desert. All those projections about how we'd all be buying our groceries over the Internet—it just wasn't happening the way they had thought it would.

"There has to be another way," I said, already knowing the hollowness of that statement.

"Let me know when you find it," she said dryly. "Meanwhile, I'll be working on my résumé. I have a feeling we're next."

Everybody was outsourcing and downsizing. It never seemed fair to the ones who found themselves on the butcher block, but you know, in reality—well, that's *reality.* Companies all over technology-related industries were being hit hard. They were trying to be creative, trying to find ways to save as many employees as they could, so they were selling off little units like ours. It's not possible or probably even appropriate for a company to place loyalty to a few over the good of everyone.

"Really," she said bitterly, "there is no such thing as loyalty in this environment, because it simply isn't pragmatic. It isn't businesslike. 'Job security' is a myth, no matter what level you're employed at. This department is just part of the chess game. It's nothing personal."

But it felt personal to me.

"Jane, I cannot leave Ericsson," I told her. "This company—my whole career—I mean, maybe something could be worked out to let me stay on somewhere else in the company."

"Oh, I'm sure it could," she nodded. "They're never going to lay you off because of who you are. You're a huge asset. In fact, you're one of the reasons the buyer was interested." I thought she was talking about the fact that I was a top-producing global account manager, in charge of their biggest bread-and-butter account. But then she added, "I mean, c'mon! You're Lance Armstrong's mom!"

The sale went through, and I was contracted to the buyer for six months, after which I was to return to Ericsson in a different capacity, but you know, it just wasn't fun anymore. You'd show up every morning, thinking, *Who won't be here today? Oh, no! They can't let him go.*

He has a new baby on the way. Or, *Not her! She just moved her parents here from Houston.* Every day felt like we were just waiting for the rug to be pulled out from under our feet.

~

The engineering department was the next to go. They could get it done cheaper by sending it all back to Sweden.

"What about taking an early retirement?" Ed asked. "Have you ever considered just staying home and being . . . home?"

"No!" I said. When had I ever had the luxury of considering anything but supporting my household?

"Well, *would* you consider it?" he asked.

"I don't know. I'm not sure it's in my makeup to be the full-time wife or the Junior League, tennis club kind of person."

But once the seed of the idea had been planted, it started to grow. It started to appeal to me. And when I set it up next to the idea that someone who was the sole support of his family was going to be laid off so the company could keep Lance Armstrong's mother, it became a no-brainer. With my wedding day coming closer, I sold my house and prepared to phase out of my job, and the only thing that kept me from feeling like I was stepping off a cliff was the solid warmth of Ed Kelly's arms around me.

Leaving Ericsson was one of the most wrenching things I've ever had to do. I came to the company when I was young and inexperienced, and they were a small family group. We were both just beginning to discover our place in the world. As they grew to be a major supplier in this country, I grew to be a more capable, more confident woman than I'd ever imagined I could be. The terrific people I worked for over the years had nurtured and mentored me, opening doors that allowed me to grow; they not only changed my life but gave me the opportunity to do the thing I most wanted to do: make a difference. We'd come full circle. I realized I'd done everything I was meant to do here, and it was time to move on. The nature of my life was changing, and the nature of the company was as well. It actually worked out perfectly that the two transitions came at the same moment in time.

I felt almost guilty about the idea of having my days to myself. I couldn't even imagine what that was going to be like. But I knew this about myself: I would adapt. Despite all my big talk to Lance when he was growing up—set goals, form a strategy, follow through—I never really had a plan for myself. The last time I thought I could chart a course for the universe and a plan for my life, I was planning to have a baby girl and name her Erica, and you see how that worked out. So I never planned. I just rolled the dice. And that's not scary at all when you're feeling lucky. Whatever was coming my way now, I couldn't help but feel enormously optimistic about it. I'd never been so full of hope. Ed and I started building a new home for ourselves, and I looked forward to creating a peaceful sanctuary there for me and my husband.

~

My wedding day dawned clear and warm. A perfect Dallas summer day. And it was my day. Of course, my first thought was, *Oh, how I wish Lance was here!* I held him close to my heart the whole afternoon. Still, it was good to know that the people who came were there because they cared about me and Ed. Being Lance Armstrong's mom is the most important thing in my life, but having a moment of my own felt fine.

"I'm sorry I won't be able to make it," J.T. told me on the phone that morning.

He tried to make some excuse about this thing came up and da-da-da, but I could hear in his voice that the chemo was taking its toll.

"Frances is going to be there!" he said. "I told her take lots of pictures and kiss the bride for me."

"We'll miss you, J.T."

"I'll miss you too, Linda. And I miss that son of yours. Tell him to call me sometime, will you?"

"Sure," I said.

"What's he up to, anyway?"

"Oh, he's eating, sleeping, and breathing nothing but the Tour right now. Training hard. I'm so excited for him."

"Yup. Us too. Tell him we'll be tuned in every day."

"I'll tell him," I promised, though I suspected Lance already knew.

Our wedding was the sort of relaxed, lovely day I doubt many couples have when they're young and just discovering what the whole world means. When two people have shouldered the seasons and passed through a few of life's refining fires, they know what those vows mean, and the ceremony takes on a poignantly wise quality.

Naturally, Ed and his son were knockout handsome, his daughters were drop-dead gorgeous, and if ever there was a day in my life when I felt like a princess, this was it. Debbie and Daddy and Alan were there with their families, and my mother had bought a rose yellow dress that looked so pretty on her, it made me smile when I saw it. You just don't go out and buy a rose yellow dress unless you feel *something* good about your life. If I didn't know better, I would have thought she was having fun. The whole day—which stretched into a long evening of music and celebration—was just about as close to absolutely perfect as you can get living on the real-life side of the television screen.

After the reception, we left for a seven-day cruise in the Caribbean, then came home to the lake house, where our honeymoon lasted the rest of the summer. We lived there until our home was finished. It was fabulous. I was at summer camp, and I was in hog heaven, I wanna tell you what! I would sit there at the kitchen table and watch those hummingbirds and look out over the water, and there were days when I didn't even get dressed or put my makeup on until noontime. Ed would go off on a business trip, and I'd go out golfing by myself, and I didn't just play one ball—I'd play two! I met up with some of the old codgers who lived around there, and they'd call out as soon as they saw me.

"Hey, Linda! C'mon and play! Why dontcha play two balls? We're holdin' you up."

And I'd drive that sucker out over the water and they'd clap and we'd all laugh.

I wanna tell you what. It was one awesome summer.

And I feel guilty admitting it, but I really didn't miss the thrill of my daily work as much as I thought I would. Truth be told, I didn't even think about it. Isn't that terrible? Of course, my girlfriends missed me, and they'd call and say, "Aren't you getting bored?" But I wasn't. I was just so, so *happy*. I just rode off into the sunset with my Prince Charming.

In a Mercedes convertible.

Life is good.

~

J.T. had gone far above and beyond courage, fighting the cancer that simply would not retreat. He'd had chemo, radiation, and bone marrow transplants, and when none of that worked, he went beyond allopathic care to alternative medicine. He never wanted to discuss the details at great length. Only on occasion he'd talk about going to Arkansas to see this specialist or reading up on this clinical trial in Houston.

"Linda, I have a claim to fame today!" he told me. "I have maxed out my insurance. I'm the guy who got his money's worth, by God! And I had my steroids today, so I'm loaded for bear. Some lady tried to give me some crap about it, and I let her have it."

"Oh, J.T.!" I laughed, trying to picture it.

"I do love my steroids! They make me tell it like it is," he declared, but then his voice softened. "And they also make me tell you how I feel. They make me want to tell you that I love you. Always have loved you and that boy of yours. You're a great lady. It's good to see you so happy, Linda. You deserve it."

I couldn't speak for the lump in my throat.

"I should have made him call you more often. When he was living up here, I mean."

"Oh, you did fine," I said. "You were his surrogate mother. And I owe you a debt of gratitude, J.T. You stood by him from the bottom up. And you were one of the few people who really cared about him without having anything to gain from it. If it hadn't been for you—"

J.T. cleared his throat gruffly.

"Oh, now don't get all sloppy on me," he said. "Who's the one on drugs around here?"

I checked in on him periodically while we were at the lake house and tried to get him and Frances to go to lunch or something, but he was either busy or making up excuses so I wouldn't know how sick he really was.

The first day of October 2002, he called me to tell me that he was in the hospital.

"We've got the hospice people coming. And I just wanted to give you a call to tell you that I love you."

"*Oh, J.T.!*" I didn't even know how to respond. "J.T., I . . . I love you too. And I'm getting in the car right now. I can be there in a couple hours."

"Oh, no, no, no—don't do that. I'm fine. Scotty's here, and Frances is home getting the whole place all set up. Give me a call later, and I'll let you know how it's going."

After we hung up, I went and put my arms around Ed's neck and told him about the conversation.

"That's probably the last time you'll talk to him," he said gently.

"But he sounded fine," I said. "He was speaking as clearly as I am right now."

"Linda, he was calling you to say good-bye."

"No! He said to call back," I insisted. "So I'm going to do as I'm told. First, I'm going to get hold of Lance, then in a couple hours I'm going to call J.T. back."

But Lance's answering machine picked up the call at his house, and when I called J.T.'s cell phone a little later, Scotty answered.

"Scotty . . . where's your dad?"

"The ambulance is taking him home," Scotty said. "He wanted to die at home."

"What can I do?" I asked.

"Well, get hold of Lance, I guess. And then . . . I'll keep you posted."

My hands were trembling when I dialed Lance's number again. Someone picked up. The phone clattered against a countertop and the noise of a party welled up in the background. This was October 1, I realized. The next day would be Lance's "carpe diem" day—the sixth anniversary of his cancer diagnosis. It had become his tradition to celebrate the occasion with a big blowout, but when I hadn't heard anything about a party this year I figured—

"Hello?"

I was startled by the unfamiliar voice.

"Who is this?" I asked.

The person said something, but I didn't quite catch it.

"Is Lance there?"

"He's out swinging on the rope with Ethel," she said.

"Who?"

"His mom!"

"This *is* his mother," I said. "And I need Lance to call me back immediately. It's urgent."

"Sure, no problem." The phone clattered again and disconnected.

I paced until almost midnight, pressing my hand against the knot in my stomach. Then I checked the battery on the phone and lay down with the handset next to my pillow.

Before I even realized I was dozing off, I was suddenly aware of being wide awake, swept in one swift breath from deep oblivion to absolute clarity.

Normally, when you wake up in the night, you hear a sort of ambient humming in the house—clicking and settling or maybe the wind at the window. But when I awoke, there was a seamless quiet around me.

It's okay.

Without a sound, the words passed across my heart. A profound peace filled me like a cup running over, and without knowing where it came from, I felt the unshakable knowing of two things: J.T. had died. And everything was going to be all right.

Oh, there's always that bittersweet quality to life, isn't there? The day J.T. died, my son celebrated six years of life that can only be described as a bonus.

Ed and I drove down for the service, and it was such a great service. So many people whose lives had been touched and blessed by this very good father, mentor, and friend. Standing in the churchyard after the funeral, Lance looked shell-shocked and sorrowful, the lesson he'd learned plainly etched around his eyes. Some of his oldest friends were the pallbearers. Boys he swam and rode with, shared adventures and got in trouble with.

There they stood. The fireball boys. All grown up.

Lance came over to me, and I hugged him hard, hoping the lingering feeling of that profound peace would flow to him.

"He wanted to tell you good-bye, son," I said. "And that he loved you."

Lance nodded against my neck.

"It's just so so sad."

He nodded again.

"I've lost a good friend."

"Mom," Lance said, holding me at arm's length. "*We've* lost a good friend."

"Yes," I said. "You're right. I'm sorry. And Lance, I think J.T. wanted you to know . . . everything's going to be all right."

I held him close for another moment, then watched him walk away—willing him to stay upright, wanting him to live his own life, and incredibly proud of how he had learned to fly.

~

"There's a story," says my hippie girlfriend, "about a man named Moses, but it really begins with the story of his mom."

"Oh?" I say, smoothing sunscreen over my shoulders. My hippie girlfriend holds out her hand, and I squeeze a dollop into her palm.

"In a place and time when her baby boy was not even supposed to exist," she goes on, "this mother looked at her son, and the Bible says, 'She knew he was special.' She refused to listen to a world that tried to tell her he was nothing. She protected him with all the substance of her strength. She worked hard, carefully preparing a vessel for his escape. And when it was time, she let him go. She watched as he drifted down the river and far away, helpless to change the course of his destiny, but knowing with her whole heart that he would find his way, and that he would take a little bit of her farther out into the world than she could imagine. And *that*," she concludes, "is the power of *mom*."

I haven't seen my son parting the Red Sea lately, but I have seen him cross oceans and battle formidable adversaries. So I feel like I must have done something right. Or maybe I was just lucky.

"What ever happened to her?" I ask.

"I don't know," says my hippie girlfriend. "This was the Bronze Age. She probably had eighteen more children, baked bread on a rock, and died very young."

We look at each other and laugh out loud.

I suppose that's a likely scenario. But I'd rather believe she found a destiny of her own. Or better yet—she *created* one.

And I'd like to believe she lived happily ever after. I think she deserved that.

FIFTEEN

SOMEDAY WE'LL BE TOGETHER

Peggy Kelly gave me two great gifts.

One was a man who'd been trained to appreciate a good woman. The other was Barney, the brown-eyed beagle who was at her side the last several years of her life. I loved him as soon as I saw him, and he and Sam were buddies right away. They teamed up to bring out this ridiculously silly side of me.

Ed's daughters used to exchange glances when they caught me doing my squeaky little doggy voice and saying things like, "Yes, Barney loves his mama! And Sammy loves his mama! Doesn't he? Yes, he does. 'Cause we gives him treatses and his baffees and *kee-kee-kee-kee-kee. . . .*"

Ed would just stand there and shake his head.

"You know," says my hippie girlfriend, "sometimes I think your voice actually goes high enough where only dogs can hear it."

"I can't help it!" I tell her. "I'm a nurturer by nature. Although I used to have cats instead of dogs. Lance and I even tried to potty-train our cat one time."

"Oh, really? How'd that work out for ya?"

"It didn't," I admit, "but we gave it a good effort."

And that's what counts, isn't it? A good effort. Your *best* effort. You're a hard-ass about the good things as well as the bad. As relentlessly loving as you are relentlessly tough.

Love-struck creatures like Barney and me are quick to latch on and slow to let go. Ed's daughters were the opposite, and I could respect that. After all, I was their stepmother, and *stepmother* is synonymous with *evil hag. Interloper. Intruder.* And worst of all—*not Mom!*

Fortunately, I still had the phone number of that extremely insightful therapist.

There was a lot of level-finding and soul-searching to do that first year or so. Difficult moments for everyone. I formulated my strategy early on: I'd just keep on coming back until I wore them down. I would love them and love them until they simply couldn't come up with a legitimate excuse not to love me back.

As you can imagine, this worked about as well as potty-training a cat. It took me a while to realize that they didn't have to love me. Loving somebody is about what flows out of your heart, not what comes back. It isn't something you can find or build or badger into existence. Sometimes it's like a note in a bottle. You toss it out into the water, willing to let the tide take it wherever it's going to go.

~

I made Sharon Barlow's gumbo on Christmas Eve, and this is not your run-of-the-mill, suburb-dwelling gumbo. This stuff will burn your house down if you're not careful, so the algebra involved in expanding this recipe to feed twenty-five was making me a little nervous. Still, nothing makes me happier than the nurturing act of home cooking. I get into it.

The first thing you have to have for seriously superincumbent gumbo, of course, is a substantial roux. That's like the grandma's house where all these diverse ingredients are going to come gather and hopefully have a good old time together. Blend four or five tablespoons of flour and an equal amount of butter. Give them a good romance—crank the heat high and keep things stirred up. Season with salt and pepper. When the roux is the color of a penny (not burned!), reduce the heat, toss in about one and a half cups of diced onion and the same amount of diced celery, and cook those until tender. Now it's time for the rest of the gang to show up. Toss in:

Two 16-oz. cans Mexican-style stewed tomatoes
Two 7½-oz. cans Rotel
One 10-oz. package frozen okra
8 bay leaves
½ tsp. garlic salt
½ tsp. Tabasco pepper sauce (or more)
4 cups water
2 cans crabmeat (not cold)
½ lb. flake lump crabmeat (cold)
2 containers Joey oysters

Don't be shy. Dump everything in there to duke it out, simmering on low for about two hours. Every once in a while, you'll want to peek in there, stir things up, and add a little gumbo filé (which you'll find in the spice section of any self-respecting southern grocery store) until you've put in five or six tablespoons (or whatever feels right). No need to be control-freaky about it. Have faith that it'll be fine pretty much on its own until people have arrived, coats are piled up on the bed, the table is set, and everyone's been hugged. Then dash in and add two pounds of shelled shrimp (frozen raw). By the time you've figured out who's sitting next to whom and what everyone wants to drink, the shrimp should be cooked. Sit everybody down, say grace, and start passing out plates of this amazing mélange over steamed rice.

Ed and I went to Christmas Eve mass at St. Elizabeth's. My idea of God doesn't seem to fit in with any organized religion, but I love the beauty of the ritual, the framework for spiritual expression, the music, and the ancient meaning of mass. The cathedral was glowing with candlelight and goodwill. Standing in the middle of it with this good man I loved, I felt blessed.

I'd already started the gumbo before the service, and we went straight from church to pick Lance up at the airport. Sadly, he and his wife had divorced earlier that year, but she was supportive as he went for and won his fifth Tour de France victory. Over the autumn, time worked its healing art. He found his laughter again when he started seeing Sheryl Crow and was bringing her to share the holidays with us. It was wonderful to see him so happy and so grounded. By the time we got back to the house, the whole place was filled with rich fragrances and lots of merrymaking. My gumbo was flaming hot—I miscalculated on the Rotel—but that just seemed to add a little extra spice to the night.

We listened to music, drank champagne, opened presents, and took pictures. Jeff set up his camera on a tripod and set the timer to take a picture of the whole assembly, and we scrunched close together so we'd all fit in the frame. As Jeff dove into the shot, the flash captured us there—*my family*—together, in a moment I wanted to last forever.

~

The next morning I cooked breakfast while all the kids went out for a walk. Lance rode along beside them for a while, then wheeled off to ride through his old stomping grounds.

"It really hasn't changed at all," he told me when he came back, but I couldn't tell if that made him happy or sad. "Whole place smelled like up dog."

"What's *up dog*?" someone asked.

"Not much, dog!" Lance grinned. "What's up with you?"

A groan went up from around the sunlit kitchen. Mo glanced over the top of her newspaper and eyed Lance standing there in his Spandex bike shorts.

"Hey, Sporty Spice," she said.

Lance responded by sitting on her lap and making a loud farting noise.

The Cleavers we are not.

What we are is a fabulous stew, a multigenerational gumbo—born, blended, and bonded into something richer and more colorful than those grainy old black-and-white ideals. Something to which no rules can be applied. Something better than I ever thought of wishing for.

On Mother's Day, I received a card from each of Ed's children, and inside Mo's was written:

Dear Linda,

You know how much we try to forget about Mother's Day, but this year you deserve to be honored. Thank you for being a shoulder to lean on and one of the best friends a girl can ask for. Thank you for being you—and being such an amazing stepmother. I am so glad you and Dad found each other. Your love is overwhelming. Hopefully you know how much you are loved back! Thank you for being in my life.

Love, Maureen

So I take it back. Peggy Kelly gave me more than just two great gifts. So much more. I've only begun to know.

~

I am still floating. My hippie girlfriend doesn't know it, but there's a big butterfly right over her shoulder.

"So how was *Letterman*?" she asks. "Did you have fun?"

"I guess," I tell her. "It was a Mother's Day thing. 'Top Ten Pieces of Advice I Gave My Celebrity Child.' I was celebrity mom number ten."

"Who else's mom was there?"

"Well, Beyonce's mom. She was great. And then somebody from MTV and a guy from *Saturday Night Live*. And that young girl who's a big rock star. I can't think of her name."

"Cool," she says absently.

"Yeah," I sigh, "but the thing is—here I was, mom number ten, so I was going to kick off the whole thing, and when they handed me the card with what they wanted me to say . . . well, it was kind of stupid. It said, 'Hey, son, with all that tenacity and perseverance, you should be a paperboy!' or something like that."

"Oh, dear. That is kind of stupid. What did you do?"

"I handed it back to the guy and said, 'That's stupid. I'm not saying that.' "

"*No way!*" My hippie girlfriend practically falls off her chaise, she's laughing so hard. "Oh, my Lord! You are my hero, Linda Armstrong Kelly! You see, stuff like that—*that* is why I love you. Who has the balls to do stuff like that? Anybody else would be too mind-boggled by their fifteen seconds of fame. You just kill me."

This wasn't exactly the response I got from the producer, but it never even crossed my mind that I should be afraid to speak up. Why would I be? There's no way I was going to say something that would be an embarrassment to me or my son. And anyway, it was for their own good. They came back a little while later with something much funnier: "That whole 'win the Tour de France five times in a row' thing? My idea!" It got a big laugh.

"Let's play a game," says my hippie girlfriend. "I'll say a word, then you say the first three words that pop into your head."

"Oh, I love that game!" I tell her. "I love words. I always wished I had good diction and a big vocabulary."

"You do," she says. "I think you're articulate."

"Thanks." (I make it a practice to say "thanks" when I receive a compliment, even if I don't believe it.)

"Ready?"

"Go for it."

"Dallas," she says.

"Hmm . . . big . . . beautiful . . . fast."

"Baby."

"Oh! Priceless, precious, wonderful, perfect, funny, love, joyful, sweetness. Did I say precious? Especially precious."

"Money."

"Necessary. And kind of . . . evil. And a blessing. I guess that doesn't make sense."

"Lipstick."

"*Very* necessary . . . red . . . beautiful."

"Sex."

"Awesome!" I couldn't help giggling. "And loving . . . and what's that thing you always say? Human comfort. I like that. I'm going to adopt that phrase."

"Judgment."

"Yuck, I hate that. Judgment is wrong. And it's unfair. And it's—I don't know what the word would be, but it's so *quickly done*. It's like people size you up in two minutes. Not even minutes. Seconds!"

"Gift."

"A gift is a talent. I guess it could be a possession, but I like to think of it as a talent. And it's free. No strings attached."

"Happiness."

"Oh, happiness is . . . gratitude . . . and shelter. Happiness is just that moment of sweetness that you feel."

"What's your sweetest moment so far?" asks my hippie girlfriend.

I let my hands drift across the shimmering surface of the water and allow my mind to drift back a few weeks. I woke up in Paris, and I was in love. Feeling a little stiff from sitting on the floor with my grandchildren the night before.

Today is the first day of the rest of my life, I said to myself. And the rest of my life was looking good. Closing in on fifty, I still had simmering on the back burner several unexplored ambitions that, for whatever reason, had never found their moment. With Ed's encouragement, I started lifting lids, stirring things up a little—lending my voice and energy to charities, accepting invitations to speak to corporate audiences, opening my heart and mind to the questions life seemed to be asking, and listening for the still small voice that tells you when you've finally grown into your mission in the world.

Later that day Lance won his fifth consecutive Tour de France victory, and the whole world was watching. But for me, the sweetest moments weren't found at the finish line. Spending a rare and precious evening with my grandchildren vividly brought back a particular brand of sublimely silly joy I knew when Lance was little. I taught Luke to leg-wrestle while Ed ordered dinner. Grace and Isabelle ran around naked, and I chased after them with a bath towel. We read books and danced and talked about frogs, and then we all fell asleep, thoroughly exhausted and thoroughly content.

My son is a man in perpetually forward motion, but now—after thirty years of never asking any questions about what was certainly a questionable childhood at times—he looks at his children, and he wonders.

"Did I do that when I was two?" he wonders when Luke is being impossible, and hearing Grace and Isabelle giggle, he wonders, "Did I laugh out loud when I was a baby?"

True to form, he is gathering the information he needs to put forth the best effort he possibly can deliver. He's in it for the long haul. I can't wait to see him in action when the climb gets steep. This is the easy part, I suppose. The beginning, when everything is possible.

"How old was I when I started reading?" he wonders. "How long did I use training wheels?" His children, as children do, have brought him back to who he is.

Yes, you did that, I want to tell him. Yes, you laughed. You were four years old when you started reading. You couldn't wait to get those training wheels off. And if you should ever wonder enough to read this book, my beautiful, beautiful blue-eyed boy, *yes, yes, yes*—you brought me back to who I am.

I've reached that moment—and I think it's called *maturity*—when you feel neither indebted nor unrewarded; when you have forgiven and asked forgiveness; when wrong and redemption have finally found their balance and counterbalance; when you finally see how everything that left a scar on your heart also left a blessing.

Looking into the eyes of my grandchildren, I see how past and future eventually become one. My child has children of his own. And he is a good father. Being a grandmother reconnects me to my maternal self. Seeing my son so dynamically take hold of his life sets me free to explore my own. I am poised at a starting place. I've set my goals and put some hard-climbing time into my training.

Waking from a dream of Paris, I am ready to begin.

AFTERWORD

France, July 2004

The afternoon sun poured down on the winding road to Besançon, turning the morning rain to steam. An estimated half million people had turned out to see if the impetuous American would lay claim to one of Europe's great traditions. Lance was one of only five cyclists to win the race five times. If he won this year he'd be the first man ever to win six.

My stomach was killing me.

After a two-hour train ride from Paris we walked about a mile to the secured area near the finish line, and I positioned myself with an optimum view of the Jumbotron. Lance would be the last rider to depart the starting point, but every once in a while they flashed up images of him stretching and making conversation with fans, riders, and support people.

I placed my hand just below my rib cage and leaned against Ed's sturdy shoulder. Lance was having a phenomenal Tour so far. He'd taken the yellow jersey in the second stage, as if to announce his unmistakable intention, but then strategically dropped back in the standings. He was gathering his forces, conserving his energy. A dashing young rider named Voekler swept into the lead and kept it, giving France a true hero to celebrate. But the mountains were there on the horizon. And the mountains belonged to Lance.

Outdoor Life Network was running Tour de France news and features almost nonstop, advertising the coming of "The Cyclism" and showing *The Lance Chronicles*, a sort of reality show about the training and technology that made the U.S. Postal team the world's greatest cycling machine. For two weeks before I left for France, I was glued to the live coverage, clutching poor Sammy and shouting at the television. There was a firestorm of controversy over doping in the days just before the race, and I couldn't have been more proud of how Lance handled himself.

"The tallest tree catches the wind," he said philosophically.

But the stupidity and dishonesty of some people drove me up the wall, and the false statements and rumors brought out the protective barracuda mommy in me. I just don't understand that eagerness to tear someone down when they've worked so incredibly hard to get to the top of their field. I worried about the negative energy. I worried that someone might try to hurt him. In addition to a few breathtaking pileups in which almost half the peleton hit the ground, not to mention the rain, cobblestones, and windy cliffs of Brittany—well, who knows what sort of squirming logic is in some people's heads. I couldn't forget that as Lance's friend Eddy Merckx rode toward his sixth Tour victory, a fan (for lack of a better word) stepped out from the crowd and punched him in the stomach, slamming him to the ground—costing him the race and causing him serious injury.

Watching the teams weave through those narrow village streets—oh my God, it looked like there was a Chinese dragon writhing on either side of the riders; some great monster made of a thousand grasping hands and gaping mouths. Of course, the majority of people wished my son well, but some did not. Thousands of people had been camped out along the roads for days, drinking and waiting for the teams to skim by. The Germans who had come to France to support their favorite son, Jan Ullrich, were a strident, hard-partying crowd. Some bystanders spit on Lance and shook their fists as he rode by. It about killed me to watch that happening and not be able to do anything about it. Seeing it all on television made me feel farther away instead of closer.

Lance hardly looked up. He took stage after stage. Hands in the air, huge grin on his face, he sailed across the finish lines in a blaze of sweat and glory. It was clear, the commentators agreed, that if he remained uninjured, the 2004 Tour belonged to Lance Armstrong. But that was a painfully big *if* for me. Lance wasn't taking anything for granted either.

"I'm really careful about counting toward six," he said after his victory on the Alpe d'Huez. "I'll do that on the Champs-Elysées."

I didn't want to jinx him. I couldn't even bring myself to go out and buy a yellow shirt. I ended up borrowing one from my golfing buddy Debbie Schroeder.

The longer stages that wind through the quaint villages and stunning countryside require a great deal of strategy and forethought. Time trials are another matter. There's only one way to win: go fast! The time trial at Besançon was the second-to-last stage—the defining moment.

Ed and I flew into Paris and took the train from there. As we wound our way up into the French Alps, we saw graffiti scrawled on walls and roads along the path the Tour had followed:

MERCI, ARMSTRONG!

ALLEZ LANCE!

GO GO TEXAS!

The day we arrived in Besançon, the morning newspaper featured a large photo of a jubilant Lance on the front page, along with a headline proclaiming him to be the "new cannibal" who was chewing through his competitors the way Merckx, the original cannibal, used to do.

But as competitive as my son has always been, his fiercest rival has always been himself. It wasn't enough to beat the other guys (although he takes no small joy in whooping their pants off). He always wanted to reach a little further than his grasp, beat his own best time, dig a little deeper, try a little harder. That's an attitude that especially comes in handy at a time trial.

Riders reeled across the finish line all afternoon. A bank of cameramen formed in the middle of the run-out area, their ranks swelling as it came closer to the time when the top contenders would take their places on the starting ramp. Family and friends were gathering too, bringing with them an atmosphere of total love and support.

Ed squeezed my hand as Lance prepared to rocket down the ramp. My heart fluttered when I saw his face on the giant screen. He didn't look as drawn and road-weary as many of the riders justifiably did at the end of this grueling three-week event. He looked fiercely focused, but his eyes had that joyfully mischievous sparkle I love. He seemed calm, determined, and on a fundamental level—happy.

The signal was given, and Lance launched forward, busting out with good old Green Machine go power. A roar went up from the crowd.

I still love to stand there and watch him fly, agog at that energy level and in love with every muscle and bone in his body. Since I was seventeen I've been staring at him with that same sense of wonder, that feeling of "Where will you go next?" Not because he's an icon, but because he's my kid. Every mother in the world knows exactly what I'm talking about.

~

You know what wears me smooth out? Those people who say the moon landing wasn't real. They say that it was a hoax, perpetrated in a television studio. They just can't wrap their heads around the idea. A man actually setting foot on the moon—well, that just isn't possible, for the simple reason that no man has ever done it before. They don't want to accept that the wall between what can and cannot be done is made of nothing more substantial than steam rising from the pavement in the wake of a morning thundershower.

My son flew across the finish line in Besançon, beating the best time, winning the stage, and securing his sixth Tour de France victory. He swept me into a big sweaty hug, but we didn't say anything. What on earth was there to say? This was his man-on-the-moon moment. He was standing on ground no other man had ever set foot on, and no other man will anytime soon. Even if some young guy comes out of nowhere and beats him (which some young guy most assuredly will someday), Lance will always be the first. For a minimum of six years (but probably a lot more than that) he will be the touchstone for every up-and-comer who ups and comes. He'll have this mile marker in cycling history, a place in legend from this moment on. If I was any more thrilled I'd be on the moon myself. In addition to the rush of love and outpouring of pride I felt as his mother, I was inspired as a human being. I felt privileged to be there bearing witness as this amazing young man pushed back the boundaries of what is possible.

So where do you go from the moon? I guess if you're lucky you go home again. The people who loved you enough to show up are there waiting for you long after the crowd has disappeared. That's the real victory. Because triumph is more than a race well run. The true essence of triumph is in a life well lived, and we can truly taste it only when we've learned to love that life for what it is; to relish the ride with all its hills and valleys.

Strengthened by experience and uplifted by love, we learn to hope. And having won the day, we push on toward tomorrow.

Since the Lance Armstrong Foundation was created in 1997, it has raised more than $75 million in funding for cancer survivorship programs and grants, helping thousands of people with cancer live strong. You can support the LAF by volunteering, donating, or raising awareness. For more information, call the Lance Armstrong Foundation at (512) 236-8820 or visit *www.laf.org.*